ARCHITECTURE RESEARCH BUILDING

>> ARCHITECTURE RESEARCH BUILDING

ICD/ITKE 2010/20

ACHIM MENGES / JAN KNIPPERS

BIRKHÄUSER
BASEL

>>ACKNOWLEDGEMENTS

The projects presented in this book are not the work of two protagonists; rather, they are the result of intensive teamwork by the large number of people involved, without whom none of this would have been possible.

Our very special thanks go to the scientific staff at our two institutes. Their creativity, competence and passion are indispensable prerequisites not only for the projects described in the book, but also for the long-standing success of the teaching and research at the ICD and ITKE. This applies equally to the students involved, to whom we also pay special tribute for their courage in engaging in the open-ended and risky experiment of the various research pavilions.

We would also like to thank all our partners from industry and science for their valuable contributions and cooperation, which make us hope that there will be many more joint projects.

As we are dependent on financial support from private sponsors and above all public funding bodies, our thanks also go to them for the trust placed in us.

Special thanks, too, to the University of Stuttgart for its extraordinary support on many different levels. Its scientific environment, transcending disciplinary boundaries, is an essential prerequisite for our work.

Achim Menges and Jan Knippers
Autumn 2020

University of Stuttgart
Germany

ICD
Institute for Computational
Design and Construction

itke
Institute of Building Structures
and Structural Design

>> CONTENT

INTRO
PREFACE

RETHINKING **ARCHITECTURE**

INTEGRATIVE **RESEARCH**

EXPERIMENTAL
BUILDING

EXTERNAL
POSITIONS

PROSPECTS
FOR RESEARCH AND PRACTICE

OUTRO
ANNEX

>> ARCHITECTURE RESEARCH BUILDING

In architecture, technical-constructive and sociocultural aspects are inseparably interwoven and mutually dependent. Since digital technologies have penetrated design and construction, however, a certain perplexity and lack of vision on the part of those involved in creating and constructing the built environment can be observed. The question arises as to how this fundamental change can be understood not only as a technical development but also as a significant cultural change. With our works we attempt to contribute to answering this question. At the same time, we are aware that ours can only be a partial view and that we are venturing down just one of many possible paths.

There are many reasons for us as architects and engineers to advance our research and buildings together. On the one hand, this cooperative approach is due to the academic environment of the University of Stuttgart, which we both consciously chose, and which is characterized by a culture of interdisciplinary collaboration between architecture and engineering sciences that has developed over many decades, whose outstanding representatives – Fritz Leonhardt, Jörg Schlaich and especially Frei Otto – are an inspiration for our work. Otto's design method of form-finding was an important starting point for us, as was the lightness of his buildings, which so effortlessly overcome the banal yet often thematized dialectic of the efficient versus the expressive.

Some of our research pavilions have their origins in a time when the previously widespread euphoria for ostensibly "digital architecture" gave way to general disillusionment. By the end of the first decade of the twenty-first century, a large number of buildings had been completed whose digitally generated forms collided heavily with their predigital construction methods. Aggravated by the contemporaneous global financial crisis, the bitter aftertaste of excess clung to them. Otto's buildings are entirely different, combining architectural elegance and constructive effectiveness in an astonishing way, suddenly appearing more contemporary than contemporary architecture. This achievement was recognized when he was awarded the Pritzker Prize in 2015. But we also found the tribute remarkable from another point of view: Otto was awarded the highest honors in architecture even though each of his most famous buildings had a second architect or engineer. What was being honored, therefore, was the overarching and architecture-defining contribution, which was essentially based on his research activities.

Besides an appreciation for architectural research, an enthusiasm for the enriching moment of interdisciplinary work and a fascination with lightweight structures, another essential motivation for our work and the buildings presented in this book is our conviction that digital technologies will significantly change architecture. As we know from history, a common initial reflex when dealing with new technological developments is to use them to imitate former technologies. However, the sole goal cannot be the digitizing and automating of predigital building approaches or the optimization of processes, the increase of productivity or the mere extension of the canon of architectural forms. Rather, the focus must be on exploring new possibilities and using the means of our time to take into account the complexity of qualitative and quantitative aspects that make up a building.

Besides architectural quality, spatial articulation and the sociocultural contribution, there is also the overriding challenge of drastically improving the ecological efficiency of building processes and building systems. This will only succeed if the possibilities of digitization are systematically researched and employed. We are fully aware that the same digital technologies that allow the exploration of more sustainable building practices and new architectural approaches can also be used to reinforce conventions, strengthen standardization and monopolize data. It is therefore necessary to actively, critically and at the same time positively shape the changes brought about by digital technologies. Who should be on the front lines in this if not architects and engineers?

We are aware that such positive shaping and investigation of new possibilities requires considerable effort, which in the context of digital technologies once again also raises the question of research in architecture. In practice it is becoming increasingly difficult to sound out new possibilities and follow research paths. Conformity with recognized rules of engineering is increasingly demanded via the legal, insurance and construction industry frameworks. Architectural and construction practice is increasingly limited to the current recognized state-of-the-art as defined in standards and other building regulations. This contradicts the demand for more innovation through research, which by itself creates new knowledge beyond the conventions. Thus, if practice allows an ever-smaller share of research, it can be concluded that in return research must integrate a higher share of practice. By this we do not mean applied research, but an architecture-specific understanding of basic research. In addition to the research of methods and processes, we understand building and architectural research as an increase in knowledge with regard to technical-constructive as well as architectural-cultural questions. This requires societal change, which is laborious and uncomfortable, but ultimately essential.

With this book our aim is to provide an insight into ten years of joint efforts in this matter at the Institute for Computational Design and Construction (ICD) and the Institute of Building Structures and Structural Design (ITKE) at the University of Stuttgart. The book is divided into three parts: The chapter "Rethinking ARCHITECTURE" explains the means, processes and research approaches available to us with the aim of making a positive contribution to architecture and advancing it in a future-oriented manner with the help of digital technologies. The complex framework conditions to which future construction will be exposed, along with the synergies and interactions between various research levels and the advantages of integrative and interdisciplinary approaches, are summarized in specialist articles in the chapter "Integrative RESEARCH." The "Experimental BUILDING" section gives insight into a selection of jointly realized ICD/ITKE projects as the vehicles and objects of our research from 2010 to 2020. In their respective positions, colleagues who have accompanied us on our path in different ways reflect on the range of our projects in the context of current architectural discourse. All of us are concerned with ARCHITECTURE RESEARCH BUILDING.

ACHIM MENGES
ICD – Institute for Computational Design and Construction, University of Stuttgart
—— 220

JAN KNIPPERS
ITKE – Institute of Building Structures and Structural Design, University of Stuttgart

>> ICD AND ITKE, UNIVERSITY OF STUTTGART

The structure of German universities differ significantly from those of many international academic institutions. A German university is organized into schools, so-called faculties, that are aligned along the classical academic disciplines. A faculty is in turn structured into subunits, for example, departments or institutes. The Faculty of Architecture and Urban Planning at the University of Stuttgart is divided into a total of 14 institutes covering the entire range from architectural theory to urban planning. These are responsible for certain elementary teaching areas but are otherwise free and independent in their orientation in teaching and research.

The two institutes – the Institute for Computational Design and Construction (ICD) and the Institute of Building Structures and Structural Design (ITKE) – are first and foremost responsible for basic teaching tasks in the faculty's bachelors degree program: the ICD for geometry and computer-aided design (CAD); the ITKE for the design of building structures. The ICD was founded by Achim Menges after his appointment in 2008 in response to the growing importance of digital design and fabrication methods. Since then, the teaching and especially the research activities at the Institute have been continuously expanded. The ITKE, on the other hand, teaches the canonical contents of building structures, and dates back to the nineteenth century when the teaching of architecture began at the University of Stuttgart. Initially almost exclusively focused on teaching, the Institute did not develop its extensive experimental research activities until Jan Knippers was appointed in 2000. For their basic teaching tasks the institutes are provided with modest personnel resources by the university. The approximately twenty research associates at each institute are financed almost exclusively from external research funds acquired by Menges and Knippers through very competitive procedures. Currently, the largest and most important project is the "Integrative Computational Design and Construction for Architecture (IntCDC)" Cluster of Excellence, whose funding by the German Research Foundation (DFG) is approximately 45.5 million euros for the period 2019–25. A Cluster of Excellence is the most important and extensive bloc funding award provided by the DFG. The IntCDC Cluster of Excellence was the first cluster in the field of architecture and construction to win this prestigious competition covering all scientific fields. In addition to the ICD and ITKE, many other institutes are represented in the IntCDC Cluster of Excellence, with more than 130 scientists representing different areas of the University of Stuttgart and Max Planck Institute for Intelligent Systems, mainly from the fields of architecture, civil engineering, production and systems engineering, robotics, computer sciences, and the social sciences and humanities. The common research goal is to use the full potential of digital technologies to rethink design and construction and enable groundbreaking innovations by means of systematic, holistic and integrative computational approaches. The Cluster of Excellence ties in directly with the preliminary work

1] When the moisture content in the material is reduced, the spruce cone opens up without requiring metabolic energy. This principle of motion is being researched at the ICD within the HygroSkin project.

2] The elastic deformation of strelizia during pollination served as a model for the development of the FlectoFin at the ITKE.

of the ICD and ITKE – for example, the two BUGA pavilions at the Federal Horticultural Show in Heilbronn in 2019 would not have been possible without it. Menges is the director and Knippers the deputy director of the Cluster of Excellence.

The teams of the two institutes are staffed differently according to their specialist areas. At the ICD, the majority of employees work in architecture, but also in computer science or design, while at the ITKE, the majority are engineers and some are architects. Accordingly, the employees of the two institutes contribute complementary competences to the joint projects: The ICD contributes computational design methods and digital fabrication processes, while design and analysis of the structures and testing of the materials and building components are carried out by the ITKE.

It is not only the competences of the ICD and ITKE that complement each other, but also their overarching perspectives and views. These result not only from the technical orientation of architecture and civil engineering, but also from the different personal backgrounds of Menges and Knippers.

The different but complementary institute cultures can be illustrated by the example of research on adaptive systems for architecture based on deformation mechanisms. Contrary to the collaborative works presented in this book, this research area is investigated at both institutes largely independently of each other and in different ways.

The ICD is pursuing the topic of the passive, hygroscopic actuation of layered wood composite elements, so-called bilayers. When its moisture content changes, wood reacts by shrinking and swelling perpendicularly to the grain. This material behavior is usually regarded as a disadvantage, which can be counteracted by laminating layers of wood at right angles to each other. In contrast, the passively actuated bilayers investigated by the ICD show how this natural behavior of wood – following models from nature, such as the spruce cone – can be used for kinematic, adaptive elements. This behavior can be employed in 3-D-printed, multilayered structures made of synthetic materials, which can achieve complex shapes and motion sequences and are highly scalable. In the case of the Urbach Tower, the process was used for the production of curved, cross-laminated timber boards with a length of 14 m. These were then frozen in their deformation state by laminating two curved layers and applying a locking layer. They then no longer deform with a change in humidity.

In cooperation with the Plant Biomechanics Group of the University of Freiburg and the DITF Denkendorf, the ITKE is developing actuated compliant fiber composite elements with the aim of realizing robust and low-maintenance kinetic facade claddings. These should have just a few mechanical components such as bearings or

3, 4] The Meteorosensitive Pavilion project of the ICD transfers the relationship between environmental conditions and material characteristics into a changing spatial experience. HygroSkin is closed when it rains, and opens by itself when the weather improves. Here, the material itself is the machine, which does not require any external energy supply.

joints. The idea originally arose from the study of plant movements. Since the kinematics, in contrast to common shading mechanisms, do not require a straight rotation or translation axis and instead are based on elastic bending deformation, the elements can be used on double curved surfaces. The fiber composite components offer sufficient stiffness for external applications to absorb wind loads and can also be covered with functional layers such as flexible photovoltaics or light-reflecting or -redirecting membranes. Besides the development of the kinematics, the research at the ITKE focuses on the investigation of the material composite with regard to durability and fatigue. The actuation is carried out by a pneumatic mechanism, which is very robust, integrated into the multilayered material compound and thus protected against the weather.

The passively actuated hygroscopic mechanisms of the ICD arose from conceptual reflection on the natural behavior of wood. In other words, the research initially questions the conventional views of the material shaped by industrialization and standardization. This is juxtaposed with a different material culture in which architectural form, structure and performance are derived from the intensive examination of the inherent properties of the material. In the case of hygroscopically actuated systems, the material itself becomes a programmable machine, which raises not only technical but also conceptual questions. It is not without reason that much of the ICD's work in this field, such as the HygroScope for the Centre Pompidou in Paris or HygroSkin for the FRAC in Orléans, were projects first shown in a cultural context.

On the other hand, the development of the actively actuated fiber composite elements of the ITKE – for example, the FlectoFin and FlectFold projects – is oriented towards the large-scale application of built architecture. This applies not only to the high-performance material composite, which can safely carry even high wind loads over a long service life, but also to the active actuation, which leaves the user in control of the motion state, as is desired in most applications in practice. A pneumatic system is used for the drive, which requires the supply of external energy, but only very low air pressures, meaning that it is therefore not only resource-efficient but also low-maintenance and durable. The elements are very simply laminated and pressed flat, so that even larger quantities can be produced economically.

It is precisely the combination of these different views and approaches that distinguishes the joint ICD/ITKE projects: the questioning of established architectural and building conventions on the one hand, and the goal of pursuing concrete ideas that can be scaled and transferred to the requirements of real architecture on the other.

5] The FlectoFin was the ITKE's first flexible facade shading made of fiber composite laminates.

6] The FlectoFold represents the further development of the FlectoFin into robust and durable flexible facade shading made of fiber composite components.

RETHINKING ARCHITECTURE

>> EXPERIMENTAL ARCHITECTURE FOR THE TWENTY-FIRST CENTURY

GEORG VRACHLIOTIS

"Today it makes sense to begin a discussion about the role of science with the structural sciences," the physicist and philosopher Carl Friedrich von Weizsäcker wrote in his 1971 book *The Unity of Nature*, where he made the following additional diagnosis: "The mathematization of the sciences is one of the characteristics of today's scientific development. A physicist, population biologist and economist can use the same mathematics."[1] With the term structural sciences, Weizsäcker tried to grasp not only pure and applied mathematics, but also those interdisciplinary branches of science commonly known as systems theory, cybernetics or information theory.[2] He thus named those model sciences that form the technological foundations of our present-day digital society. But it was no coincidence that Weizsäcker published his reflections on the structural sciences in a collection of essays in which he made the idea of nature the subject of philosophical considerations. He suspected that the structural sciences were referring to a new tendency in the natural sciences, according to which processes and forms in nature could not only be digitally analyzed, but also simulated and finally synthesized again, that is, reproduced and manufactured.

At the time, Weizsäcker could not yet have foreseen the extent to which this development would expand both the methodological foundations of the natural sciences and the self-image of architectural design.

COLLECTIVE THINKING BETWEEN COMPUTER AND ECOLOGY

Two developments in particular shaped the 1970s: the popularization of the computer as a new tool and medium on the one hand, and the beginning of the modern ecology movements and thus the politicization of nature on the other. Both had impacts on architecture, though technological and ecological thinking barely touched each other in building practice.[3] When Weizsäcker published his book, the foundations for the transparent tent landscape were being laid for the 1972 Munich Olympic Games. And when Donella and Dennis Meadows, together with Jay Wright Forrester, sparked an international debate on the global destruction of the environment with their study *The Limits to Growth* – published the same year – the roof construction for the Multihalle in Mannheim was in its planning stage.[4] Although neither project had an explicit ecological connotation, it cannot be denied that conceptual considerations of sustainability played a certain subliminal role. The question of architecture's possible social contribution to this debate gradually began to come to the public's attention.

Stuttgart succeeded in establishing itself as an innovative center of an architectural avant-garde in which the idea of lightweight structures opened up access to both the technological and ecological debates. Although lightweight construction was regarded as an

innovative and interdisciplinary branch of research, it tended to take up a more marginal position within the architectural scene. While in many places the poetic monumentality of brutalism or the playful aesthetics of colorful postmodernism were celebrated, in Stuttgart researchers were making small models from soap bubbles, observing the flow behavior of sand and considering the connections between biology and building.[5]

A lively collective of thinkers emerged around the unconventional architect Frei Otto. The most influential were the civil engineers Fritz Leonhardt and Jörg Schlaich, the geodesist Klaus Linkwitz and the computer scientist John Agyris.[6] This group, unique in the history of the twentieth century, shaped entire generations of architects and engineers with its experimental thinking; and can therefore undoubtedly be mentioned in the same breath as Achim Menges and Jan Knippers.[7] In a certain sense, both men make reference to Frei Otto's concepts and methods, with his decades of research on the processes of form-finding in nature also providing inspiration.

1, 2] Frei Otto photographing a model for the Munich Olympic Park, Atelier Warmbronn, ca. 1968

3] Frei Otto, nighttime photograph of the Tanzbrunnen (Dance Pavilion) at the 1957 Bundesgartenschau (Federal Horticultural Show), Cologne

However, Menges and Knippers are by no means uncritical of the former idea of lightweight structures. They do not succumb to the temptation of credulously transferring the idea of lightweight structures from its history to our present, nor do they see lightweight structures as the sole answer to the ecological questions of our time. Rather – and this is where the independence and originality of their work is to be explored – Menges and Knippers combine lightweight structures with methods of computer-aided design and robotic manufacturing. They are thus researching the foundations for a completely new and integrative design process located between architecture, structural framework, materiality and digital fabrication.

FROM THE PHYSICS OF NATURE TO DIGITAL FABRICATION

Many of the pavilions and prototypes developed by Menges and Knippers over the past ten years do not fit into any of the epochal categories so familiar to us, nor do they work with the numerous style labels with which we repeatedly attempt to classify the built environment. Thus, the pavilions may also elude traditional architectural criticism. Instead of questions of design, Menges and Knippers are concerned with exploring the material-cultural dimension of architecture – on the one hand, in order to reposition the concept of resource between nature and technology, and on the other, to be able to better investigate the physical dimension of nature with the help of the digital. Materiality is thus not something that has to be forced, for better or worse, into an already fixed form, but something that can serve as a starting point for the design process itself.

What at first sounds like an academic gimmick turns out, on closer inspection, to be an elegant attack on nothing less than the historically established hegemony of geometry.

What we are dealing with here is a radicalism in thinking similar to that attributed to Otto. This is particularly evident in one of Menges and Knippers' latest building project, the BUGA Fibre Pavilion. Realized in Heilbronn in 2019, it represents a small structural revolution despite its scale and temporary use. On the basis of bi-

4] ICD/ITKE University of Stuttgart, BUGA Fibre Pavilion at the 2019 Bundesgartenschau (Federal Horticultural Show), Heilbronn

onic research on chitin and cellulose, they developed a new type of fiber composite construction system made of light glass and carbon fibers for the pavilion's load-bearing structure using digital fabrication. The BUGA Fibre Pavilion thus once again allows the experimental thinking and innovative power of the 1960s and 1970s to reemerge.

RESEARCH INSTEAD OF A GENIUS CULT, COOPERATION INSTEAD OF AUTONOMY

"Among today's various advances to make technology more natural, the discovery of the laws of nature that explain the relationships between form, material utilization, load-bearing capacity and function plays an important role," Otto noted in the early 1980s in the founding document for the research association Natural Constructions – Lightweight Construction in Architecture and Nature.[8] It is not entirely clear which of the various advances he was referring to, but the centrality, for him, of the "discovery of the laws of nature" and his understanding of the term "technology" in terms of both craftsmanship and apparatus become clear when one studies his physical model experiments. His turning to the physical model was not based on a scientification of architecture in the narrow sense of the natural sciences, but on an architectural interpretation of forms found by experiment. Experimentation thus served to investigate causal relationships and as a method of form-finding. Inspired by the variety of forms in nature, early on Otto began to investigate the structure of cells and bones, trunks and stalks, diatoms and spider webs, water vortices, soap bubbles, termite mounds and bird nests. He developed instruments for researching self-organizing processes in nature, measuring tables for determining the course of forces, apparatuses for researching pneumatic construction forms and fine-mesh net models for optimizing complex tent structures. Otto's research became relevant as a social innovation because he continually succeeded in questioning – and overcoming – architecture's traditional claim to autonomy. He saw the importance of technology. But although as an architect Otto was thoroughly open to technological progress, he made no secret of his skepticism about computers: "I am not at all against digital processes, but emphasize the importance of understanding what we are doing. Solving problems with software programs not specially written for the particular problem we're dealing with may lead to a lack of understanding of what is shown on the screen. Something may look perfect on the monitor, but that does not mean you understand it or that it functions in real size."[9] Given the university environment where Otto conducted his research, such a statement may at first seem surprising. At the University of Stuttgart from the late 1960s onwards, he had access to one of the most powerful mainframe computers available at the time. Following the thoughts of Weizsäcker, one might even think that Otto, faced with the technical power of the new structural sciences, wanted to justify himself and his working methods. To some around him, working with soap bubbles and suspended models seemed increasingly outmoded in view of ever more powerful computer simulations.[10] But both enormous computing power and precise on-screen visualizations seemingly failed to impress him. In view of his early works, however, his skeptical attitude makes sense. Through his many collaborations with architects, engineers and biologists and after decades of model-based empirical work, Otto had acquired a valuable knowledge of materials and processes that could not simply be transferred to computer simulation. Switching from the analog model to digital modeling therefore didn't make sense in his eyes. Since then, as is well known, architectural production has moved on significantly, and once again we are dealing intensively with a wide range of materials and substances. With the refocusing on the physics of nature, the history of experimental thinking about the links between architecture, art and science is thus once again brought to the fore.

THE NEW NEED FOR EXPERIMENTATION

Almost 50 years have passed since the publication of *The Limits to Growth* and the construction of the roof landscapes in Munich and the Multihalle in Mannheim.

Today's architecture is hardly imaginable without computers, but it only gains its conceptual originality from a productive distance to the world of the digital.

One of Menges and Knippers' main achievements has been the initiation of both epistemological and technological discourses bringing together architecture, structural engineering, lightweight structures and

5] Teamwork to install the dome for the pneumatic model of the Arctic City project, Atelier Warmbronn, ca. 1971

digital fabrication. With their pavilions, Menges and Knippers have impressively demonstrated that it is possible to gain access to the public through fundamental research in architecture.

In this sense, Menges and Knippers' research and building projects function like reflection machines that challenge us over and over again to question our existing thought patterns. The radical nature of their research lies in the fact that they are not only interested in building in a new way, but also in being able to think in new ways. Understood in this way, research can mean the production of scientific knowledge, but it also can be the intellectual starting point for a joint discourse about the future of society.

How can digital fabrication contribute to ecological building? And what does it mean to design as an architect and as an engineer in a society that is seeking a balance between the datification of all areas of life, the social challenge of urbanization, climate change and an increasingly important awareness of resource limitations?

We are looking for new models of building – socially, politically, culturally, but also technically, that is, with digital production techniques. In view of the ecological challenges of the future, it is therefore particularly important not to lose oneself in socially romantic images of the past. In the spirit of Otto, now is rather the time to strengthen experimental thinking and reinterpret it for the digital age.

The point is not to acknowledge the era's failures, but to develop new questions and narratives for a common ecological future out of its methodical optimism – a future where we are once again faced with the challenge of making architecture socially relevant through experimentation.

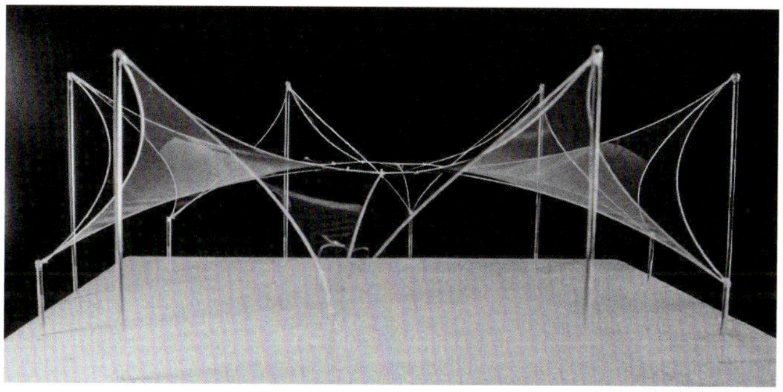

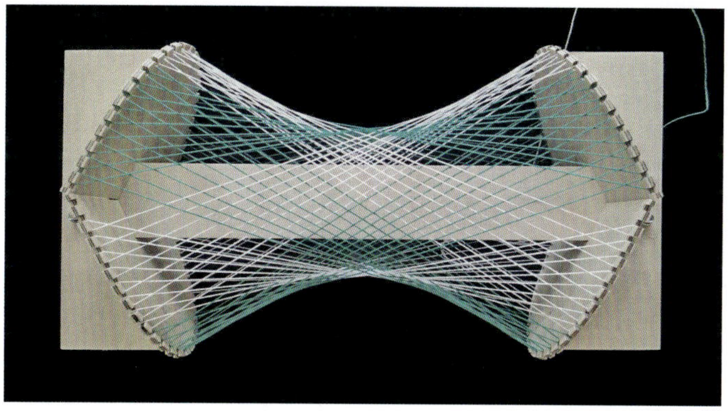

6, 7] A soap bubble model of the Tanzbrunnen, Entwicklungsstätte für den Leichtbau EL (Development Center for Lightweight Construction) Berlin, by Frei Otto (top); and a yarn model of the BUGA Fibre Pavilion by ICD and ITKE (bottom).

GEORG VRACHLIOTIS

Prof. Dr. / Professor of Architecture Theory at the Karlsruhe Institute of Technology (KIT) / Dean of the KIT Faculty of Architecture / Director of the Architecture Collection (saai | Southwest German Archive for Architecture and Engineering)

—— 223

→ [1], [2], [3], [4], [5], [6], [7], [8], [9], [10]: —— 224

>> RETHINKING ARCHITECTURE DIGITALLY

People spend 87 percent of their time in buildings. These form the physical space and material framework, as well as the basis for the sociocultural context in which a large part of our lives takes place. Architecture develops its social significance as well as its ecological and economic relevance through the active design of the built environment. How this design takes place and shapes our environment is directly related to the intellectual and physical creation of architecture, that is, the processes of design and construction. Digital technologies now allow us to question the previous interactions through which these processes of generating and materializing form and space have taken place since the Renaissance. A major focus of the research presented in this book concerns the question of how, in the context of the digital world and digitization, we can think differently about material and materializing in architecture.

Focusing on digital technologies is not an end in itself, though: it is part of a search for answers to some of the pressing questions facing the architecture of tomorrow.

The construction and operation of buildings are central causes of man-made energy and resource consumption, pollutants emission and waste production. We must significantly reduce the consumption of finite, mainly fossil resources for buildings and carbon dioxide emissions if we are to achieve the goals of the United Nations Climate Convention. At the same time, rapid urbanization requires that the productivity of design and construction processes be drastically increased. If we do not want to fall back on the repetitive design and monotony of the serial building of the last century, we need new methods and processes that match architectural diversity and quality with digital design methods and building processes. The challenge is to build significantly more, while consuming fewer resources.

Today's design and construction is firmly linked to the idea of a process chain: at the beginning there is the formal idea and spatial concept of the architects, followed by the technical processing of the engineers, prefabrication in the workshop and finally implementation on the construction site. Even though the reality is usually much more complex, with numerous cross-linkages and iteration loops, common practice is organized along this chain. However, this traditional process has the effect of limiting the degree of innovation because each link in the chain processes the information it receives from the previous one using its own methods, and then evaluates it according to its own criteria before passing it on to the next.

Breaking up this linear and hierarchically organized process is therefore the key to releasing genuine innovations that go beyond incremental increases in the efficiency of existing design methods and building systems. Only if all the project participants in design and implementation communicate with each other in an open and hierarchy-free process right from the start, and the different levels influence each other, can something really new be created.

Digital technologies offer the opportunity to fundamentally change the building industry. At present, research and development is mostly focused on data consistency between the various subareas of design and construction. Otherwise, the digitization of the individual subareas largely takes place separately. This in most cases leads to isolated findings and fragmented improvements to already existing design procedures, production processes and building systems, with little influence on the aesthetic and functional qualities of the resulting buildings. Thus, the scientific examination of digital technologies also requires a new approach to the fundamental question of research in architecture.

1, 2] The ICD/ITKE team during the design of the BUGA Fibre Pavilion for the 2019 Bundesgartenschau (Federal Horticultural Show) in Heilbronn (top).

Our research at the ICD and ITKE aims to examine the possibilities of digital technologies for architecture in an integrative and interdisciplinary way and to reflect critically on them. The focus is on the question of how new digital technologies can be used not only to optimize essentially predigital processes and systems, but also to develop new approaches for design, planning, production and construction.

Our goal is to develop genuinely digital building systems and methods that enable an architecture that fully reflects digitization as a fundamental technical and, above all, sociocultural change.

In this sense, the ICD/ITKE buildings presented here test a radical counter-model to current design and construction practice. They show how a fundamental and knowledge-oriented process can generate solutions that are outside of established typologies of architecture, construction and structural design, and yet are still convincing in terms of both their functional performance and architectural expression. This can only be achieved with the full utilization of the potential of digital technologies for deep integration, with all the disciplines and competences involved from the outset.

Detours and dead ends are not only unavoidable; they are also an enriching part of the process. An essential aspect of future-oriented architectural research is therefore the investigation of digital technologies, not as a continuation of existing methods and processes, but rather a starting point and vehicle for rethinking design and construction. This is not about the unconventional as an end in itself, but exploring alternative approaches that do justice to the possibilities and means of our time. It is about taking the epochal change brought about by digital technologies as an opportunity and shaping its disruptive potential both critically and positively.

>> COMPUTATION INSTEAD OF COMPUTERIZATION

Digital technologies and their relation to design and construction have been researched for more than half a century. What is remarkable about this is not only the long time period, but also the fact that concepts such as parametric modeling and rule-based design were developed and investigated at a very early stage. Initially, however, this required extensive computer equipment only present at select academic institutions and a few companies.

It was not until the invention of the microprocessor and the personal computer in the early 1980s that the hardware prerequisites were created for wider practical application. However, during the subsequent development and expansion of computer-aided design (CAD) the focus was on the digitization of the activities of the technical draftsman. As a result, the change from analog to the digital creation of plans had no conceptual impact on the fundamental approach to design. This initially was beneficial for the commercial success of the CAD applications because it meant no uncomfortable rethink was needed.

The situation also essentially didn't change when applications for the creation of complex geometries became more accessible in the early 1990s. Technologies such as NURBS and mesh modeling, previously only used by highly specialized and proprietary CAD applications, for example in the automotive industry, could be converted into generally accessible and easier-to-use software applications. This was taken up by architects to complement two-dimensional drawing with three-dimensional modeling. The possible canon of forms was thus considerably expanded from basic geometric elements to free-form surfaces. The resulting, sometimes provocative new forms of architecture, either enthusiastically received or deeply despised depending on an individual's point of view, continue to shape the general idea of so-called digital architecture to this day. Despite their new form language, the buildings could not hide the fact that the seemingly radical designs originated from a methodically conventional design process. Also, behind the digitally generated, double-curved facade there is usually still a conventional predigital structure.

Since the 2010s, the approach to digital technologies in architecture has continued to change. Following parametric free-form architecture, primarily promoted by architects but often perceived as excessive, digital technologies are now being applied by architects and specialist planners primarily to increase the efficiency of the design, planning and construction processes. These include generative design, whose aim is the automated generation of design variants; and building information modeling (BIM), which aims to increase data consistency from design through to building operation using database-based modeling. In combination, these two approaches allow for the faster iteration of design variants, rapid implementation of design changes, cross-disciplinary work in one model, and integrated tracking of design information throughout the building life cycle. At the same time, however, existing conventions are consolidated, standards are strengthened and conventional design thinking is not called into question. For technical and conceptual reasons, BIM manifests existing standardizations and also requires new ones. Thus, the conventionalization of construction is further strengthened at a point in time that in actual fact requires a critical rethink instead.[11]

The core concept of "digitization" needs to be questioned. The word suggests that the purpose of digital technologies is merely to digitize previously analog methods, processes and systems. Here, it is of critical importance to differentiate between the notions of computerization and computation.

Computerization in the aforementioned sense refers to the automation, mechanization and conversion of entities or processes that are already given and precisely defined in nondigital approaches.[12] This applies to a large extent to the use of digital technologies in architecture: with the introduction of conventional CAD applications, the pen and drawing board were digitized by the mouse and screen. Modeling in three-dimensional space was then also computerized. BIM now digitizes design using standard construction elements, products and details, and transfers them into database-based modeling. From a conceptual point of view, computerization is an evolutionary stage of existing approaches.

Computation, on the other hand, represents a genuinely digital approach.[13,15] In contrast to computerization, the focus here is on opening up undetermined, vague or insufficiently defined spaces of possibilities and solutions, which can only be determined generatively and exploratively by computers using algorithmic and logical methods. In architecture, computation and its application in computational design and computational construction allows conventional approaches, established processes and traditional typologies to be questioned and rethought.

Computation forms the basis for the research of genuine computational design and construction whose specific characteristics and logics are derived from digital means and possibilities and do not represent a linear development of the predigital concepts, as has mostly been the case up to now. [14,15]

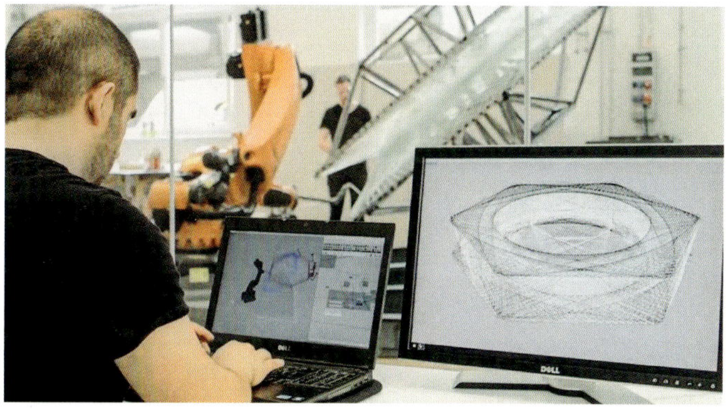

1, 2] Fundamental and open-ended research on the possibilities of digital technologies leads to genuinely new building systems, as shown here in the Elytra Filament Pavilion on the Vitra Campus in Weil am Rhein (top).

→ [11], [12], [13], [14], [15]: 224

>> RESEARCH-BASED BUILDING AND BUILDING-BASED RESEARCH

Architecture makes ideas and findings visible. It can transform new methods of design and simulation and the results of materials research and advances in robotics and manufacturing technology into structures and spaces that can be experienced. The pavilion is the appropriate means for this. It allows selected questions to be examined in a targeted manner without having to meet the multitude of functional, economic and legal requirements that make innovations in architecture so difficult.[16] At the same time, however, it requires actual implementation on a scale corresponding to that of a building. It then becomes apparent whether an idea is promising enough to be worth further development in the interests of broader application. The foundations for a new culture that is both digital and material are also laid.[17]

The ICD/ITKE research pavilions are located at the interface between university teaching and research and thus also represent an educational experiment. The aim is for a team of students, researchers and professors to investigate the potential of digital technologies for a higher degree of integration and innovation on the basis of a specific question, and to do so jointly and openly. This is intended to raise awareness of this topic and inspire the next generation of professionals. Right from the start, the projects have been designed in such a way that both the technical and architectural aspects play an important role. In the course of an academic year, an inductive research approach was used for a process that extends from the initial concept to full-scale realization of a pavilion structure in order to research new design methods, production processes and construction systems. The project team covers all the necessary

1] Students and staff in front of the ICD/ITKE Research Demonstrator 2018

2] The ICD/ITKE Research Demonstrator 2018 was created at the interface of fundamental biological research, architectural exploration, application-oriented engineering development and integrative teaching.

areas as an integral part of the investigation, from the development of the necessary software and hardware technologies, material tests and load tests to the building application and verification procedures. From 2011 onwards, this has been supplemented by biomimetic research together with scientists from the University of Tübingen.

While until 2012 the ICD/ITKE research pavilions were implemented as semester projects within the framework of general architecture teaching, the astonishing level of interest – especially from abroad – prompted us to develop them into a key component of a new, international and research-oriented course of study, the Integrative Technologies and Architectural Design Research (ITECH) Master's Program. This is open to students of architecture and civil engineering, as well as related engineering sciences, computer science and natural sciences. It therefore cultivates the interdisciplinary and integrative character as well as the format of research-based learning and teaching-based research we consider an indispensable part of contemporary and sustainable education for future architects and construction professionals.

The research pavilions are vehicles for the generation of new approaches and concepts, allowing for their technical and architectural exploration as well as their testing and verification on the basis of full-scale realization.

As such, they are located solely in the academic context, where we simultaneously act as researchers, designers, builders and clients. The developments, which started with the research pavilions as structural proof-of-concepts, were then taken up to the next level in various further projects and worked on by larger scientific project consortia involving industrial partners and actual clients. Notwithstanding the aimed-for innovations, it was also necessary at all times to meet all the requirements of the building projects with regard to site-specific conditions, fixed and usually very ambitious budgets and time frames as well as the necessary approval procedures. Based on the experience gained with these experimental buildings, the transfer to general architecture practice has now begun.

At the heart of this book is the presentation of our joint research using selected projects developed over the last decade. Despite multifaceted cross-references and intertwined lines of development, they fit as individual components of an overall research endeavor. Common to all projects is integrative and mutually informative research into design methods, fabrication processes, construction systems, building materials and biomimetics. The focus is different in each case, but the same development lines are present in all projects and also interwoven across projects. These cross-references and connections, in all their ramifications, form a multifarious but at the same time unifying moment for our scientific and architectural work over the last ten years.

→ [16], [17]: 224

>> RESEARCH STRANDS AND DEVELOPMENT LINES

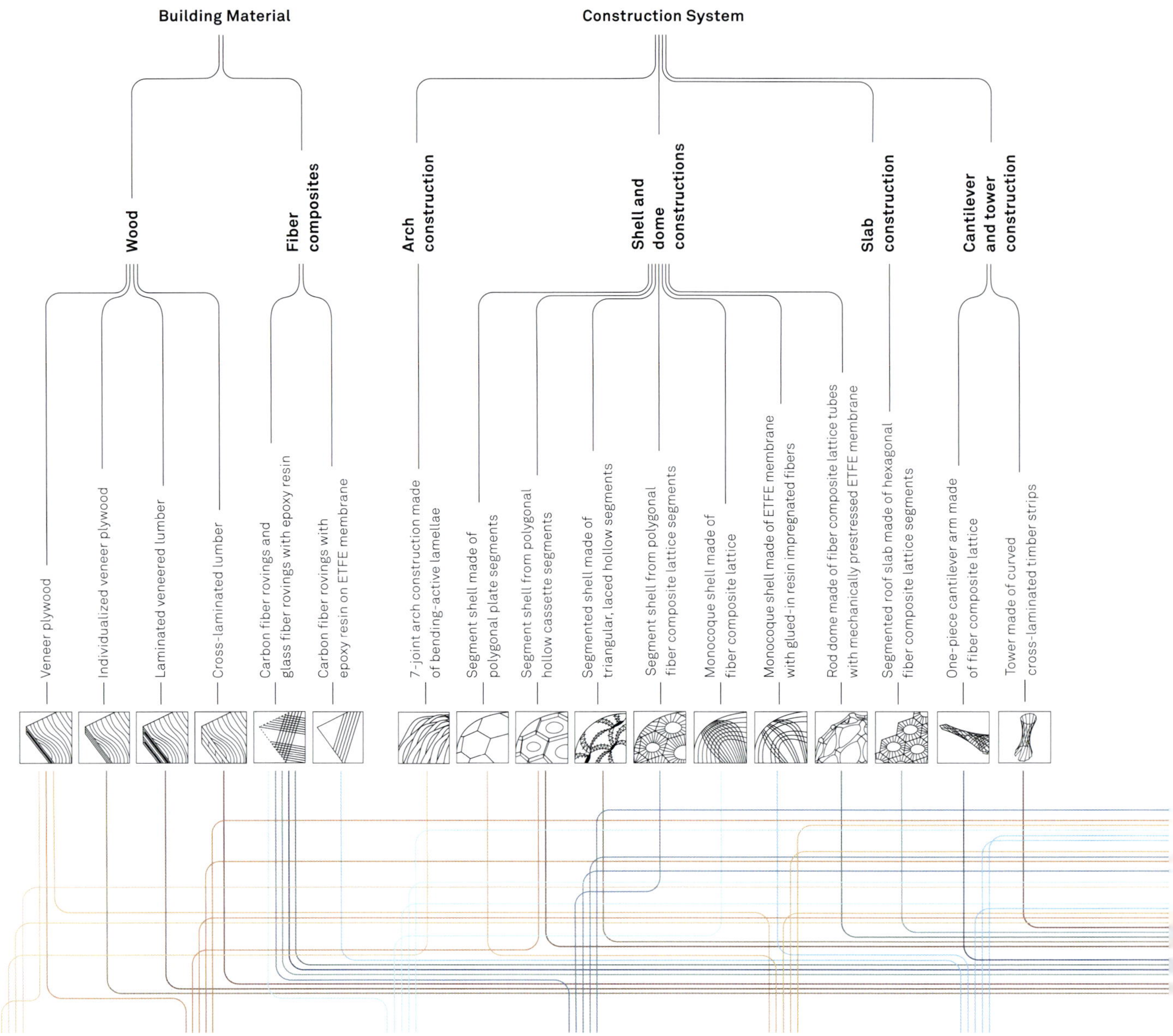

ICD/ITKE
RESEARCH PAVILION
2010
46

ICD/ITKE
RESEARCH PAVILION
2011
56

ICD/ITKE
RESEARCH PAVILION
2012
68

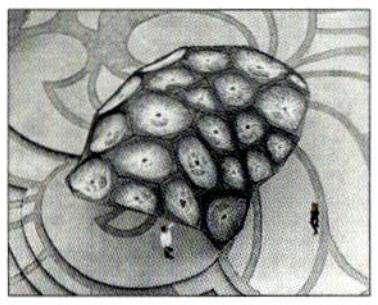

ICD/ITKE
RESEARCH PAVILION
2013/14
78

LANDESGARTENSCHAU
EXHIBITION HALL
90

ICD/ITKE
RESEARCH PAVILION
2014/15
102

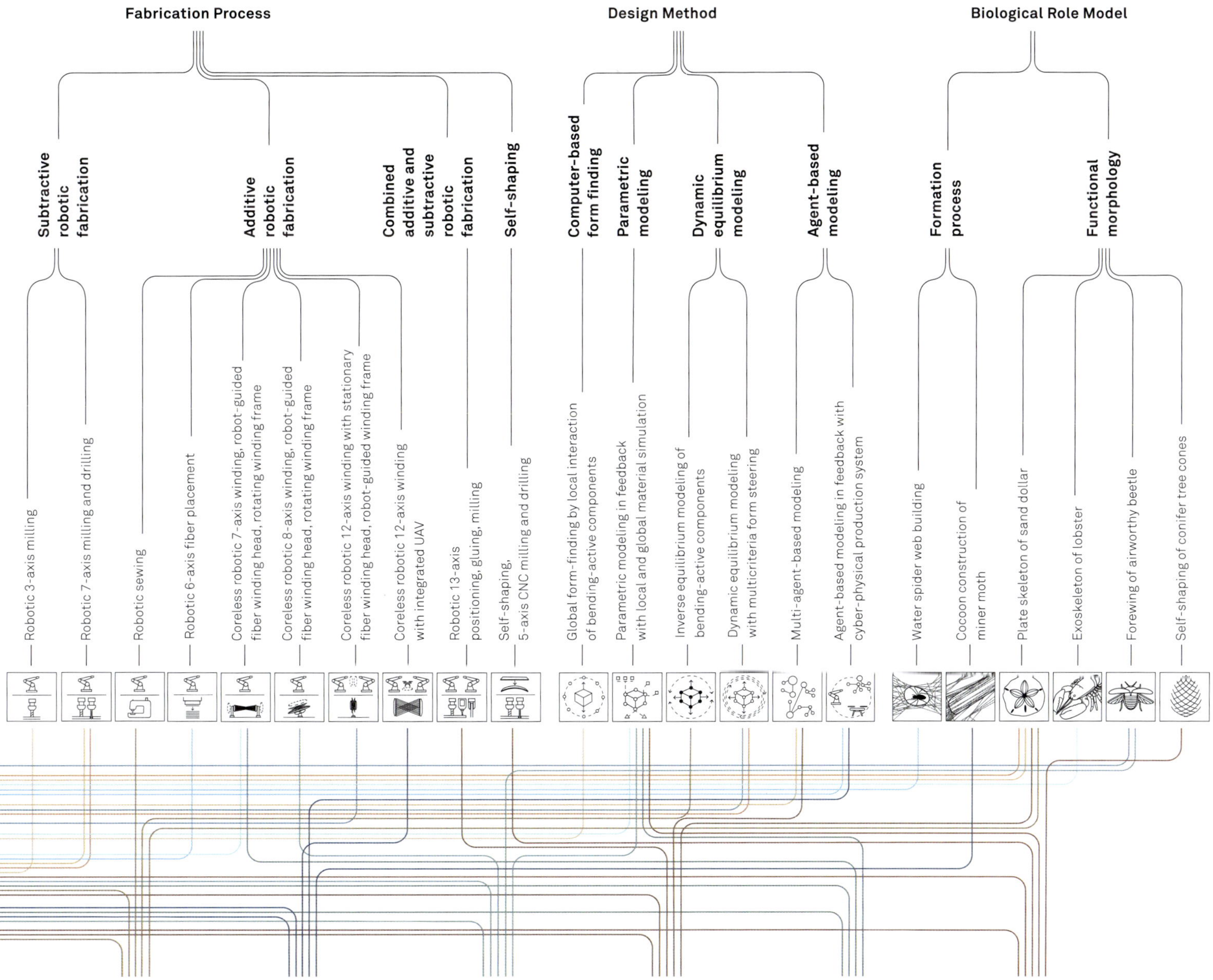

ICD/ITKE RESEARCH PAVILION 2015/16
—— 114

ICD/ITKE RESEARCH PAVILION 2016/17
—— 126

ELYTRA FILAMENT PAVILION
—— 136

BUGA WOOD PAVILION
—— 150

BUGA FIBRE PAVILION
—— 162

URBACH TOWER
—— 176

INTEGRATIVE RESE ARCH

>> INTEGRATION OF FORM, MATERIAL, STRUCTURE AND SPACE

The connecting element between design and construction is the drawing or architectural plan. The modern construction plan came into being between the thirteenth and fifteenth centuries. With the development of perspective and parallel projection during the Renaissance period, the conditions were created for the transformation of the medieval master builder into the modern architect, whose design activity is no longer directly integrated into the building process. Symptomatic of this change was, for example, Leon Battista Alberti's call for the separation of the processes of design and construction.[18] The notational format of the representational drawing therefore plays a decisive role. It generates the architectural intent and at the same time gives the instructions for its implementation. Because of this central role, architecture is considered one of the art forms that depend on a system of notation.[19] However, it is precisely in this dematerialized system of the geometric drawing and plan that a fundamental convention of architectural thought is laid down, namely the primacy of geometry and its hierarchical relationship to materialization.

Conventional design thinking prioritizes the geometric form and considers the material as its passive recipient for implementing the form. Naturally, most architects claim to design according to the materials used. However, the specific materiality is mostly assigned to preconceived constructional, structural and spatial typologies that remain in the conventional hierarchy of form and material. Construction is understood as the subordinate step of transforming a planned form into a material one. Meanwhile, this concept has become deeply rooted not only in architectural practice, but also in the legal frameworks that regulate the professional world.

This contrasts with approaches that treat design and construction in the context of digital technologies in an integrative manner from the outset. Computation makes aspects of the material world accessible that were previously far beyond the designer's intuition as well as beyond the grasp of conventional forms of notation.[20] The computer represents a direct interface between the virtual and physical worlds, allowing material behavior to be activated during the design process. Computation is thus not limited to purely digital processes, but instead the notion of material computation includes the possibility that the materials themselves can generate specific forms or even be programmed.[21] This approach of the material-specific, combined design and construction process takes up and expands on Frei Otto's design method of "finding form."[22]

ICD/ITKE RESEARCH PAVILION 2010
⟶ p. 46

The ICD/ITKE Research Pavilion 2010 is a clear example of the design-integrated feedback of material and form. Here, the integration of the elastic behavior of wooden lamellas into the design process has been used to create a new type of bending-active architecture. The material remains no longer the passive recipient of a previously geometrically defined shape, but instead becomes an active agent in the design process. The same applies to the materialization process. Due to the high degree of integration, no conventional, geometric construction plan is necessary – or even possible. The components are joined in a procedural sequence, whereby the architectural shape of the pavilion emerges by itself on-site through the elastic material behavior.

It is not only the design-methodological development that is interesting, but also the changing understanding of aspects such as form complexity, the simplicity of a construction process, the effectiveness of a structure and the authenticity of the material expression. In the course of further research, this integrative approach has been continuously deepened, ranging from targeted differentiation of the material behavior in the ICD/ITKE Research Pavilion 2015/16 to programming the material in the Urbach Tower so that it takes on a specific shape entirely by itself.

ICD/ITKE RESEARCH PAVILION 2015/16
→ p. 114

URBACH TOWER
→ p. 176

In another research field, the focus of investigation is on how the materialization process can become design-generative in the context of digital production technologies.[23] The initial realization was that switching from process-specific CNC machines, which in most cases are an automated variant of conventional manufacturing processes, to generic manufacturing units such as industrial robots means that the fabrication process itself can be designed in such a way that there is design-integrated feedback between the materialization process and the form to be materialized. On the one hand, this enables the design-integrated conception of new manufacturing processes, such as the coreless, robotic winding of large-format, fiber composite components, conceived for the ICD/ITKE Research Pavilion 2012. On the other, it also requires appropriate design methods.

ICD/ITKE RESEARCH PAVILION 2012
→ p. 68

LANDESGARTENSCHAU EXHIBITION HALL
→ p. 90

An agent-based modeling system was developed for the Landesgartenschau Exhibition Hall at the State Garden Show 2014, in which the generative behavior of each component agent reacts to the specific possibilities and limitations of a production environment. The decisive factor here is that this feedback can take place not only offline – that is, anticipating production – but also online. This means that during manufacturing, processes are carried out in direct response to sensor data from the production environment. These cyber-physical production systems change the understanding of the materialization, that is, the production of architecture.[24] Instead of defining a clear set of instructions – whether in the form of a construction plan or a predefined set of machine control code – before the building process begins, the focus is on designing the process-related machine behavior. The ICD/ITKE Research Pavilion 2014/15, which was used to investigate a cyber-physical fiber-laying process on a shape-changing pneumatic mold, is an example of this.

ICD/ITKE RESEARCH PAVILION 2014/15
→ p. 102

In such behavior-based manufacturing, data is continuously collected and fed back to the manufacturing robot. This means that new information is gained and additional knowledge generated during the production process. In the course of production, this feedback leads to the design constantly evolving until the construction process is completed.

→
[18], [19], [20], [21], [22], [23], [24]:
—— 224

>> BIOMIMETICS AS SCIENTIFIC LATERAL THINKING

In the coming decades we will have to drastically intensify our construction activities due to rapid urbanization and the growing world population. The collapse of the Earth's ecosystem can only be prevented if we use significantly fewer resources than in the past for the construction and operation of buildings. Building more with less is therefore a key challenge for the architecture of tomorrow.

For natural structures, the low consumption of resources is a decisive advantage in evolution. In addition, natural structures show further characteristics that can also play an essential role in future construction. All plant and animal structures are ultimately based on the use of solar energy. In order to reduce energy consumption, they can adapt to changing climatic conditions, both during the course of the day and the year, as well as during their lifetime. They are robust, which means they can withstand disturbances without becoming completely out of balance. If damage occurs, they are able to repair it themselves. They mainly use those substances that are present in the immediate vicinity. At the end of their life span, they disintegrate again into basic building blocks that, as part of a cycle, form the basis of life for other, new living beings.

Many of these natural properties are also desirable for architecture. The criteria of biological evolution and developmental goals in architecture are similar, but the strategies for their implementation are diametrically opposed.[25] In architectural design, complex technical challenges are broken down into individual subtasks, for which optimized individual solutions are then developed. A straightforward example is a wall. It essentially consists of a structural layer, an insulation layer, waterproofing and external cladding. Each of these layers is optimized to perform the function assigned to it. This means that a large number of different materials are used, such as mineral building materials, petroleum-based plastics, metals, wood and much more. These components, which differ in composition and properties, usually have a simple, repetitive geometry and are joined together to form a functional whole.

In contrast, natural structures display an almost infinite variety of structuring possibilities.[26] They use a few polymeric basic building blocks – for example, in the form of proteins, polysaccharides or nucleic acids – which are almost exclusively made up of the same light chemical elements: carbon, hydrogen, oxygen, nitrogen, phosphorus and others. In the course of evolution, mutation, recombination and selection have resulted in highly differentiated structures from these basic building blocks. From the macroscopic organism down to the individual molecules, each structural component consists of smaller elements, each made up of similar basic building blocks. Thus, multifunctional structures are created from weak-efficiency basic modules, which are adapted to diverse and sometimes contradictory requirements. They not only carry loads, but also transport nutrients and water. They catalyze chemical reactions, recognize molecular signals and are capable of a variety of self-x-functions, such as self-organization, self-adaptivity, self-healing and self-cleaning. The basic principle of all biological systems is the effective conversion of energy into physiological performance, a goal that is also pursued in a broader sense in architecture.

Almost all biological systems use fibrous structures – for example, cellulose in plants, chitin for the outer skeletons of insects and collagen in the tendons and bones of mammals – in order to achieve very finely tuned structural properties and thus high efficiency through fiber orientation, layer composition and packing densities of the fibers. Biomimetics therefore plays a special role in the development of a resource-efficient fiber composite construction method.

ICD/ITKE RESEARCH PAVILION 2012

→ p. 68

A linear transfer of such functional principles from biology to architecture will only be possible in very rare cases. The technical possibilities are still far from able to reproduce the natural structures created in the course of evolution lasting 3.8 billion years in all their complexity. The transfer to architecture is also usually associated with the challenge of scaling, not only in terms of size, but also in terms of the loads to be carried, the expected service life and other criteria relevant to architecture.[27] A key difference between biological and technical structures is still that the former must be viable throughout the entire growth process. The morphology of natural structures is inseparably linked to the process of their formation.

Architectural analogies to biological growth were only created through the introduction of additive manufacturing processes.

ICD/ITKE RESEARCH PAVILION 2013/14

→ p. 78

The fiber composite structures shown in the pavilions are in static equilibrium during robotic winding. The physically possible forms provide the framework for the design and optimization space both when growing in nature and in additive manufacturing.

Biomimetics analyzes the principles of form, structure and function of nature and looks for possibilities to transfer these in an abstract form to architecture and construction technology.[28, 29] Architects and engineers are required to deal with structures that elude the usual criteria of architecture. Current construction approaches are primarily geared towards simple and reliable implementation, and therefore always use the same methods, processes and systems. The examination of natural constructions brings into question these firmly established strategies.

ICD/ITKE RESEARCH PAVILION 2011

→ p. 56

The interaction between biologists and architects not only concerns the sharing of knowledge, but also the exchange of methods of scientific work. The natural sciences bring digital imaging methods such as magnetic resonance tomography into the collaboration. In return, engineers' numerical simulation methods provide a deeper insight into the functional principles of biological systems. Two scientific cultures meet that could hardly be more different – in biology the focus is on analysis and understanding, while research in architecture and engineering is focused on transfer to application. Biomimetics brings these different perspectives together and requires everyone to go beyond the limits of habitual thought patterns. Therein lies the actual potential for generating real innovation.[30]

→ [25], [26], [27], [28], [29], [30]: 224

>> STRUCTURES BEYOND TYPOLOGIES

The approach to load-bearing structures in architecture as practiced today was constituted in the second half of the nineteenth century. The rapid growth of railways required the construction of large numbers of halls and bridges. They had to be built quickly and safely for previously unknown loads and spans. Neither the architects nor the early pioneers of iron construction could achieve this with their experimental trial-and-error approach. Within a few years, the methods of graphic and analytical statics were developed. Mathematics and mechanics replaced intuition and experience and became the design tools of engineers. This led to a new self-conception that was fundamentally different not only from that of architects, but also from previous generations of engineers. As a result, new structural typologies such as truss girders and pin-joint arches were created in the middle of the nineteenth century that were then used and are still used for almost all bridges and halls. In complete contrast to the entire history of building and construction, safety wasn't achieved through mass and stiffness, but through hinges and rotations, as they allow for the reliable calculation of internal forces. This new, analytical approach allowed engineers to design previously unthinkable enabled spans and loads. At the same time, the variety of structural forms was reduced to a few calculable and standardized typologies, which since then have been reproduced. Structural predictability became the dominant design criterion for engineers.[31,32,33,34]

Following the introduction of numerical analysis methods in the 1970s and computer-based production chains at the turn of the millennium, the possibilities for the design and calculation of structures considerably expanded. Today, multiple statically undetermined load-bearing systems no longer present a challenge for structural analysis. Computational design and fabrication chains enable individualized components and thus complex designs. Architectural diversity and structural performance are constantly increasing. Underlying them, however, are almost always the same structural typologies of the nineteenth century: frames and arches, trusses or triangulated grid shells, to name but a few. The reason for this is that the calculational prediction of the load-bearing capacity is still an indispensable prerequisite for every structure. In this respect, the construction industry differs from other technological fields such as automotive engineering. There, the development of new vehicles takes place primarily by means of prototypes and extensive test runs. Simulations are seen as a method for reducing high expenditure on experiments, but not as a substitute for them. In the building industry in contrast, the following applies: what cannot be calculated also cannot be built. In practice, this leads to the constant use of the same structural concepts, which are only incrementally improved in research. The room for innovation is thus drastically reduced.

One aim of the ICD and ITKE's research and experimental buildings is to use integrative, computational design and fabrication processes to overcome the limitation to a few, firmly established and recurring structural typologies.[35] The structural and ecological efficiency of the load-carrying system is to be significantly increased. We not only consider the weight of the construction, but also include the manufacturing and assembly processes in the evaluation. The paradigm of lightweight construction is thus interpreted in a new and more comprehensive way. [36,37,38]

ICD/ITKE RESEARCH PAVILION 2010 ⟶ p. 46

The ICD/ITKE Research Pavilion 2010, which consists of a seven-joint arch construction, can be cited as an example. According to nineteenth century theory, this system would be unstable and thus unbuildable. However, it is possible by varying the arrangement of the joints over the surface of the shell to ensure that local weakening does not result in global instability. The geometric variation of the components – made possible by digital fabrication – is in this case the prerequisite for the stability of the construction.

ICD/ITKE RESEARCH PAVILION 2011
⟶ p. 56

This is similarly true for the segmented wooden shells realized as part of the ICD/ITKE Research Pavilion 2011. The segments are only connected with low bending stiffness. Only through the geometric variation of the elements and their trivalent arrangement on the shell surface, where three joints meet at one point in each case, does a stable shell result despite the actually weak connections.

Additive manufacturing processes represent a fundamental challenge to the design processes practiced today.[39] They allow a very high differentiation of physical and chemical properties. On the one hand, these characteristics enable highly efficient structures, which, on the other, elude reliable structural analysis due to their complexity. There are simulation methods that describe complex physical phenomena from the micro to the macro level. However, if the input parameters for material and geometry cannot be reliably determined, the calculations of deformation and strain, and thus the load-bearing capacity, cannot be reliably calculated.

An example is the robotic winding process for fiber composite structures, a large-scale additive manufacturing process. The wound structures are extremely light as the fibers are only laid along the main load paths. A reliable prediction of the load-bearing capacity by simulation methods is virtually impossible, as this depends on a large number of parameters. Aspects such as the contact between the different layers of the fiber rovings, the pretension and cross-sectional geometry of the freely spannig and partly compressed rovings, the degree of curing of the resin, etc. can hardly be reliably determined. Alternative strategies for the verification of the load-bearing capacity that integrate calculations and component tests in a consistent, safe and reliable process must be developed.

ICD/ITKE RESEARCH PAVILION 2013/14
⟶ p. 78

This also influences the design of structures. Since load tests on the overall structure are only possible in exceptional cases, this leads to modular constructions such as those developed in connection with the ICD/ITKE Research Pavilion 2013/14, in which the experimentally determined load capacity of the individual components can be related to an assessment of the load-bearing capacity of the overall structure.

As a further consequence of the limited calculability of the load-bearing behavior, the permanent monitoring of supporting structures will increase in importance. This requires not only reliable methods of structural monitoring – for example, with integrated fiber optic sensors – but also construction systems whose load-bearing properties can be quickly and reliably adjusted in the event of unexpected behavior. Here, too, locally installed winding units in combination with modular designs offer new and as yet unexplored possibilities for localized reinforcement and reconfiguration.

The fiber composite structures produced with the robotic winding process developed by the ICD and ITKE show how additive manufacturing processes enable unprecedented structural efficiency. At the same time, however, they also partly refer back to the premodern era, in which the load-bearing capacity of building structures was primarily developed and validated experimentally.

⟶ [31], [32], [33], [34], [35], [36], [37], [38], [39]: 225

>> INNOVATION WOOD

Most of the construction materials available today are specially developed and industrially produced to meet the particular requirements of the building industry. Wood differs from these materials in many ways. It grows as a functional plant tissue of trees, consisting mainly of cellulose fibers, hemicellulose and lignin. These biological origins define the properties of wood.

The perception and use of wood as a natural building material has undergone considerable change over the course of time. Local availability and the relatively easy, manual workability meant that wood was the main material used in the preindustrial age, not only for building but also for the majority of other artifacts. With the advent of industrialization, this changed over the course of a few decades. Wood was replaced by more advanced materials such as cast iron, steel, glass and ultimately concrete, which were better suited to the possibilities of industrial production and the resulting changes in manufacturing processes. These technological and sociocultural changes required an increasing degree of standardization and norms. The biological variability and the resulting heterogeneity of wood led to its perception as an inferior, less efficient and less reliably planable and usable material.

At present, the perception of wood as a building material is changing again, especially in view of the extremely high consumption of resources in the building industry and the considerable challenges this entails. Wood is being rediscovered as one of the few naturally renewable building materials that also has an extremely low level of embodied energy and can even store carbon dioxide. One of the oldest building materials is therefore also currently considered one of the most sustainable and future-proof. Digital technologies make it possible to rethink the way we use wood.[40] An interesting aspect here is the questioning of the established idea of material-oriented design, which is currently based to a considerable extent on the use of semi-finished products and their industrially specified formats, and the transfer of these into established structural typologies and design approaches. In contrast, a major focus of research at the ICD and ITKE is to develop new architectural possibilities from the specific characteristics of the material itself. This was examined by means of examples of typical wood properties, including elasticity, anisotropy (direction-dependent differences in material properties), hygroscopicity (the ability to absorb humidity and bind water) and the excellent machinability of wood.

Compared to other building materials, wood is characterized by its elasticity, that is, its relatively low stiffness combined with relatively high strength. Wood is thus very well suited for construction approaches in which flat and therefore easily manufactured components are transformed by bending into a curved state, which often offers higher performance and an expressive state. However, with a few exceptions, such as Frei Otto's form-found wooden grid shells or procedural, indigenous construction methods, it is rarely used in architecture. This is essentially for two reasons: On the one hand, the elastic behavior cannot be captured with the prevailing, purely geometric design techniques and notational formats. On the other, conventional approaches to achieving stability in structures rely on maximum stiffness. The ICD/ITKE Research Pavilion 2010 by contrast shows how the integrative use of computational design and simulation approaches can lead to a new type of bending-active structure made of elastic wood lamellas that goes beyond existing construction and structural typologies.

ICD/ITKE RESEARCH PAVILION 2010 ⟶ p. 46

A similar approach was taken up in the ICD/ITKE Research Pavilion 2015/16 and extended by the strategic use of the anisotropy of wood. Anisotropic materials are materials that exhibit different properties in different directions. Due to the cellular structure of wood, in which cells are mainly arranged parallel to the trunk axis and the cellulose fibers in the relevant cell walls are in turn similarly oriented, the mechanical properties parallel and transverse to the main fiber direction are very different.

ICD/ITKE RESEARCH PAVILION 2015/16
⟶ p. 114

While plywood lamellas with homogeneous stiffness distribution and thus uniform bending behavior were used for the ICD/ITKE Research Pavilion 2010, component-specific wood laminate strips were produced for the ICD/ITKE Research Pavilion 2015/16. By varying the grain direction of the individual lamellas, it is possible to adjust the stiffness so that a precalculated shape with different bending radii emerges by itself during the bending process. To this end, the strip ends are brought together by a robot and then sewn. This new joining technique strengthens the pressed laminate and enables very efficient joining, as the wood fibers are not damaged and only displaced by the needle. Here, the integration of the elasticity and anisotropy in the design and construction results in a new type of segmented shells made of elastically bent, extremely thin-walled wooden strip segments.

Another characteristic of wood is its hygroscopicity, that is, the ability to bind moisture from the environment. In traditional timber construction this characteristic is usually considered a special challenge or even a deficit compared to other materials since changes in the moisture content of wood lead to changes in shape. A piece of wood may swell or shrink by up to ten percent perpendicular to the main grain direction as the moisture content increases or decreases across. To avoid this, wood is usually dried before processing and use in construction.

In contrast, in the context of the Urbach Tower it was investigated how the hygroscopicity of wood in combination with its anisotropy and elasticity can be used to activate planned self-forming behavior. Using the parameters of initial moisture content, fiber arrangement and layering, the wood can be programmed to curve into a predetermined shape during the normal industrial drying process. In the case of the Urbach Tower, these are 14 m-long, load-bearing cross-laminated timber elements. This requires not only a sufficiently accurate simulation of the material behavior, its integration into a computational design process and a direct link to the digital manufacturing, but also alternative design thinking for timber construction.

URBACH TOWER
⟶ p. 176

In a parallel and, in many projects, overlapping development strand, the excellent workability and machinability of the wood were considered. In combination with high-precision digital fabrication, these allow complex, form- and force-fitting connections to be incorporated directly into the material, thus enabling the design of new joining techniques and building systems. In the course of various research and construction projects – beginning with the ICD/ITKE Research Pavilion 2011, and continuing with the Landesgartenschau Exhibition Hall 2014, as well as the BUGA Wood Pavilion for the Federal Horticultural Show 2019 – a new type of wooden segmented shell construction was researched and its architectural expression and structural efficiency continuously developed.

LANDESGARTENSCHAU EXHIBITION HALL
⟶ p. 00

BUGA WOOD PAVILION
⟶ p. 150

In the course of both development strands, therefore, new, genuinely digital timber construction systems were created that are directly derived from the properties of wood and only become possible through an integrative, computational approach.

>> INNOVATION FIBER COMPOSITES

The famous House of the Future was built by the Monsanto Chemical Company in Disney World, California, in 1957. The construction consisted of a sandwich construction of prefabricated half-shells. Paper honeycombs foamed with polyurethane (PUR) formed the core of the sandwich, while its top layers consisted of polyester resin reinforced with glass fibers. In the years that followed, a whole series of plastic houses similar to the House of the Future were built, representing a vision of future building. In terms of public interest, these buildings were a great success. They attracted large numbers of visitors and are still featured in numerous publications today. Nevertheless, they had virtually no impact on the general development of architecture and building technology. There are many reasons for this: the lack of experience in design, poor execution, and the incomplete development status of the materials, causing structural damage. Plastics' resulting reputation as inferior construction materials still exists in part today. During the first oil crisis in 1973–74, crude-oil prices rose, and as a result plastic houses, already expensive, were rendered economically uncompetitive. At the same time an awareness of the finite nature of natural resources was awakened, so that plastic houses were also considered ecologically questionable. Moreover, the industrially manufactured living cells, as realized in the plastic houses of the 1960s, offered virtually no possibilities for individual adaptation to user requirements. This was because the associated production process, the lamination of sandwich panels on molds, did not allow for geometric variation with reasonable effort.

In today's architecture, fiber-reinforced plastics only play a role in niche applications. In many other areas of technology – where weight and shape are relevant – they are used in large quantities for mechanically highly-stressed and safety-relevant components, for example, in aircraft construction or wind turbines. Fiber-reinforced composites also offer many possibilities in the building industry that go far beyond conventional material systems, such as the well-known lightweight construction potential due to a favorable strength-to-weight ratio. In addition, very precise adjustment of the mechanical properties can be achieved via the orientation, layering and packing density of the fibers. The fiber types, resin systems, additives, fillers and coatings can be combined in almost infinite variety, so that not only the physical and chemical properties but also the visual and haptic qualities can be varied. The processing of fiber composites takes place at comparatively low temperature and pressure. This enables the integration of numerous functional components into the material composite, such as heat-storing phase change materials for the optimization of building physics' properties, sensors for monitoring temperature, strain and damage, and actuators for active control of the component geometry using pneumatic cushions or piezoelectric materials.[41]

When it comes to fiber composites, much experience has been accumulated in many areas of the technology. The key to its dissemination in architecture therefore lies not in the optimization of the material system, but in the development of suitable fabrication processes. Architecture's main focus is not on the highest-possible precision or maximum performance as in aircraft construction, but on the possibility of producing large and robust components with individualized geometry in a simple and resource-efficient manner. Due to this special requirement profile, transferring manufacturing processes from other technological areas into construction holds little promise. Instead, different processes specifically adapted to the requirements of architecture are needed.[42]

It was against this background that the robotic, coreless filament winding process was developed, first used in the ICD/ITKE Research Pavilion 2012 and later further developed in various forms. Resin-impregnated, wet fiber strands, so-called endless rovings, are stretched freely in the space between frames during the process. The component is then tempered in an oven. After the resin has cured, the winding frame is removed, leaving a pure fiber composite structure. The number and orientation of the fibers can be easily adapted to the respective structural load of the component, with the number of fibers laid being precisely as required for the load-bearing capacity.

ICD/ITKE RESEARCH PAVILION 2012
⟶ p. 68

The mold-making normally used for laminating, which often consists of petroleum-based foams and is in many cases associated with a large amount of ecologically questionable waste, is eliminated by the coreless winding. The process produces no offcuts and hardly any waste. The actual materiality of the fiber plays only a minor role in the coreless winding process. Not only can glass and carbon fibers be processed, but also natural fibers and bio-based resin systems. Depending on the material combination, recycling at the end of the service life represents a challenge. Glass-fiber-reinforced plastic can be completely recycled. Cement manufacturers use the calorific value and the mineral components to save natural resources. The carbon-fiber-reinforced plastic poses greater problems. The fibers clog filters, and their electrical conductivity can cause short circuits in the usual recycling processes. The development of suitable disposal methods is therefore an important next step for further dissemination of the fiber composite construction method.

From an architectural point of view, the question of how fiber-reinforced composites can influence design is interesting.[43] In many fields of application, the materials are regarded as amorphous, at least in part because, in most manufacturing processes negative or positive molds are technically required, which are decisive for the resulting shape of the component. In contrast, coreless winding not only allows the material to be transformed into new, spatial fiber lattice constructions, but also gives the fibrous material its own tectonic expression, thus unfolding an architectural articulation from the material itself.[44,45] The winding process has been tested in several research pavilions, and the structural performance of the components convincingly demonstrated – for example, in the BUGA Fibre Pavilion.

BUGA FIBRE PAVILION
⟶ p. 162

Future integration into the building structure is not only about the interfaces to the building envelope, wall, floor or technical installations, but also about the development of hybrid construction methods in which robotically wound elements made of cost-intensive fiber composites are combined with conventional materials such as wood, steel or concrete in such a way that each material can make use of its specific advantages.

⟶
[41], [42], [43], [44], [45]:
___ 225

>> FROM EXPERIMENTS TO APPROVED BUILDING SYSTEMS

Each ICD/ITKE research pavilion started with a question, for example: How can load-adapted shells be assembled from prefabricated segments? Can fiber composite structures be produced without the usual mold-making? Are pneumatic molds for fiber composite constructions possible? How can drones compensate for the limited reach of robots? At the beginning of the examination of each question, there were no concrete specifications for the architectural shape or for the technical implementation. Both were developed in an open-ended process, which in the case of all the pavilions involved detours, setbacks and, above all, a great deal of effort on the part of everyone involved. Each pavilion pursued an idea that initially seemed promising for larger-scale application and the requirements profile of real construction tasks. However, this expectation was not fulfilled in all cases to the same extent.

In deciding which of the ideas developed in the pavilions to take up for a client, criteria that are of secondary importance in the context of research (such as reliable cost planning, construction time and the ability to meet building code requirements) also played a role, in addition to the convincing architectural implementation. What was surprising, for example, was not so much that the wooden segment shells developed for the first time in the ICD/ITKE Research Pavilion 2011 turned out to be very promising, but rather that the modular ICD/ITKE Research Pavilion 2013/14 made of wound fiber composite components also proved to be very convincing in terms of both fabrication reliability and the performance of the structure.

In transferring research findings to the construction practice, both functional challenges and process-related hurdles must be overcome. The ICD/ITKE research pavilions are based on the parallel and mutually influential development of design methods and fabrication processes. This approach runs completely counter to the separation of design and execution, which is the paradigm of building practice today. The tender processes and the distribution of tasks and liabilities are strictly organized along this dividing line. Strategic partnerships between designers and contractors for the development of new technologies are virtually impossible. Alternatives to this are design-and-build models, which, however, primarily pursue the goal of maximizing profit on the part of the contractor and minimizing risk on the part of the client. Standard contractual constellations are not only highly unsuitable for the implementation of innovations, they even hinder them. In the current construction environment it is consequently often difficult to interest contractors in innovative and thus risky projects.

For the pavilion buildings realized by the ICD and ITKE outside the university context, innovative and cooperative contractual constellations were therefore required. These involve a contractor as a cooperation partner and thus have the effect of avoiding a real competitive situation between different providers of construction services, as is usually mandatory under procurement guidelines for cost optimization. In some cases, such as the Elytra Filament Pavilion in the Victoria and Albert Museum in London, production took place at the university itself. The success of this project subsequently led to the establishment of a spin-off company that now offers the robotic winding of fiber composite structures as a construction service. It has already been involved as a cooperation partner in the production of the subsequent BUGA Fibre Pavilion.

ELYTRA FILAMENT PAVILION
⟶ p. 136

However, the biggest hurdle on the long road from research to practice is that research pavilions are by definition outside the generally approved state of the technology. From the point of view of a client or user, this is initially associated with technical and financial risks and therefore requires considerable communication skills and transparency on the part of the designers. In almost every case, clients must be prepared to accept that the usual liability must be reduced, since statements on durability and longevity are only possible to a limited extent. Furthermore, new construction methods are not covered by standards or building code, but must of course still meet the usual safety requirements and be approved by the building authorities. This aspect is given little attention in the usual discourse on architectural research. Ultimately this means that the building authorities must be involved as a partner in the design process from the very beginning. And it also means that the structure must be developed in such a way that the load-bearing capacity can be verified experimentally with reasonable effort.

The presented fiber composite structures, in particular, are a long way from being compliant with any building code and regulations in the foreseeable future. Due to their complex material structure, they elude reliable structural calculation of failure states, so that the proof of load-carrying capacity can only be achieved by means of tests. The ICD/ITKE Research Pavilions 2012 and 2014/15, for example, are architecturally and structurally convincing, but sufficient safety can only be demonstrated by means of a load-bearing test on the overall structure. Consequently, this would mean that the structure would have to be built at least twice: first for the relevant load-bearing test for the construction authority, and secondly for final use. For this reason, the modular approach of the ICD/ITKE Research Pavilion 2013/14 was pursued instead, since its individual components could be tested at reasonable cost. The experimentally determined load-bearing capacity of the individual components can then be used to make a reliable statement about the load-bearing capacity of the overall structure.

BUGA FIBRE PAVILION
⟶ p. 162

Statistical evaluations and safety considerations are to be taken into account in the design of the test series: the higher the number of tests and the lower the deviation of the results, the higher the applicable load capacities. The construction must not only carry the expected loads, but also an additional safety margin. This covers all uncertainties for load, material and construction, which are naturally higher for each new construction method than for those tested over many years. The more uncertain the assumptions for the structural properties (while taking into account all influencing parameters, such as aging and manufacturing tolerances), the higher this safety margin must be. Conversely, the more established a construction method, the lower the safety factor. For a conventional steel structure, an overall safety factor of about 1.5 to 2 is sufficient, while for a less proven construction method, significantly higher safety factors should be applied. In the case of wound fiber composite structures, these are around a factor 4 to 5. This means that each component is only allowed to fail in the test at five times the load that it is likely to have to bear later under maximum loads. The timely further development of verification procedures for new construction methods and materials acceptable to the building authorities is therefore of considerable importance for the transfer of innovative research achievements into construction practice. Not only does statistically verified data on long-term behavior need to be determined, there is also a need for verification procedures that integrate and take into account tests and structural calculations in a verified theoretical concept of safety.

LANDESGARTENSCHAU EXHIBITION HALL
⟶ p. 90

BUGA WOOD PAVILION
⟶ p. 150

All these interrelationships show that complex barriers need to be overcome on many levels in order to transfer an idea that has been successfully tested in an academic context into architectural practice. This calls for the involvement of numerous competencies and, above all, a long-term effort.

EXPERIMENTAL BUILDING

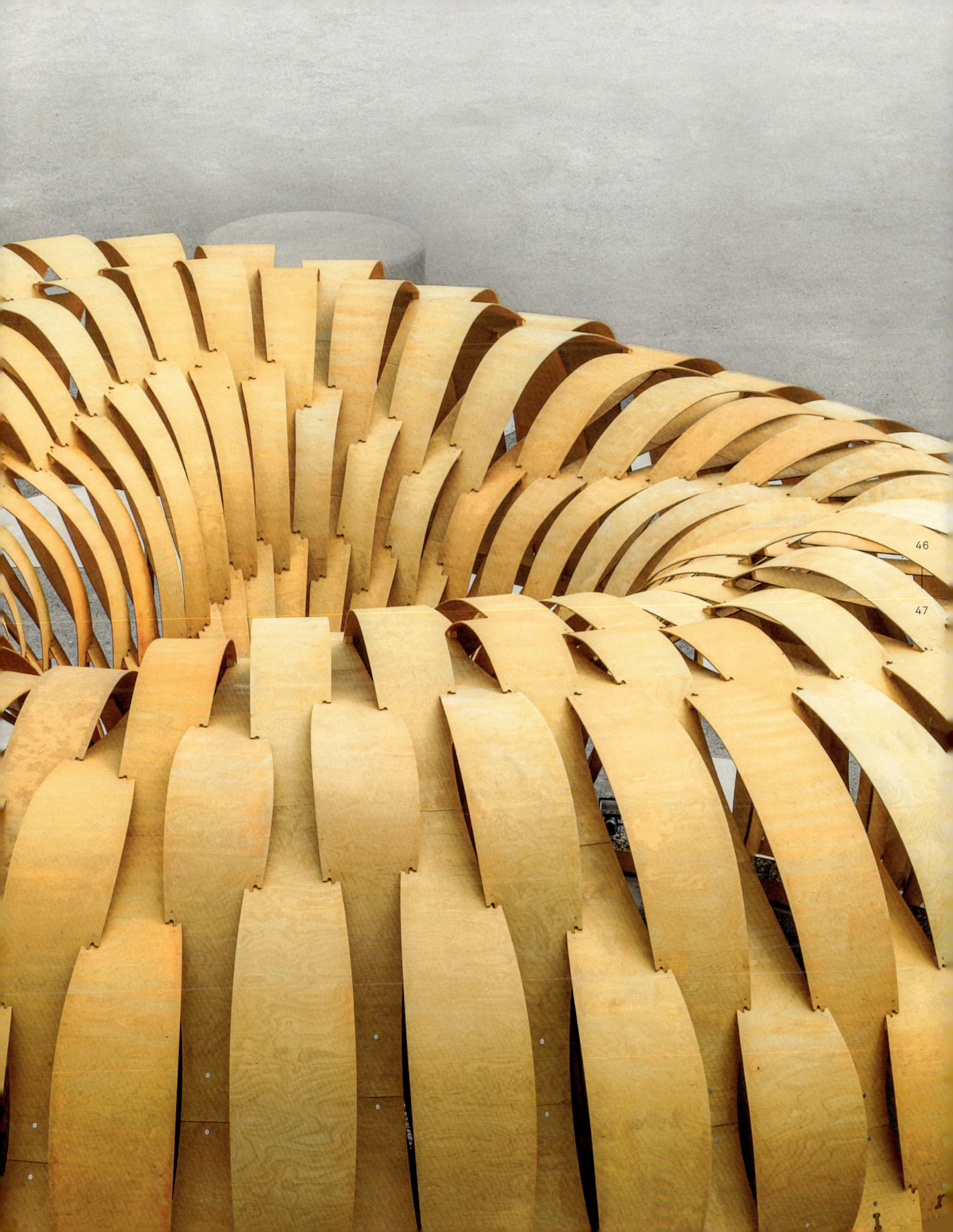

>> ICD/ITKE RESEARCH PAVILION 2010

University of Stuttgart

Points of light dance across the floor. The exterior shimmers through the open mesh of the filigreed wood structure. Passersby are amazed by the unusual object. Soon they will get used to the futuristic structures erected annually by teams of students and researchers from the ICD and ITKE on the campus of the University of Stuttgart, and later at other locations as well.

NOVEL BENDING-ACTIVE STRUCTURE

In the summer of 2010, an elegant pavilion made of curved plywood strips was the prelude to a series of experimental architecture over the following ten years. A characteristic feature of the building was its filigreed lamellar structure, which exploited the possibilities of wood as a construction material by means of computational design, simulation and production processes, thus demonstrating methods of lightweight construction in 2010. Together with students, the researchers used the project to investigate how the numerical simulation of structure and material behavior leads to new architectural and constructive possibilities based on the elastic bending behavior of wood. The result was a light and aesthetically pleasing pavilion structure, creating a spatial atmosphere in the interior like that under large deciduous trees with their characteristic play of shadow and light. The color of the wood and the seemingly irregular interlacing of the strips enhanced this natural character. At night, the pavilion was illuminated from the inside, and the entire structure shone in warm light.

SPACE-CREATING, LOAD-BEARING STRUCTURE MADE OF EXTREMELY THIN AND LIGHT WOODEN STRIPS

The construction principle and aesthetic form-finding are mutually dependent and based on the behavior of the bending-active load-bearing structure. The wooden strips were coupled in such a way as to achieve a division into segments subject to tensile and bending stress whereby each tensile segment elastically holds the adjacent bending segment in form. By bending the birch plywood strips, 10 m long but very thin (6.5 mm), the self-stabilizing construction is put under internal stress. A stable equilibrium system is created, which

1, 2] The Research Pavilion 2010 was ICD and ITKE's first experimental building on the University of Stuttgart campus.

3] Simulation model: One strip alone would be much too thin for the span of 3.5 m. The system only becomes load-bearing when braced together.

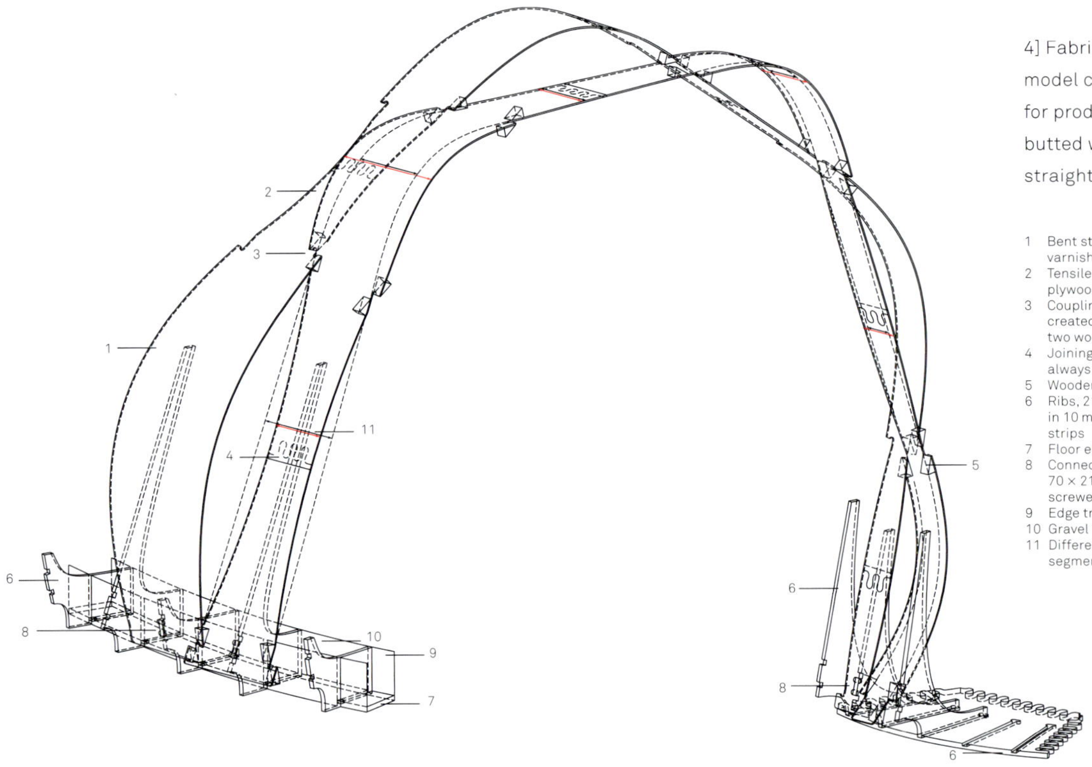

4] Fabrication model: The geometric model contains all the data needed for production. The lamellas were butted with glued tenons in the straight tensile-stressed sections.

1 Bent strip segment, 6.5 mm birch plywood, varnished
2 Tensile-stressed strip segment, 6.5 mm birch plywood, varnished
3 Coupling detail, hooked edges in the strips were created with the cut and connected rigidly by two wooden wedges.
4 Joining detail, semirecessed tenon joint; joining always on tensile-stressed strip segments
5 Wooden wedge, spruce, varnished
6 Ribs, 21 mm birch plywood, varnished, recessed in 10 mm groove, 6.5 mm spigot for fixing the strips
7 Floor element, 21 mm birch plywood, varnished
8 Connection detail, strip was placed with 70 × 21 mm recess exactly on the frame and screwed down
9 Edge trim, 4 mm birch plywood, varnished
10 Gravel filling
11 Different parameters for the shaping of the segments

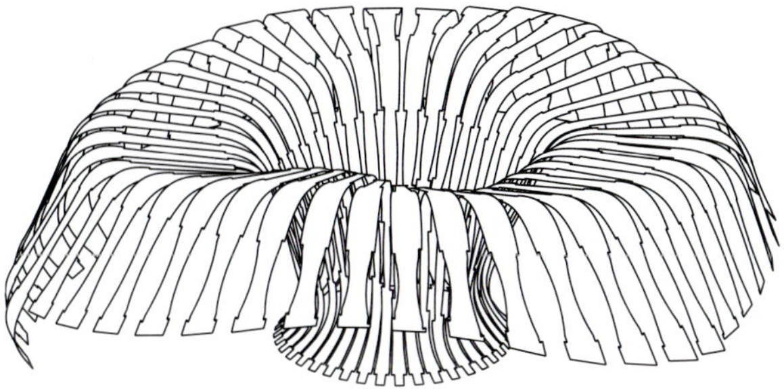

5] Pairs of strips:
Part 1 (top) and Part 2 (bottom)

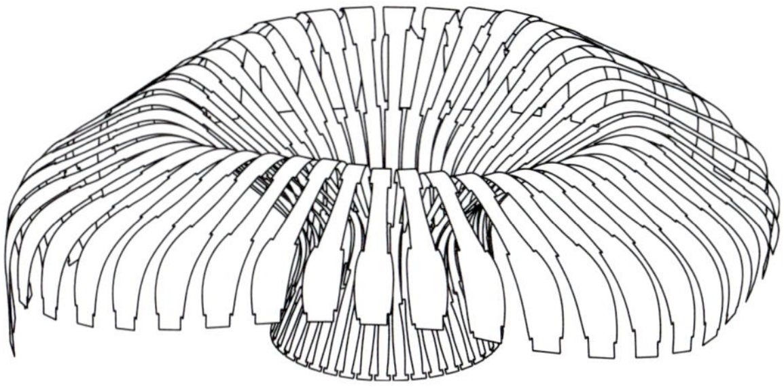

ICD/ITKE RESEARCH PAVILION 2010

University of Stuttgart, Campus City Center
Realization: Design studio with students, scientists and researchers

PROJECT INFORMATION

Completion: June 2010
Floor area: 70 m^2
Volume: 20 m^3

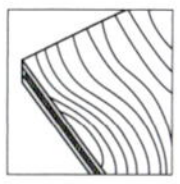

MATERIAL
Veneered birch plywood

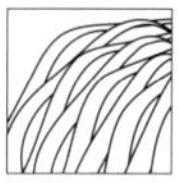

CONSTRUCTION
Radially arranged 7-joint arch construction made of bending-active lamellae

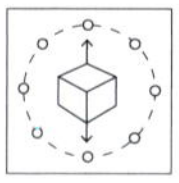

DESIGN
Global form-finding by local interaction of bending-active components

FABRICATION
Robotic 3-axis milling

→ **PROJECT PARTICIPANTS**
—— 206

→ **REFERENCES**
[59], [60], [61], [62], [63]:
—— 225

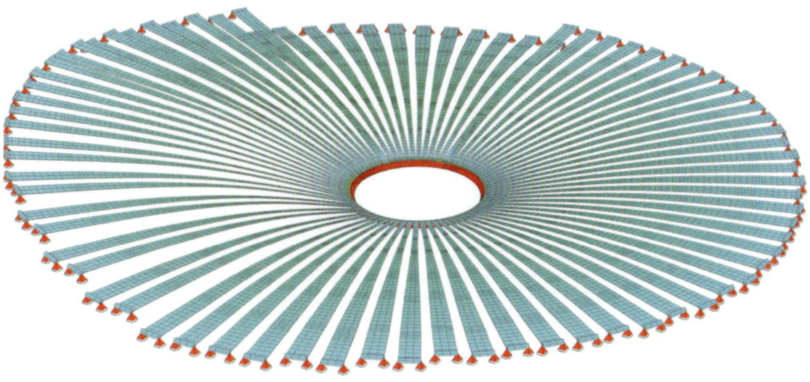

6] Form-finding: The design model was transferred to the structural model. The exact geometry of the pavilion resulted from the simulation of the bending process.

turns the soft strip segments into a stable load-bearing structure. In total, the pavilion consisted of 80 interconnected wooden strips and formed a torus with an outer diameter of 10 m and a span of 3.5 m. To generate the necessary length of the wooden strips, they were joined at the tensile-stressed strip segments with semirecessed tenon joints. Birch plywood strips subject to tensile and bending loads were connected to each other by means of cut-in hooks at their edges and fastened to each cut by two wooden wedges. This required 40 differently shaped spruce wedges. With additional elements such as frames, connecting details, edge cladding, and pegs that anchored the strips in the floor element, a total of more than 500 geometrically different parts had to be produced.

ROBOTIC FABRICATION BASED ON A COMPUTATIONAL MODEL

The parametric simulation under all of the given geometric and physical conditions allowed the exact bending and load-bearing behavior of the coupled strips to be calculated. This model enabled the geometric shape to take into account the bending stresses, and additionally was used to dimension the structure under wind loads. The data and results obtained from the information model and simulation were translated directly into the machine code of the digital fabrication system, and so the large number of individual parts could be manufactured with a perfect fit in the robotic production facility at the University of Stuttgart. The students then assembled the pavilion on the university campus.

7, 8] Structure and detail of the bending-active timber construction: The flat strips took on the pre-calculated shape by themselves during the joining process.

9] Exterior view: The irregular distribution of the connection points was generated in such a way that a stable overall system was created despite local weak spots.

11] Detail: The entire bending-active system, which was both load-bearing structure and skin, consisted of only 6.5 mm-thick wooden strips.

12] View: At night the construction's lightness became particularly apparent.

10] Top view: The complete structure of the pavilion was illuminated from the inside.

>> ICD/ITKE RESEARCH PAVILION 2011

University of Stuttgart

In the case of the wooden pavilion realized in summer 2011, the primary question was how a load-adapted and freely formed shell structure with edges and openings could be produced from prefabricated segments. For the first time, a model in nature was searched for and successfully found in the sea urchin. Both the arrangement of the plates and the principle of their joining were transferred to segmented wood construction. From August to December 2011, the temporary research pavilion served as an architectural object of interest, a space for investigation and experience in the open area between the university buildings KI and KII on the Campus City Center of the University of Stuttgart.

More than 850 individual parts were joined together to create an unusual form with two different spatial situations. The main space of the pavilion consisted of double-layered segments, which made the structure of the individual modules visible through openings in the inner layer. In an adjoining, smaller side space, the inner layer of the shell modules was completely detached, so that the constructive logic of the double-layer structure was revealed and could be experienced. After the exhibition phase on the university campus, the pavilion was dismantled and rebuilt at a new location on the premises of the Ochs company, which provided significant support for the research project.

FROM BIOLOGICAL MORPHOLOGY TO ARCHITECTURAL CONSTRUCTION

The objective of the experimental building was to incorporate the performance of biological structures into an architectural design and develop a corresponding structural and spatial material system. During the investigation of suitable biological structures, the morphology of the sea urchin (*Echinoidea*) was chosen to provide the basic principles for the biomimetic building system. The shell of the sea urchin has a modular structure of polygonal plates linked together at the edges by fingerlike calcite protrusions. The seams with these finger-joint-like connections enable the individual segments to grow without affecting the stability of the overall shell. The special geometric arrangement, in which three joints meet at one point, results in a very stable shell.

1, 2] The ICD/ITKE Research Pavilion 2011 explored the transfer of biological structure-forming principles into architecture.

This morphology of the plate skeleton was transferred to prefabricated wooden segmented shells with traditional finger joints, which allowed a form-fit connection, and implemented to the design of the pavilion. The principle is based on the fact that three plate segments always meet at just one point, enabling the overall shell structure to bear bending. The joints themselves, however, can withstand only limited bending, though they can withstand normal and shear forces. In addition to the joining and ordering system, further fundamental properties of biological structures led to the application of the principle of heterogeneity. This means that the segment sizes are not uniform, but adapt to local curvatures and discontinuities. The central segments in areas of low curvature have dimensions of more than 2 m, while some of the edge segments are only 0.5 m in size. The sea urchin segments still have the ability to take on different growth directions. This principle was also transferred to the pavilion. The segments stretch and orient themselves based on the mechanical stresses. In addition, the biological principle of hierarchy finds a correspondence. The structure of the pavilion has a two-level hierarchical structure. On the first level,

3] Biological model: Sea urchin shell

4] Seven-axis robotic fabrication unit: Digital fabrication enabled the transfer of traditional joining technology to complex geometries.

5, 6] Plate segment (left) and structure (right): The individual segments were simply stacked on top of each other and secured in position with a few bolts. In this way, non-destructive dismantling was possible later. Due to the special arrangement of the elements, a rigid shell structure was nevertheless possible.

ICD/ITKE RESEARCH PAVILION 2011
University of Stuttgart, Campus City Center
Realization: Design studio with students, scientists and researchers

PROJECT INFORMATION
Completion: June 2011
Floor area: 72 m²
Volume: 200 m³

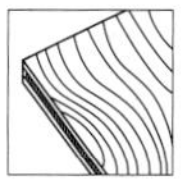

MATERIAL
Veneered birch plywood

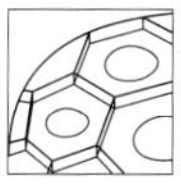

CONSTRUCTION
Segment shell from polygonal hollow cassette segments

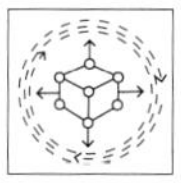

DESIGN
Dynamic equilibrium modeling with multicriteria form steering

FABRICATION
Robotic 7-axis milling and drilling

BIOLOGICAL ROLE MODEL
Plate skeleton of the sand dollar

→ **PROJECT PARTICIPANTS**
—— 207

→ **REFERENCES**
[64], [65], [66], [67], [68], [69]:
—— 225

the panels were joined into segments with a glued but flexible finger joint. On the second hierarchical level, a simple, flexible bolted connection between the segments sufficed, enabling the pavilion to be assembled and dismantled several times. On both hierarchical levels, three plates or segments meet at one point, which allows for flexible connections on both levels.

In contrast to classic lightweight construction methods, which can only be applied to load-optimized shapes, the new design principle can be applied to a wide range of structural geometry. The high lightweight construction potential of this approach is demonstrated by the fact that, despite its considerable dimensions, the pavilion could only be constructed from 6.5 mm-thick plywood panels and therefore had to be primarily secured against lifting due to wind suction.

INTEGRATIVE DIGITAL DESIGN AND MANUFACTURING

A prerequisite for the design, planning and implementation of the complex morphology of the pavilion was a closed digital chain, from the design model to finite element simulations and machine control.

The production of the plates and finger joints was carried out using a seven-axis robotic fabrication system. On the basis of the computer-generated geometric model, the generation of the machine control code (NC code) could be automated, which enabled economical production of the more than 850 geometrically different components and the more than 100,000 joints arranged freely in space. Following the robotic production, the plywood panels were assembled into segments at the finger joints, primed, and stained. The individual segments were bolted together in a detachable flexible joint butt, enabling the pavilion to be erected and dismantled several times.

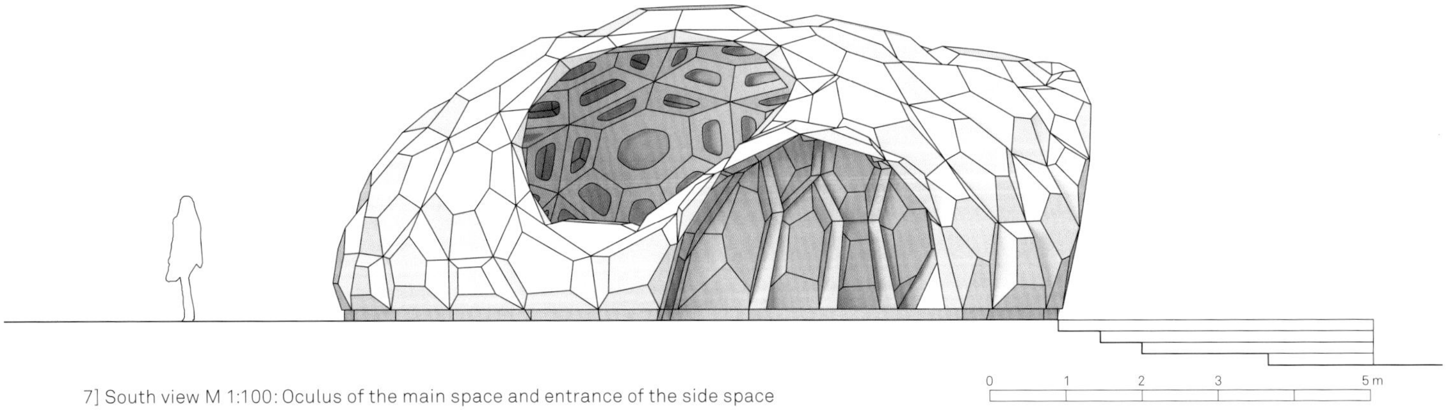

7] South view M 1:100: Oculus of the main space and entrance of the side space

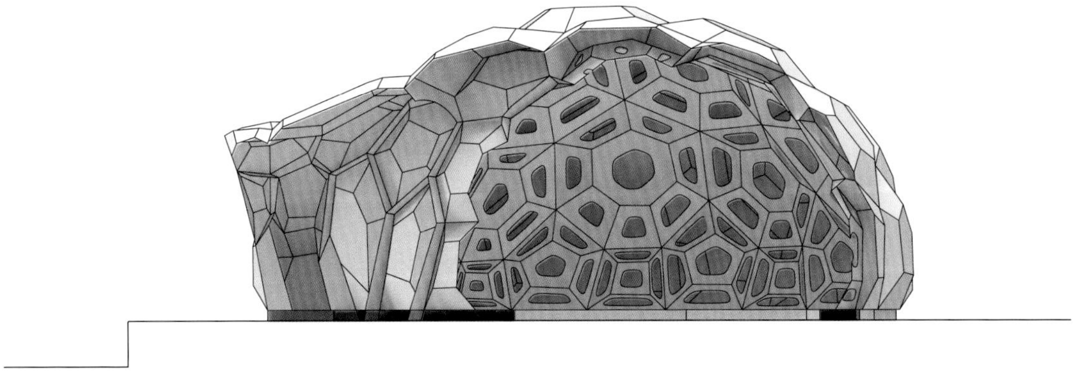

8] Section M 1:100: The constructional logic became architecturally tangible through the transition of a two-layered structure in the main space and its dissolution in the adjacent space.

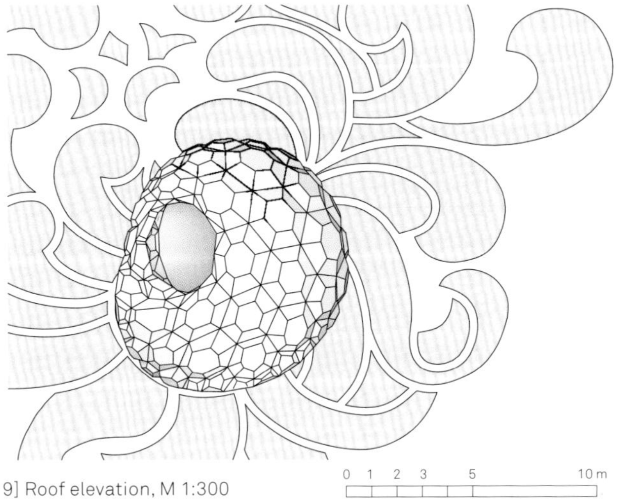

9] Roof elevation, M 1:300

10] The larger interior space was spanned by two-layered backlit cassettes, which dissolved into visible individual layers in the smaller adjacent space.

11] Exterior view at night

12, 13, 14] The pavilion consists of 850 geometrically different components and more than 100,000 freely arranged finger joints.

POSITION: **THOMAS SPECK** ON

ARCHITECTURE AND BIOMIMETICS

Approaches using bio-inspiration for a novel eco-friendly, livable and attractive architecture have won increasing interest over the last decades as much from architects and civil engineers as from material scientists and biomimetics researchers.

Biological structures and materials are interesting and very suitable role models for building construction and architecture for multiple reasons. They are typically multilayered, hierarchically structured, finely tuned and highly differentiated based on the combination of a few basic molecular components.[28]

This leads to materials and structures that are characterized by multiple networked functions and (often) possess excellent mechanical properties, a pronounced adaptability to changing environmental conditions and manyfold self-x-properties (e. g. self-cleaning, self-repair). Biomimetics has a high innovation potential and offers the possibility for the development of sustainable products and production chains. The huge number of organisms with the specific structures and functions they have developed during 3.8 billion years of biological evolution in adaptation to differing environments represents a treasure trove that is the basis for all biomimetic projects. Novel sophisticated methods for quantitatively analyzing and simulating the form-structure-function relationship on various hierarchical levels reveal new fascinating insights in multiscale mechanics and other functions of biological materials and surfaces. Additionally, recent developments in computational design and simulation together with new production methods enable for the first time the transfer of many outstanding properties of the biological role models into innovative biomimetic products at reasonable cost, which is of special importance for applications in architecture and building construction.[30, 47]

Compared to other research fields in biomimetics, architecture and building construction have a special status. They take advantage not only of specific developments in architectural biomimetics but additionally may, and increasingly do, incorporate results from other fields of biomimetics research, including lightweight constructions and materials, surfaces and interfaces, optimization, and sensor- and energy-biomimetics. An additional unique feature of biomimetic architecture is the fact that (biomimetic) buildings are typically one of a kind. This allows for testing of biomimetic developments on the prototype level under permanent use of the inhabitants. All this has resulted in making biomimetic architecture an increasingly important and innovative field. Nevertheless, bio-inspired approaches in architecture are still sparsely used, and architects, civil engineers, tenants and homeowners are still not fully aware of of the real potential of these approaches.

Very visible and successful exceptions are the biomimetic pavilions and bio-inspired facade-shading systems developed and built by the ITKE and ICD of the University of Stuttgart in collaboration with colleagues from the Universities of Freiburg and Tübingen and the DITF Denkendorf.[30,47-50] They very successfully include and combine two basic and desirable aspects of bio-inspired architecture: (1) the transfer of structurally based robust functions from biological role models, and (2) their aesthetic value and beauty. The former can be seen in the "hard approach" to bio-inspired architecture and building construction. Here the quantitative analysis of the form-structure-function relationships of a biological role model provides the basis for the transfer into novel biomimetic materials and structures with clearly defined, specifically desired, robust and resilient (multi-)functionalities. In this approach the loss of (some) of the aesthetic value existing in the biological role model is inevitable or at least has to be accepted. The latter can be described as a "soft approach" to bio-inspired architecture and building construction in which the aesthetics and beauty of the biological role model are the (main) inspiration for bio-inspired architecture.[51,52]

The biomimetic pavilions developed and built by the ITKE and ICD over the last decade not only possess the physical functionality transferred from the biological concept generators but also show a structural beauty and functional elegance similar to the highly aesthetic biological role models.

These still rare cases represent the silver bullet in bio-inspired architecture and are considered ideal solutions combining bio-inspired reliable functionality with the intrinsic beauty of the biological role models, a combination that makes bio-inspired architecture especially attractive.

THOMAS SPECK
Prof. Dr. / Plant Biomechanics Group, Botanic Garden, Faculty of Biology, University of Freiburg, Germany / Cluster of Excellence Living, Adaptive and Energy-autonomous Materials Systems (livMatS) @ FIT – Freiburg Center for Interactive Materials and Bioinspired Technologies / Freiburg, Deutschland —— 223

⟶
[28], [30], [46], [47], [48], [49], [50], [51], [52]:
—— 225

>> ICD/ITKE RESEARCH PAVILION 2012

University of Stuttgart

The investigation and abstraction of the biomimetic principle of the lobster and the subsequent technical implementation in a robotically manufactured glass and carbon fiber composite system made possible a completely new and performative load-bearing structure and tectonics in architecture. In November 2012, the first biomimetic experimental building of ICD and ITKE made of a fiber composite material was implemented with students and researchers.

The focus of the design was to transfer the fiber structure of the biological model – the outer skeleton of arthropods – to fiber-reinforced plastics in order to derive new tectonic possibilities for architecture. And this seems to have been successful: when the pavilion was opened in Stuttgart, people talked about a new construction language in which structure and form are no longer separable. Also, as the design was no longer determined by the properties of previously known materials, it signaled a possible paradigm shift in the construction industry. Instead, the desired formal and structural properties would lead to the development of a corresponding fabrication process.

The starting point for the ICD/ITKE Research Pavilion 2012 was the investigation of a fabrication method adapted to the requirements of the construction industry, namely the robotic winding of carbon or glass fibers on a rotating steel frame, as well as the associated computational design and simulation processes. Based on biological structural characteristics, a high-performance structure with a shell thickness of only 4 mm of composite laminate and a span of 8 m could be achieved.

LOBSTER EXOSKELETON WITH LOCALLY ADAPTED FIBER ORIENTATION AS A MODEL

The functional morphology of arthropods was investigated in a wide range of different subspecies of invertebrates. The exoskeleton of the lobster (*Homarus americanus*) was analyzed in detail due to its local material differentiation and served as a biological model for the derivation of biomimetic principles for the application of highly anisotropic materials. Its exoskeleton (the cuticle) consists of a soft part, the endocuticle, and a relatively hard part, the exocuticle. The cuticle is a secretion product in which chitin fibers are embedded in a

1, 2] The ICD/ITKE Research Pavilion 2012 was based on the development of a production method of robotic winding of carbon or glass fibers, highly innovative for the construction industry.

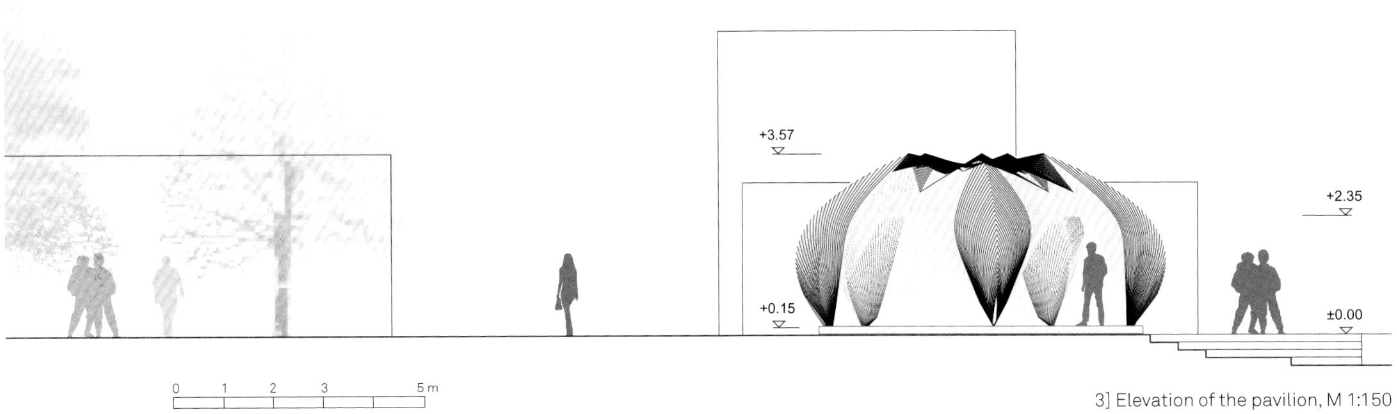

3] Elevation of the pavilion, M 1:150

protein matrix. The position and orientation of the fibers are decisive for the differentiation of the material properties in response to the respective requirements. The chitin fibers are incorporated in the matrix by forming unidirectional individual layers. However, in the areas where a non-directional load transfer is required, such individual layers are laminated together in a helicoidal arrangement. The resulting isotropic fiber structure allows a uniform load distribution in every direction. On the other hand, areas that are subject to directional stress distributions exhibit an unidirectional layer structure. This anisotropic fiber arrangement is optimized for the respective loading situation. Due to this local material differentiation, the shell creates a load-adapted and high-performance structure. The abstracted morphological principles of locally adapted fiber orientation constituted the basis for the computational form generation, structural design and fabrication process of the pavilion.

LAYER STRUCTURE ACCORDING TO THE FORCE FLOW

The principles of fiber orientation, fiber structure, and the resulting layer thicknesses and stiffness gradients of the exoskeleton of the lobster were transferred to the design of a shell structure made of a robotically fabricated fiber composite system. A robot places glass and carbon fibers impregnated in resin on a rotating steel frame, creating a layered structure. In existing fiber lay-up processes in other industries, the fibers are usually applied on a separately manufactured mold. However, mold making is costly and often uses many environ-

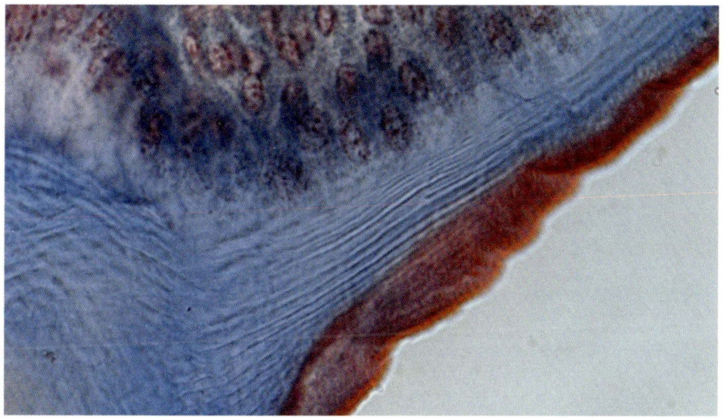

4] Microscopic section: Layered structure of the exoskeleton of the lobster with the endocuticula (blue) and the hard exocuticula (red)

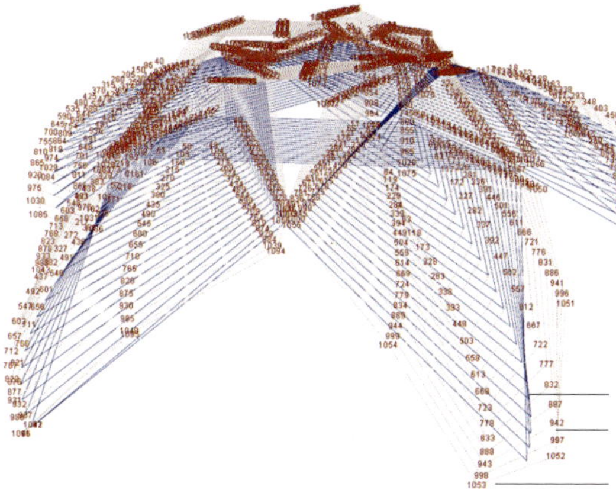

5] Integrative design and fabrication model: The position of the anchor points determines the shell geometry resulting from the winding process.

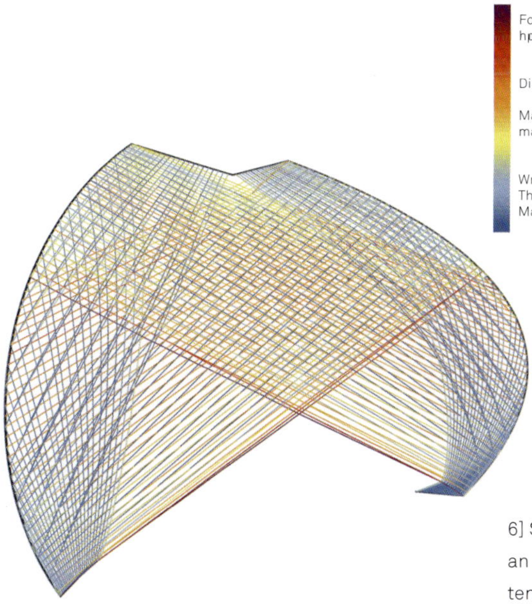

6] Simulation model: During winding, an anticlastic surface with differently tensioned fiber strands is created.

ICD/ITKE RESEARCH PAVILION 2012

University of Stuttgart, Campus City Center

Realization: Design studio with students, scientists and researchers

PROJECT INFORMATION

Completion: November 2012

Floor area: 29 m²

Volume: 78 m³

Construction weight: 5.6 kg/m²

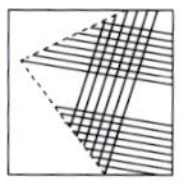

MATERIAL

Carbon fiber rovings and glass fiber rovings with epoxy resin

CONSTRUCTION

Monocoque shell made of fiber composite lattice

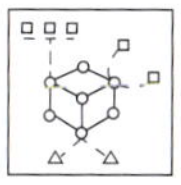

DESIGN

Parametric modeling in feedback with local and global material simulation

FABRICATION

Coreless robotic 7-axis winding, robot-guided fiber winding head, rotating winding frame

BIOLOGICAL ROLE MODEL

Exoskeleton of the lobster

→ **PROJECT PARTICIPANTS**

—— 208

→ **REFERENCES**

[70], [71], [72], [73], [74], [75], [76]:
—— 226

mentally problematic resources. Such manufacturing processes are therefore particularly suitable for larger series. In the construction industry, however, it is usually a question of unique elements, which is why a different fabrication process has been developed to minimize the effort required for mold construction. The fibers were deposited on a lightweight steel frame with defined anchor points, so that they were freely tensioned between these depositing points. From the straight segments of the prestressed fibers, anticlastic surfaces emerged that resulted in the characteristic double-curved shape of the research pavilion. On these hyperbolically parabolic surfaces, initially wound from glass fibers, the structurally effective carbon fibers were laid in subsequent windings. The pavilion thus created its own positive mold during the robotic production. In the robotic winding process, the fibers could finally be placed in such a way that they adapted to the flow of force. The simultaneous development of geometry and fiber structure enabled the form and materiality to be directly and simultaneously integrated into the design. Layer optimization made it possible to develop a highly efficient material buildup with minimal material usage.

ROBOTIC WINDING PROCESS FOR NOVEL FIBER COMPOSITE STRUCTURES

The robotic fabrication of the experimental building took place directly on the construction site in a specially built weatherproof production environment. A six-axis industrial robot was used, coupled with an external seventh axis. The robot was placed on a 2 m-high platform to extend the reach and working height to 4 m respectively. Equipped in this way, the six-axis robot laid the fibers on the temporary steel frame, which was driven in a circular motion by the seventh axis. The fibers were applied in a wet, resin-soaked state.

This setup made it possible to wind a structure of almost 8 m in diameter and 3.5 m in height with a fiber length of more than 60 km. The generation of the winding paths based on the computational geometry model, the robotic motion planning including mathematical coupling of external axis and robot, and the control of the robot itself could be implemented in a specially developed digital design and fabrication process. After completion of the robotic filament winding process and the subsequent tempering of the fiber-resin composite, the temporary steel frame was removed. The remaining thin shell of only 4 mm thickness forms a fully automatically fabricated, but locally differentiated structure. The semitransparent pavilion, which allows the structural logic to be tangible in a new way due to the spatial arrangement of carbon and glass fibers, weighs less than 320 kg despite its considerable size.

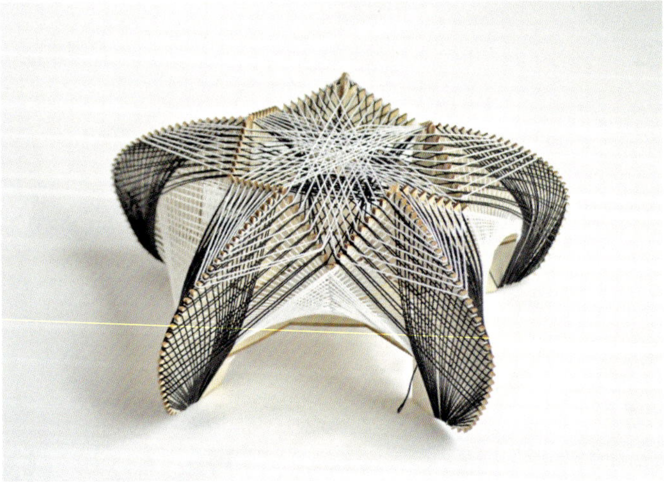

7] Working model: Physical models play an important role in the development and evaluation of geometry and winding syntax.

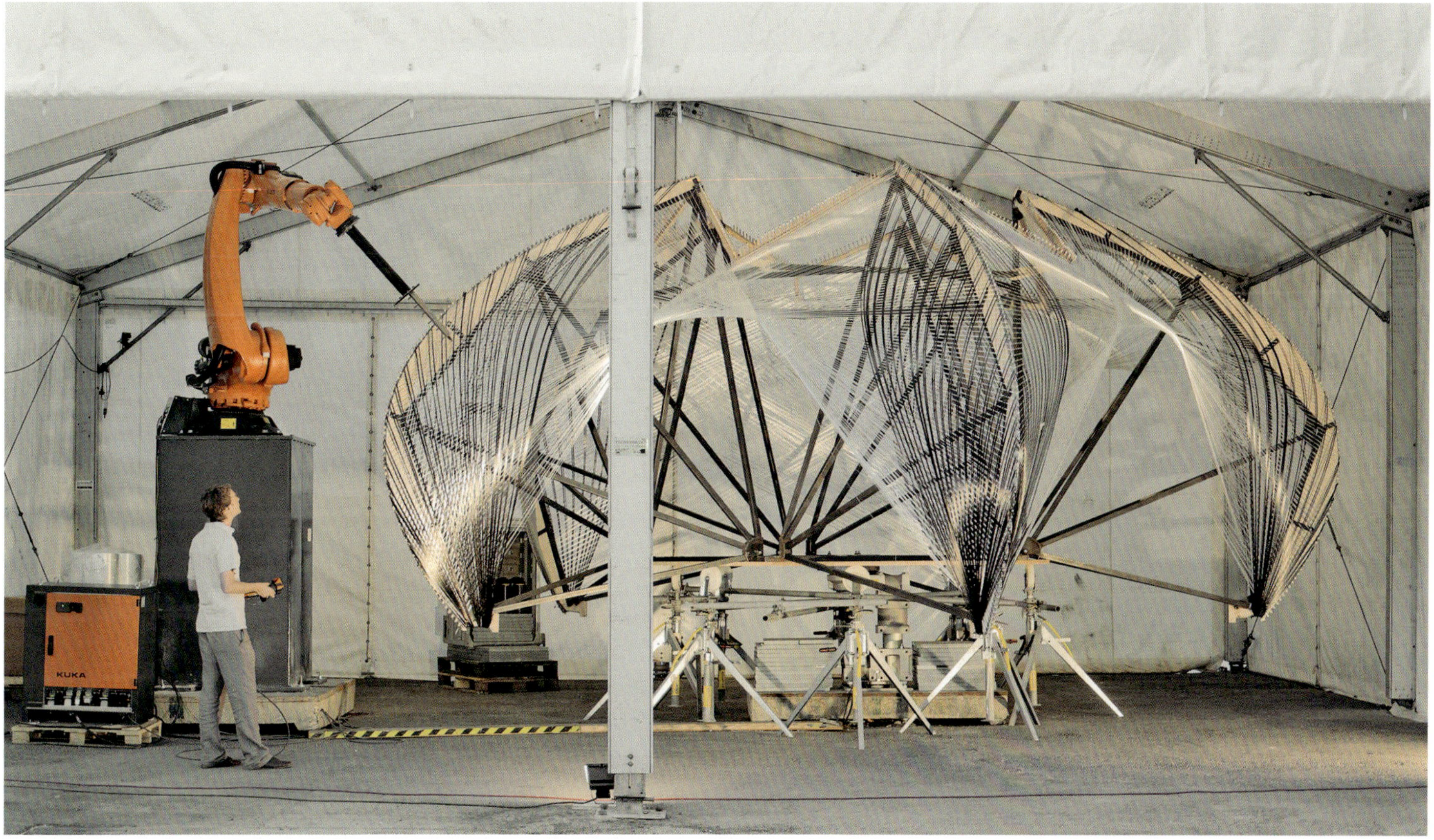

8] Fabrication setup and winding process: A robot applies the resin-impregnated fibers to a rotating winding frame, which is removed after curing.

9] Detailed view: The characteristic surface structure of the glass and carbon fiber structure results from the innovative fabrication process.

11, 12] Exterior view (top): In the robotic winding process, the shape of the pavilion emerges as the state of equilibrium between the transparent glass fibers and the black carbon fibers.
Interior view (right): This winding process leads to a new architectural expression of fiber composite constructions.

10] Top view: More than 60 km of fiber strands were robotically wound forming a thin, yet stable shell, just 4 mm thick.

>> ICD/ITKE RESEARCH PAVILION 2013/14

University of Stuttgart

The advantage is obvious: double-layered shell modules offer structural performance and enable a large number of geometric variations. To this end, the design principles of natural lightweight structures were investigated and abstracted in cooperation with the Institute of Evolution and Ecology and the Paleobiology Research Unit of the University of Tübingen.

STRUCTURE OF BEETLE WINGS AS A MODEL

The wing shells (*elytra*) of airworthy beetles proved to be a suitable model for material-efficient construction methods. The elytra are especially strong to protect the beetle's wings and abdomen, but at the same time designed to save material and weight to maintain flight capability. The performance of this natural double-shell construction is based, on the one hand, on the complex geometric shape of its load-bearing structure, and, on the other, on the specific arrangement and orientation of the natural composite material, consisting of chitin fibers embedded in a protein matrix. The variation of the fiber arrangement allows for locally adapted mechanical properties. Using microcomputer tomography, high-resolution, three-dimensional models of the beetle elytra were created and used to examine the intricate internal structures of beetle shells. The elytra morphology is based on a double-layered structure whose upper and lower shells are connected by column-like support elements with a double-curved geometry, the so-called trabeculae. Within the trabecula, the fibers of the inner and outer shells continuously merge into each other. The distribution and geometric articulation of the trabecula is highly differentiated throughout the elytra shell.

FROM BIOLOGY TO STRUCTURAL LOGIC

The comparative study of several airworthy beetle species made it possible to identify fundamental structural principles and generate abstracted structural-morphological design rules by means of computational design and simulation processes. The development had to take into account both the abstracted biological construction principles of the elytra and the peculiarities of robotic fabrication technology and integrate them into the design process from the very outset. The component

1, 2] The construction of the ICD/ITKE Research Pavilion 2013/14 is based on the double-shell structure of the wing shells of airworthy beetles.

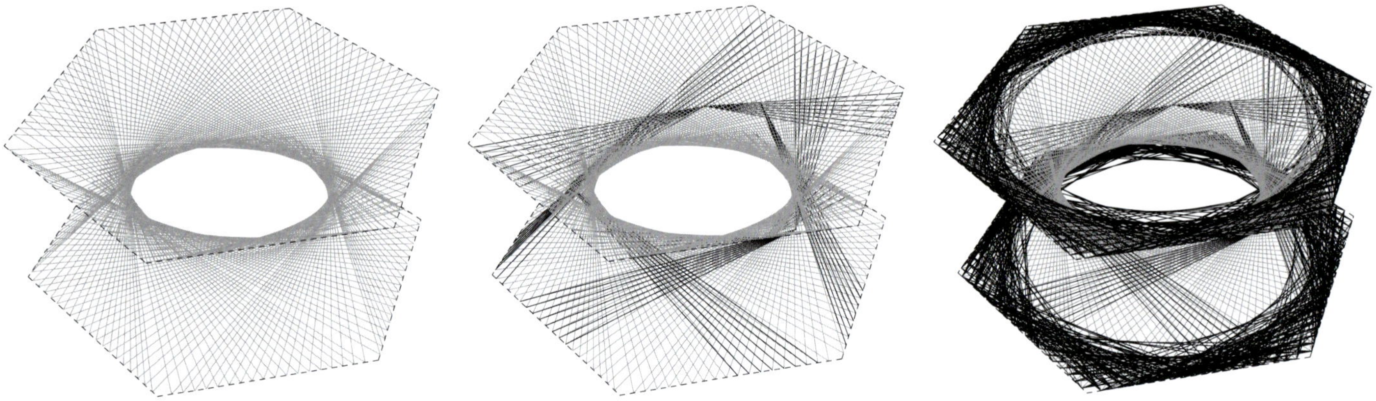

3] Layer structure: First, a hyperbolic body made of glass fibers was wound (left), onto which carbon fibers were then laid (center) and edge reinforcements applied (right).

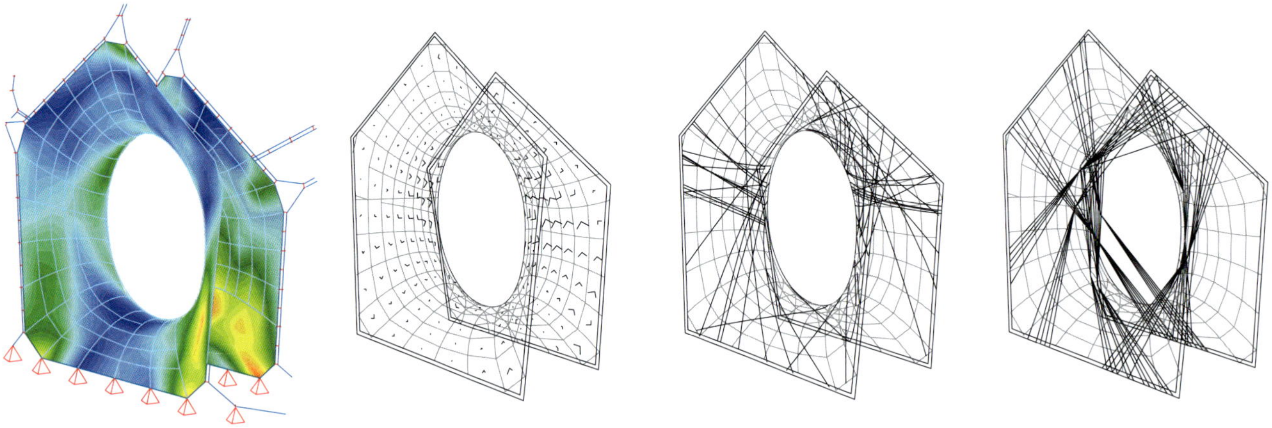

4] Simulation model: For the arrangement of the carbon fibers, the principal stress directions were determined on a shell model (left), which were then gradually converted into a winding syntax (center/right).

5] Airworthy Turtle Beetle (*Cassida viridis*)

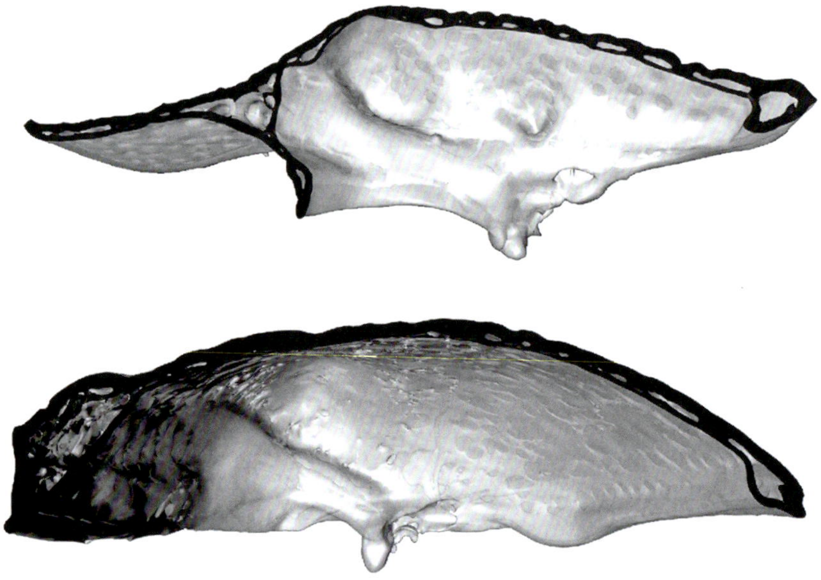

6] Microcomputer tomography: Section through the elytra of the Turtle Beetle *(Cassida)* (top) and the Willow Leaf Beetle *(Chrysomela vigintipunctata)* (bottom).

geometry of the modular experimental setup was based on the differentiation of the trabecular morphology and its fiber arrangement.

ROBOTIC WINDING PROCESS FOR DOUBLE SHELL ELEMENTS

In contrast to conventional fabrication processes where each element shape requires an individual mold, a new approach was developed that could react to complex and individually varying geometries without the great effort implied by mold construction. By means of a coreless robotic winding process, the fibers were wound onto frames (effectors) guided by two collaborating six-axis industrial robots. A fiber bobbin positioned stationary between the robots wound the anticlastic bodies, which could be removed from the frame after the resin had cured. The actual component geometry – from the two-dimensional frame to the third dimension between the frames – emerges through the interaction of the fibers laid in midair. The slender frames of the effectors can be freely adapted to the required geometries of the modules. The frames are reusable and reconfigurable after each winding process. This coreless winding process represents a material-

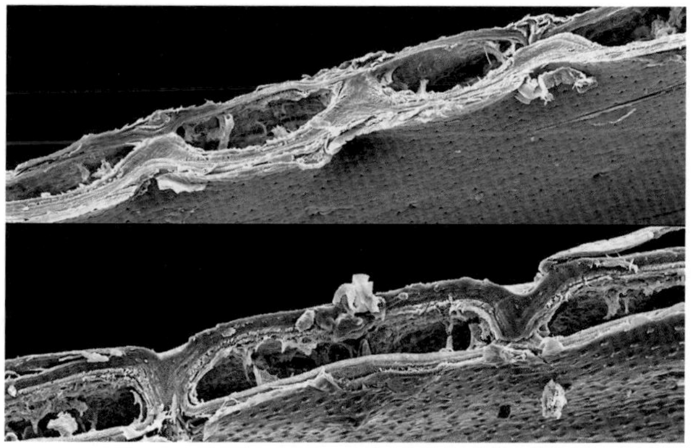

7] Scanning electron microscope image: The section through the cover wing of the Potato Beetle *(Leptinotarsa decimlineata)* shows the double-shell structure of this natural fiber composite construction.

ICD/ITKE RESEARCH PAVILION 2013/14
University of Stuttgart, Campus City Center
Realization: Design studio with students, scientists and researchers

PROJECT INFORMATION
Completion: March 2014
Floor area: 50 m²
Volume: 122 m³

MATERIAL
Carbon fiber rovings and glass fiber rovings with epoxy resin

CONSTRUCTION
Segmented shell made of polygonal fiber composite lattice segments

DESIGN
Dynamic equilibrium modeling with multicriteria form steering

FABRICATION
Coreless robotic 12-axis winding, stationary fiber winding head, robot-guided winding frames

BIOLOGICAL ROLE MODEL
Forewing of airworthy beetle

→ **PROJECT PARTICIPANTS**
— 209

→ **REFERENCES**
[77], [78], [79], [80]:
— 226

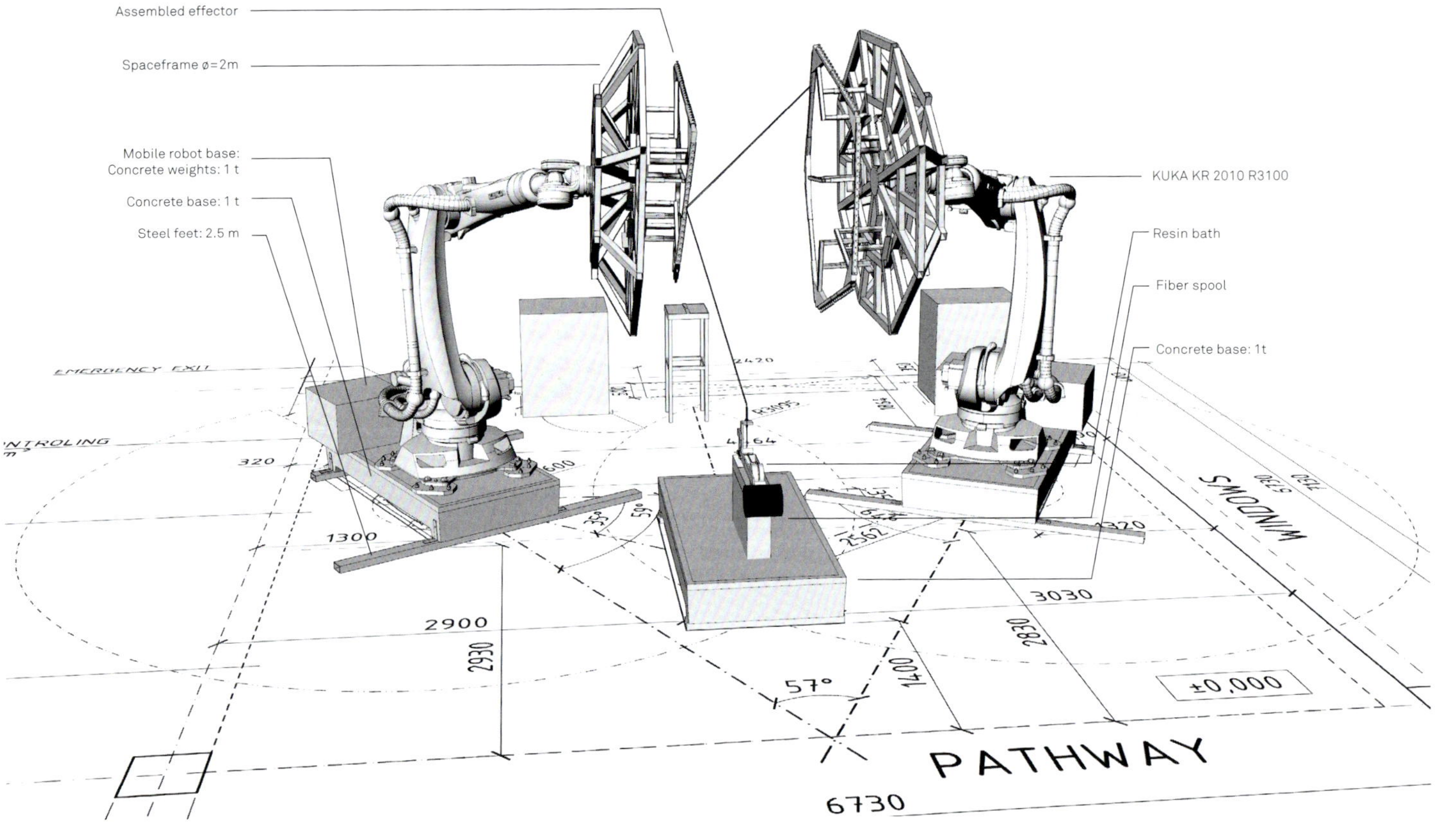

8] Model of fabrication setup: Two collaborating robots with geometrically adjustable winding frames carried out the fabrication. The fiber bobbin was arranged stationarily in between.

9] Fiber composite component: The hexagonal components had external dimensions of up to 2.6 m with a weight of only 24 kg.

10] Fabrication process: The fiber composite components emerged in midair between the winding frames.

11] Construction: The low weight facilitated the assembly of the load-bearing fiber composite components.

efficient and resource-saving manufacturing process due to its material savings and avoidance of offcuts or waste.

INTEGRATIVE FORM GENERATION AND MATERIALIZATION OF THE FIBER COMPOSITE STRUCTURE

The definition of the winding syntax is largely responsible for the link between form generation and materialization because the complex interaction of material, form, structure and production only works if the winding sequence is fully calibrated. For the technical implementation, glass- and carbon-fiber-reinforced epoxy resins were chosen. Due to their anisotropy and moldability, they are able to reproduce the complex geometry and material organization of the natural construction. The glass fibers at first create linearly tensioned lines between the frames, which interact depending on the winding sequence by depositing newly laid fibers onto already wound fibers.

This fiber-to-fiber interaction of the so-called rovings causes a mutual deformation of the fibers lying on top of each other, so that the initially straight deposited fibers combine to form complex curved surfaces. Carbon fiber rovings complement the structure according to the force flow. In this way, six different winding layers were successively applied to produce the final component.

12] Achim Menges and Jan Knippers after successfully completing the pavilion

The experimental building covering an area of 50 m² consisted of 36 different wound modules, which contributed to the material-efficient load transfer through their individual fiber layout. The largest element, with a diameter of 2.6 m, weighed only 24.1 kg. On the one hand, the overall shape of the pavilion reacted to the local conditions of the public square in direct proximity to the city park; on the other, it demonstrated the adaptability of the system, which goes far beyond a simple shell shape.

13] The construction system gave rise to an entirely unfamiliar spatial experience.

POSITION: JENNY SABIN ON

MATERIAL CULTURE

The history of modern computing may be traced back to an uncanny meeting between two simultaneously emerging disparate inventions: the punch cards that mechanized the Jacquard loom through stored memory and Babbage's steam-driven calculator, the Analytical Engine.[53] Credited with being one of the first computer programmers, Ada Lovelace intuited the revolutionary impact that Jacquard's punch cards would bring to Babbage's computer, launching the precursors of modern-day scientific computing. As Lovelace stated, "The Analytical Engine weaves algebraic patterns, just as the Jacquard loom weaves flowers and leaves."[54] Given that important aspects of the origins of computation started with woven material, how is it that it took us more than 100 years to bring matter and computation together through making and fabrication in architecture and design?

Some of the best computational designers that I know are textile designers. Whether they use computing and algorithms to organize design patterns and digital knitting processes or they work by hand and mechanical machine, the integration of parameters pertaining to geometry, pattern, material and computation are inextricably linked. So much so, that body, intuition, machine and algorithm seamlessly come together to organize and design each stitch, link and row as they form part to whole. One could argue that knitting is the first example of 3-D printing material, additively layering row by row. The intricate and boundless computational networks inherent to textile processes offer up a potent material solution to contemporary generative design processes in architecture, which frequently feature organic and natural forms of increasingly complex performance, expression and ornamentation.

In this context, perhaps our best teacher to understand the complexity of material and form, however, is nature. We need not look far to see exquisite biological examples that showcase the linkages between context, material, geometry, structure and form. Architects and structural engineers have historically looked to nature for design inspiration and models for producing and managing complexity in the built environment.

Cable nets have been inspired by the high strength-to-weight ratio of the spider web; pneumatic structures after soap bubbles; vaults after shells and eggs composed of hard and curved materials; and geodesics after radiolarian. The structural designer, Robert Le Ricolais, studied the tension networks inherent to radiolarian in order to understand the dynamic properties and qualities of closed and open "skeletal" structures. Le Ricolais professed that he had "found no better discipline in this unpredictable problem of form than to observe the prodigies created by nature."[55] Although there have been tremendous innovations in design, material sciences, bio- and information technologies, direct interactions and collaborations between scientists and architects are rare. One approach is to couple architectural designers with engineers and biologists within a research-based laboratory-studio in order to develop new ways of thinking, seeing and working in each of our fields.[56] The work of Achim Menges and Jan Knippers and their students at the ICD and ITKE at Stuttgart is at the forefront of pioneering examples of bio-inspired and bionic fibrous material systems that are carefully computed, simulated and materialized through robotic fabrication.

No longer solely privileging column, beam and arch, our definition of architectural tectonics has broadened alongside advancements made in computational design at the intersection of architecture, biology, materials science and engineering. How have these advancements impacted material practice in architecture, engineering and construction at economic, technological and cultural levels? How might we address these issues during the design process? The work of ICD and ITKE such as their ICD/ITKE Research Pavilion 2013/14 showcases possible design routes and techniques that no longer privilege column, beam and arch through a broadened definition of architectural tectonics successfully made with advancements in computational design. Designed, fabricated and constructed over one-and-a-half years by students and researchers within a multidisciplinary team of biologists, paleontologists, architects and engineers, the focus of this project is upon the biomimetic investigation of natural fiber composite shells and the development of cutting-edge robotic fabrication methods for fiber reinforced polymer structures. With an interest in exploring material-efficient, lightweight constructions, the Elytron, a protective shell for beetles' wings and abdomen, proved to be an appropriate bionic model for the generation of innovative fiber composite construction methods through biological structural principles. Overall, these lightweight structures rely upon the geometric morphology of a double-layered system inspired and informed by the Elytron beetle, then redeployed through the mechanical properties of the natural fiber composite.[57]

Importantly, the ICD/ITKE is equally committed to the communication, documentation and public dissemination of their advances in tooling and fabrication to advance the design and production of nonlinear systems via complex geometries. While the exploration of biological and nano-to-micro scaled material properties and effects at the human scale form the starting points for many of the featured projects, the disciplinary hurdles that are encountered through the production of projects across scales culminate in what is perhaps the most potent deliverable: a new model for transdisciplinary collaboration and the formation of new models of thought in the research and practice of architecture and engineering.

Just as Lovelace opened the world of digital space through woven material, the ICD/ITKE projects analogically translate the knowledge acquired by biology into computational design to generate high-performance and frequently sustainable material systems for architectural application. This has led to the development of an in-depth technical understanding of nature's inner workings for the design and fabrication of bio-inspired materials and forms that open new and deeply embedded interpretations of material culture as it relates to computation and digital space.

JENNY SABIN
Wiesenberger Professor and Associate Dean for Design, Department of Architecture, Cornell University / Director, Sabin Design Lab / Principal, Jenny Sabin Studio / Ithaca (NY), USA ___ 222

→
[53], [54], [55], [56], [57]: ___ 225

>> LANDESGARTENSCHAU EXHIBITION HALL

Landesgartenschau Schwäbisch Gmünd, 2014

The Exhibition Hall was an experimental building showcasing innovations in timber construction for the forest administration of Baden-Württemberg (ForstBW) during the Landesgartenschau (State Horticultural show) in Schwäbisch Gmünd in 2014. Since then, the permanent building has been used as an event space by the municipality of Schwäbisch Gmünd. It is thus one of the first ICD/ITKE pavilions to make the leap from research object to applied and permanent architecture.

INNOVATIONS IN RESOURCE-SAVING TIMBER CONSTRUCTION

Wood is one of the oldest building materials known to humankind. The aim of the project was to show how novel methods of digital design in conjunction with robotic fabrication open up completely new application possibilities for this material. The use of regionally available beech wood is not only in line with future forestry strategies in Central Europe, but also suitable for resource-saving lightweight wood construction due to its excellent mechanical properties. Funded by the EU and the state of Baden-Württemberg as part of the Robotics in Timber Construction research project, this is the very first building whose primary structure consists completely of robotically fabricated beech plywood plates. With a surface envelope of 245 m^2 and dimensions of approximately 17 x 11 x 6 m, the Exhibition Hall offers a floor space of approximately 125 m^2 and a gross volume of 605 m^3. The 50 mm-thin load-bearing structure made of beech plywood required only 12 m^3 of wood. The wood resources deployed were used almost entirely as the waste from the plate production was further processed into beech parquet flooring.

The interior of the Exhibition Hall is divided into two spatial zones: the foyer space and the main exhibition space. In both zones the plate structure is dome-shaped, consisting of convex polygonal plates. In between is a saddle-shaped spatial contraction of concave polygonal plates. Visitors enter the building through the lower part and are then guided through the slight narrowing of the structure to the 6 m-high main space with its large glass facade opening toward the surrounding landscape. The interior is particularly characterized by the pattern of the visible and largely untreated load-bearing

1, 2] The Landesgartschau Exhibition Hall is the first wooden shell structure that was manufactured entirely by robot.

beech wood structure with its visible finger joint connections. The geometrically determined transition from convex to concave polygonal plates further emphasizes the spatial arrangement. The construction principles, in keeping with the biological model – the plate skeleton of the sand dollar, a subspecies of the sea urchin – were derived from the differentiation of the plate form and finger joint connections. They remain visible and tangible in the interior.

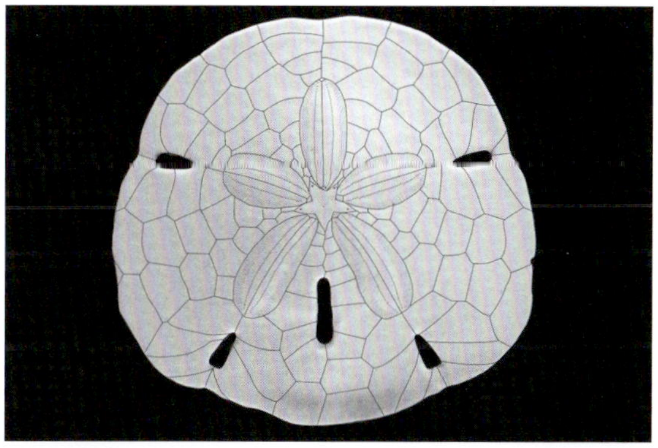

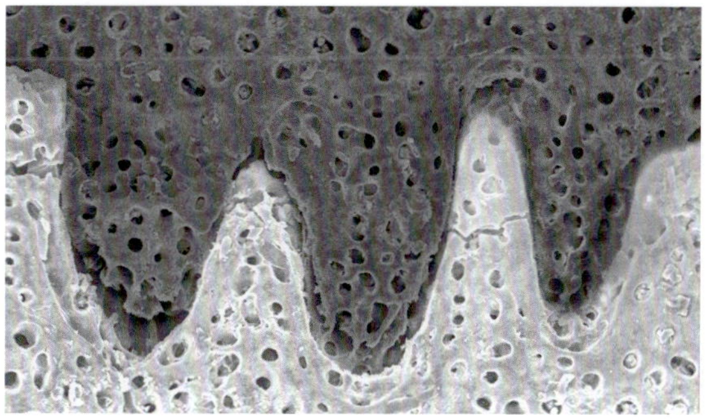

3, 4] Biological model: The outer skeleton of the sand dollar consists of interlocked individual plates (top). These are interlocked with each other at the edges of the plates, so that individual growth is possible and at the same time the stability of the whole construction is guaranteed (bottom).

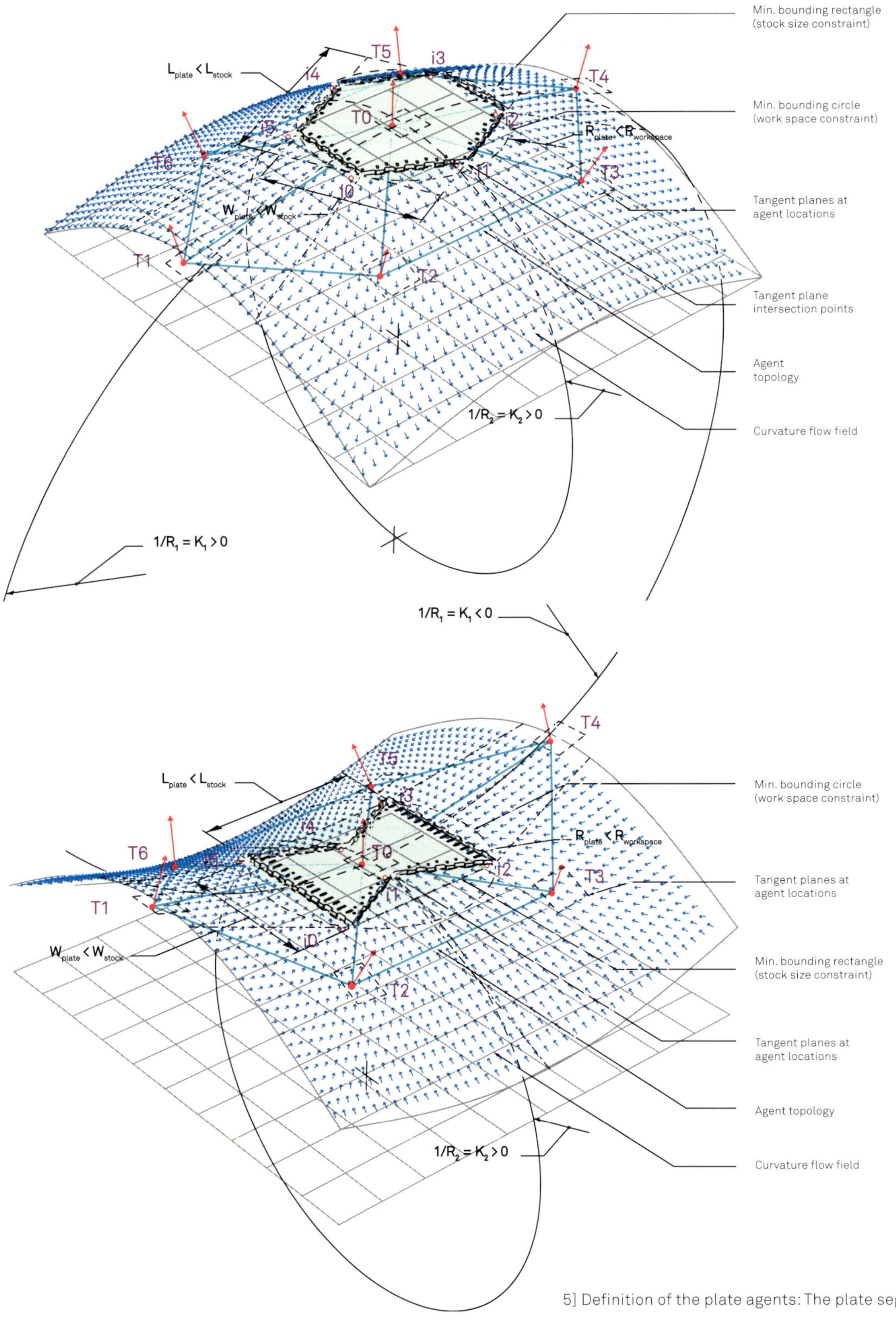

5] Definition of the plate agents: The plate segments form different geometries depending on their position in the overall system and the curvature of the shell surface.

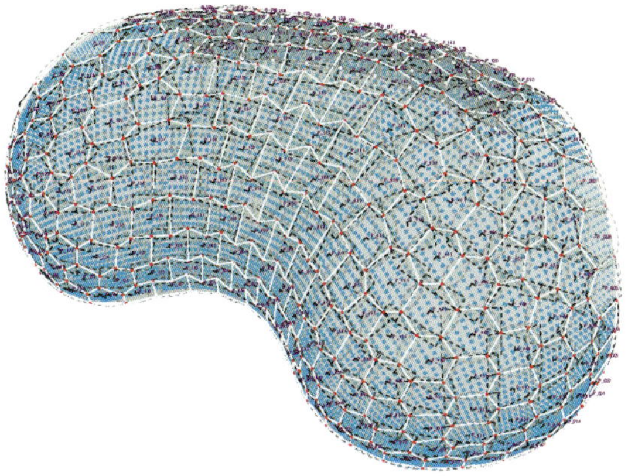

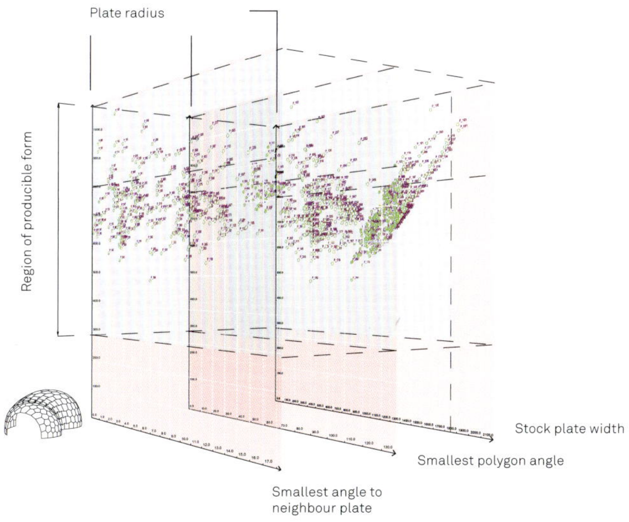

6, 7] Agent-based modeling: The behavior of the plate agents and their spatial arrangement (top) is controlled by an n-dimensional parameter space (middle).

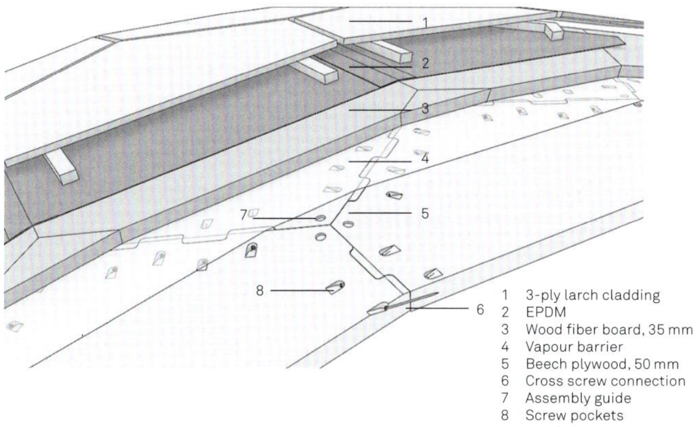

8] Layer structure:
Structural design of the wooden segment shell

LANDESGARTENSCHAU EXHIBITION HALL

Landesgartenschau Schwäbisch Gmünd, 2014
Realization: Cooperation between Landesgartenschau Schwäbisch Gmünd and the University of Stuttgart, implementing company, müllerblaustein Holzbau

PROJECT INFORMATION

Completion: 2014
Floor area: 125 m²
Shell surface: 245 m²
Weight of load-bearing structure per surface area: 37.5 kg/m²

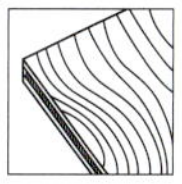

MATERIAL

Veneered beech plywood

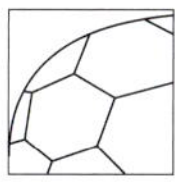

CONSTRUCTION

Segment shell made of polygonal plate segments

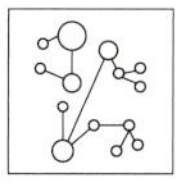

DESIGN

Multi-agent-based modeling

FABRICATION

Robotic 7-axis milling and drilling

BIOLOGICAL ROLE MODEL

Plate skeleton of the sand dollar

→ **PROJECT PARTICIPANTS**

—— 210

→ **REFERENCES**

[81], [82], [83], [84], [85], [86], [87], [88], [89]:
—— 226

BIOMIMETIC LIGHTWEIGHT WOOD CONSTRUCTION

In terms of functional integration, a basic principle of biological structures, the wood segment plates of the Exhibition Hall form the building's structure and envelope at the same time. Nevertheless, the plywood plates are only 50 mm thick. This is made possible by deriving biomimetic principles of the segmented shell structure and its connection details from the plate skeleton of the sand dollar. Natural structures in the animal and plant world usually have much more complex forms and structures than technical constructions. This "more" in form is often the reason for their particular performance and material efficiency and goes hand in hand with a "less" in material input and resource consumption. The individual plates of the skeleton, consisting of calcium carbonate, form a stable and efficient shell structure due to their specific arrangement. The characteristic formation of the plate edges shows extrusions that interlock the plates and serve as a biological model for the robotically milled finger joints of the timber structure, as first investigated for the ICD/ITKE Research Pavilion 2011.

AGENT-BASED MODELING AND ROBOTIC PREFABRICATION

A total of 243 different beech wood plates as well as all elements for the insulation, the water-bearing layer, and the top layer of larch plates were digitally designed using a tool specially developed for this research project and then fabricated by robot. In a digital simulation and optimization process, all of the elements find their position, size, and shape – in accordance with the possibilities of robotic manufacturing – by themselves. With the help of agent-based modeling, the design process takes into equal account both material properties and production conditions. The so-called agents, that is, each individual element, are assigned properties in advance and the guiding parameters – for example, the size of the plate segments or the maximum possible connection angle – are defined so that the final design process can be carried out by the design software as an assistance system. All agents arrange themselves independently in the overall model based on the predefined options. The greatest challenge and innovation for the production were the 7,600 geometrically different finger joints that give the pavilion its stability. Here, robotic production with a seven-axis system played a key role, since it offered a much higher degree of freedom than conventional computer-controlled production methods.

9] On-site assembly: Construction stage with visible waterproofing layer before installation of the wood-plate cladding

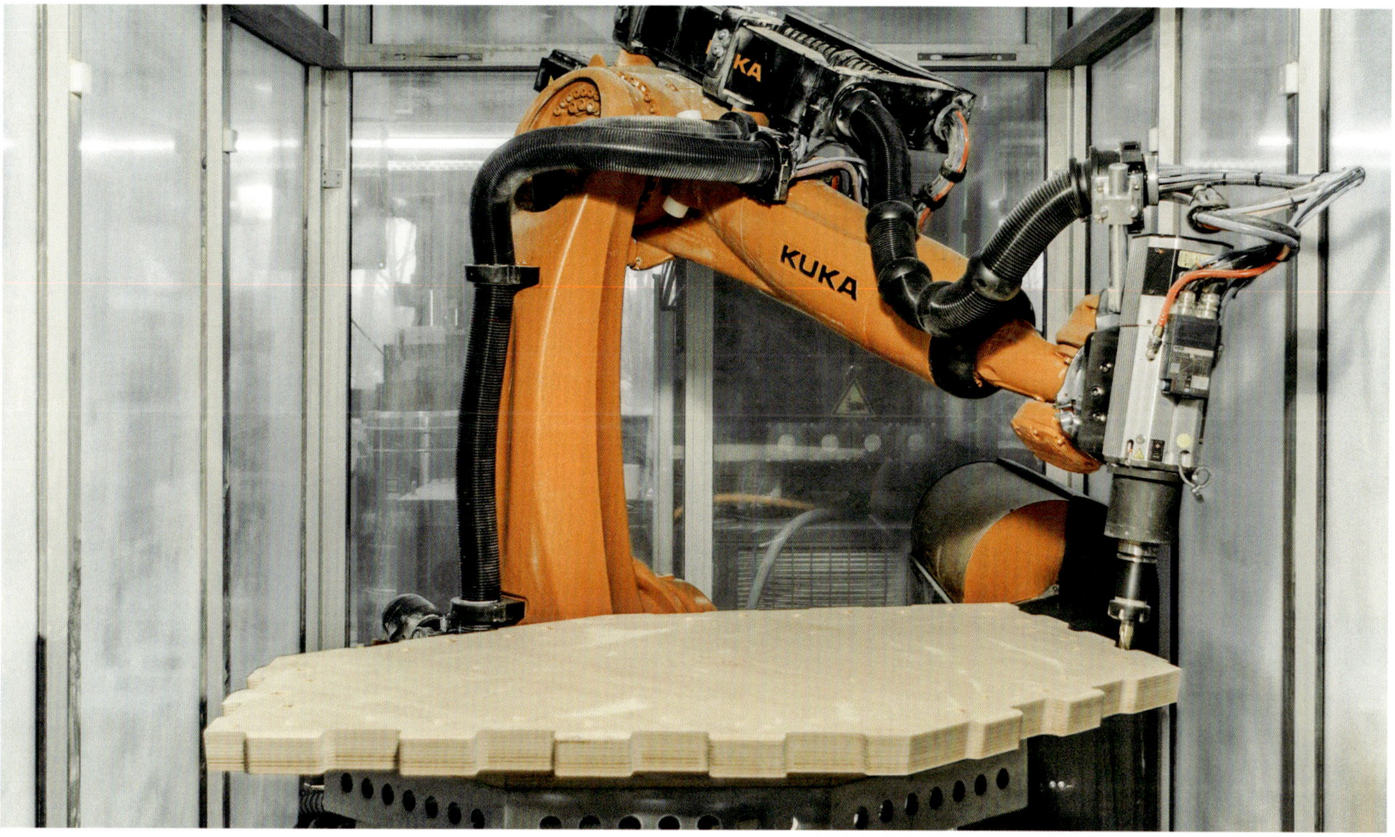

10] Robotic production of the plate segments

11] Joining of the load-bearing timber structure: The high precision of the fabrication process enabled a load-bearing system in which the forces between the plates were essentially transmitted via contact.

Despite the fact that all the components were unique, the prefabrication of the shell structure took only three weeks.

Integrated computational design and fabrication enable very high precision compared to existing processes. The quality control of the individual plates is therefore a particular challenge requiring extremely precise metrological recording by laser trackers operating in the submillimeter range. In addition, three-dimensional laser scanners are used for multiple measurements of the entire structure, enabling an analysis of the long-term behavior to be carried out. Thus, it could be shown that the average deviation of the components is only 0.86 mm. This is an exceedingly good value compared to the usual tolerances in the construction industry, particularly in view of the fact that the beech wood shell is both the primary structure and the finished surface in the interior.

Thanks to the fully integrated digital design and prefabrication, the entire building was realized in just four weeks.

12, 13, 14] Interior and exterior view of the pavilion: In the interior, the visible, load-bearing shell structure made of beech plywood panels creates the architectural expression. On the outside, the building is clad with ventilated larch plates.

POSITION:
BOB SHEIL
ON

EXPLORATIVE TEACHING

Central to the progression of architecture and engineering as research-based disciplines is a vibrant culture of experimental and explorative education. In recent years, visionary academies such as University of Stuttgart, ETH Zurich, KADK in Copenhagen, and the University College London have understood the need for this progression to develop through greater synthesis and interaction between both disciplines and each of their evolving boundaries.

Today, binding these cultures together is the greatest challenge ever to face the built environment, that of global ecological and climate repair. Such a challenge requires collaborative thinking and collaborative action, and requires new design-led transdisciplinary domains to be forged as technically expert and culturally informed networks. Of equal weight as a challenge is the vital necessity to broaden access to higher education for talented applicants from all backgrounds. Without an ethnically, sexuality and gender-diverse and inclusive profile of learners and researchers, ideas, experiences and ambitions will be limited in scope, imagination and critique.

It is increasingly common for a student entering an architecture or engineering school to say that the idea of becoming an architect or engineer is not their goal. One reason for this is the length and cost of study, what's called in the UK the "route to registration," a term that sounds like a pilgrimage, which some would say it is, as the journey can last ten years for an architect. However, what's more noticeable as a reason not to have a specific professional goal is that more and more students are seeing how an experimental and explorative education in either discipline can lead them towards many different career paths and life experiences.

The context for this is how much more than a route to registration schools with an exploratory agenda have to offer, with in some cases more than 50 percent of students taking non-accredited or post-professional programs, that is, programs that are outside the prescribed curriculum for professional qualifications. Programs in areas such as "Bio-integrated Design" or "Design for Manufacture" at UCL, "Integrative Technologies and Architectural Design Research" at ICD/ITKE University of Stuttgart, or "Computation in Architecture" at CITA Centre for Information Technology and Architecture at KADK.

Such programs tap into the host institute's full array of resources, they cut across silos and make links with departments that otherwise might not connect, or indeed might not otherwise have fully realized their vitality as breakthrough collaborators for built environment research.

Architecture and engineering departments, whether in large universities or small, have the capacity through hybrid education and collaborative research to speculate on the future of the built environment in demonstrably powerful ways. One such example is the extraordinary pavilion program codeveloped by ICD/ITKE since 2010 that has pioneered multiple new avenues of enquiry into design and fabrication processes, computational tooling, structural performance, materials science, methods of assembly, interdisciplinary participation, industry partnership and public engagement. Their work is cited around the world as exemplars in prototyping and provocation.

What makes them so influential is that the status of their projects as explicit buildings or structures is exploratory and ambiguous. They are part architecture, part structure, part complete, part fragment. In this regard they represent the power of creative synergy in research and education across architecture and engineering, and they represent the power of invention through collaboration.

Such work is reflected in other exploratory forms of hybrid education and research that have emerged in recent years, such as that between design and biochemical engineering, or performing arts, historical environments and extreme environments, and indeed in programs that span the triple domains of architectural, environmental and structural design.

In short, we are witnessing a profound and exciting step change away from constraint and convention, and towards collaboration and creativity, where the whole is greater than the sum of its parts.

BOB SHEIL
Professor of Architecture and Design through Production / Director of Bartlett School of Architecture, University College London / London, UK
—— 222

>> ICD/ITKE RESEARCH PAVILION 2014/15

University of Stuttgart

Since the water spider spends almost its entire life under water, it needs a stable air bubble to breathe. The spider first builds a web between water plants, under which the air bubble is placed. In a further step, the air bubble is reinforced from the inside with fibers. This creates a stable structure that can withstand mechanical stress such as water currents and provides the spider with a safe habitat. A particularly interesting aspect of this natural fabrication process is the adaptation to individual environmental conditions by means of fiber-reinforced structures with a minimum of necessary auxiliary construction.

ADAPTATION OF THE DESIGN PRINCIPLE

For this research pavilion the principle of the air bubble was reversed and the combination of a minimization of the mold construction in a simultaneously weatherproof envelope was investigated. The research pavilion developed from the inside out via a membrane prestressed with air pressure. An ETFE foil was used for the initially soft envelope, supported solely by the positive air pressure. An industrial robot placed in the air-supported interior reinforced the ETFE envelope with carbon fibers from the inside. To ensure adhesion between the membrane and the resin-impregnated carbon fibers, an additional adhesive had to be used. The pneumatic formwork was gradually stiffened until there was a self-supporting envelope structure that no longer needed pneumatic support.

BEHAVIOR-BASED CYBER-PHYSICAL FABRICATION

At the beginning of the design and construction process, the shell geometry and main fiber bundle locations were generated and structurally simulated using computational form-finding methods. An agent-based design method was then developed to determine and adjust the fiber position. Like a spider, a digital agent wanders over the surface and creates the robot path for the fiber flow. The agent behavior is derived from a multitude of simultaneously interacting design parameters, such as the distance and density of the fiber layers.

The changing stiffness of the pneumatic formwork and the resulting fluctuations in deformation during the

1, 2] For the ICD/ITKE Research Pavilion 2014/15 the net design characteristics of water spiders were investigated. Their behavior patterns and design rules were analyzed, abstracted and transferred into a technical procedure.

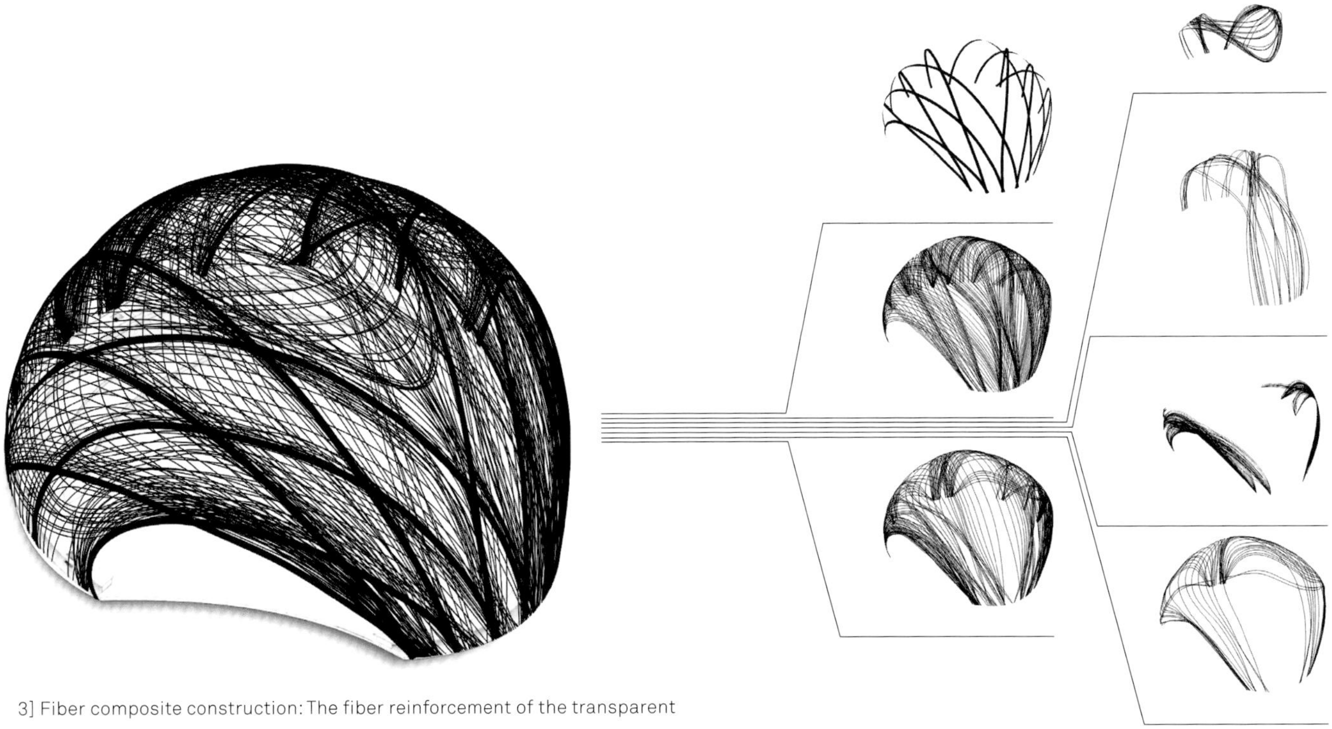

3] Fiber composite construction: The fiber reinforcement of the transparent building envelope consisted of arch-like main strands, foil surface reinforcement and edge reinforcements.

4] Principle of construction: The starting point was a pneumatically supported ETFE skin (left), which was reinforced with carbon fibers from the inside by a robot (middle) until a sufficient load-bearing capacity was reached. As a result, the air pressure could then be released and the entrances cut into the foil (right).

ICD/ITKE RESEARCH PAVILION 2014/15

University of Stuttgart, Campus City Center
Realization: Design studio with students, scientists and researchers

PROJECT INFORMATION

Completion: June 2015
Floor area: 40 m²
Volume: 130 m³
Span: 7.5 m
Height: 4.1 m
Construction weight: 260 kg

5, 6] Biological model and technology transfer: The water spider reinforces the air bubble that serves as its habitat with spider silk (top) in an adaptive construction process from the inside. This principle was transferred to a robotic fabrication process (bottom).

MATERIAL
Carbon fiber rovings pre-impregnated with epoxy resin on ETFE membrane

CONSTRUCTION
Monocoque shell made of ETFE foil with glued-in resin impregnated fibers

DESIGN
Agent-based modeling in feedback with cyber-physical production system

FABRICATION
Robotic 6-axis fiber placement

BIOLOGICAL MODEL
Water spider web building

→ **PROJECT PARTICIPANTS**
—— 211

→ **REFERENCES**
[90], [91], [92]:
—— 226

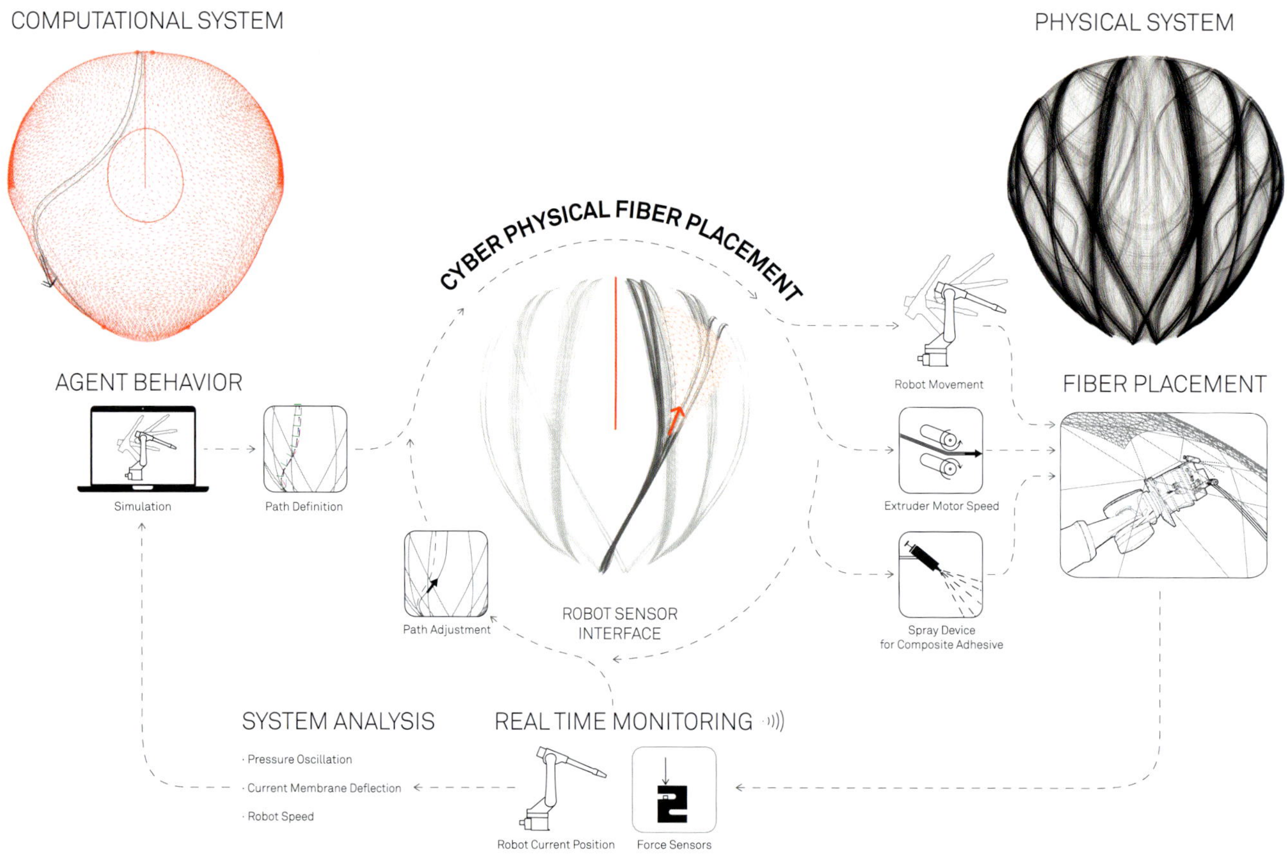

7] Diagram of the function of cyber-physical fiber laying

fiber placement process require a self-learning, adaptable control system that continuously acquires and evaluates data and adapts its behavior accordingly.

The cyber-physical system developed enables constant feedback between the real production conditions and the digital generation of the robot control code. This requires a specially constructed effector for the robot, which uses sensors to measure the contact pressure and can thus continuously adjust the robot path to ensure that the carbon fibers are placed correctly on the flexible foil. In the interest of material efficiency, carbon fibers are only applied where they are needed to reinforce the structure, completely avoiding offcuts or process waste. At the same time, the additive process turns the pneumatic formwork into a functionally integrated building envelope.

During production, nine pre-impregnated carbon fiber rovings with a total length of 45 km were placed in parallel on 5 km of robot path at an average speed of 0.6 m/min. Layered in this way, the building covered an area of 40 m^2 with a volume of 130 m^3. It was 7.5 m long, 4.1 m high, and, at 260 kg – corresponding to a weight per surface area of 6.5 kg/m^2 – very light.

8] On-site fabrication

9] Cyber-physical fabrication: During the fabrication process, the progress of the structure, the current position of the fiber placement head, and its contact pressure were recorded by an integrated sensor system that controlled the robot's behavior in real time.

10, 11] Research Pavilion on the Campus City Center of the University of Stuttgart

12] Interior view: The combination of filigreed fiber structure and transparent envelope created a distinctive spatial effect.

POSITION:
ANTOINE PICON
ON

COMPLEXITY AND CONTRADICTION IN MATERIAL COMPUTATION

In design, an approach is often all the more inspiring when it feeds upon ambiguities, tensions and even contradictions. Such is the case with the ICD/ITKE´s brilliant variations on themes such as material computation and types like the pavilion that they have contributed to rejuvenate.

To begin with, the very notion of material computation is characterized by an analytic decomposition of natural phenomena that has taken a more radical turn in the age of the computer than at the time when the application of mathematical formulas was not dependent upon digital tools. Indeed, discretization, that is, the transformation of continuous variations into a series of discontinuous values, is at the very principle of the digital. Simultaneously, material computation is permeated by a holistic vision of nature that could seem incompatible with such a decomposition.

This tension is actually rooted in a long history that goes back at least to Romanticism. How not to be reminded of the German poet Novalis's famous reference to "the great Manuscript of Design which we descry everywhere, on wings of birds, on the shells of eggs, in clouds, in snow, in crystals, in rock formations, in frozen water, within and upon mountains, in plants, in beasts, in men..."[58] at the beginning of *The Disciples at Sais*? For Novalis, nature was both written, or even coded, and profoundly unified. There is a hint of Romanticism in material computation that includes some nostalgia for the possible loss of our intuition of how "the great Manuscript of Design" is actually written. One could interpret it as a desire to recapture this deep understanding, and by the same token reestablish harmony between the spontaneous creativity of nature and human schemes.

The approach of the ICD and ITKE is also marked by a quest for performance that translates in the use of advanced materials like glass and carbon fibers, innovative assemblages and advanced robotics.

Simultaneously, the various ICD/ITKE pavilions display a poetic dimension all the more powerful in that it remains untheorized, as if the magic came as the unintended consequence of other concerns, like the quest for biomimetic relevance. This untheorized character finds its counterpart in the production of intriguing narratives regarding how a source of inspiration borrowed from the natural world becomes a structural reality.

Nothing is perhaps more telling in that respect than the story that leads from the water spider weaving its nest inside a bubble of air to the ICD/ITKE Research Pavilion 2014/15. Equally intriguing is the passage from biomimetic principles to architectural form. How is the overall form of the pavilions determined? The mobilization of optimization techniques appears only as a partial answer, especially when the form is produced through the assemblage of elements like the modular, double-layered composite fiber structures used in the ICD/ITKE Research Pavilion 2013/14. Does the form follow the from-the-inside-out principle propagated by Richard Buckminster Fuller at the beginning of his career or does it follow a completely different logic?

On that front as well, the work of the ICD and ITKE raises many questions. Its thought-provoking character stems as much from its ambiguities and contradictions as the sheer fascination exerted by its masterful staging of innovative materials, assemblages and robots.

ANTOINE PICON
Prof. Dr. / Professor of the History of Architecture and Technology / Director of Research, Graduate School of Design GDS, Harvard University / Cambridge (MA), USA

221

→ [58]

225

>> ICD/ITKE RESEARCH PAVILION 2015/16

University of Stuttgart

When it comes to developing efficient and material-saving constructions, wood is besides its characteristics as a renewable raw material a versatile material for innovative construction methods. This is due to the integration of functions – load-bearing structure, envelope and cladding in one – and to its morphological adaptability enabling it to create spatially complex structures.

NATURAL SEGMENTED SHELLS WITH FIBER CONNECTIONS

The design of the ICD/ITKE Research Pavilion 2015/16 is based – like the two previous wooden pavilions in 2011 and 2014 – on an analysis of the construction morphology of sand dollars. Previous studies had already given rise the transfer of bionic principles to architectural segmented shells made of timber plates with finger joints. In close cooperation with biologists from the University of Tübingen, two species of the sand dollar were selected that seemed particularly suitable for the technical transfer of further construction and formation principles. Detailed photographs taken with a scanning electron microscope and further literature research showed that the connections between the plate segments of the sea urchin shell consist of additional fiber connections as well as the already known finger joints. It is assumed that these elastic connections of relatively stiff plates ensure the integrity of the sand dollar's shell during the growth process, and at the same time reduce the animal's sensitivity to impact loads through their resilience.

CURVED WOOD LAMINATES WITH SHAPE-DEFINING STIFFNESS GRADIENT

On the basis of these bionic findings and the characteristic material properties of wood, a construction system has been developed which, as a two-layer structure, reproduces the shapes created in the sand dollar through secondary growth. The starting material is beech veneer, thin strips of which are laminated into flat, individually manufactured 3–5 mm-thick plywood panels. These construction elements use the anisotropy of wood to differentiate the fiber orientation of the

1, 2] For the ICD/ITKE Research Pavilion 2015/16, industrial sewing techniques for wooden constructions were used for the first time on an architectural scale.

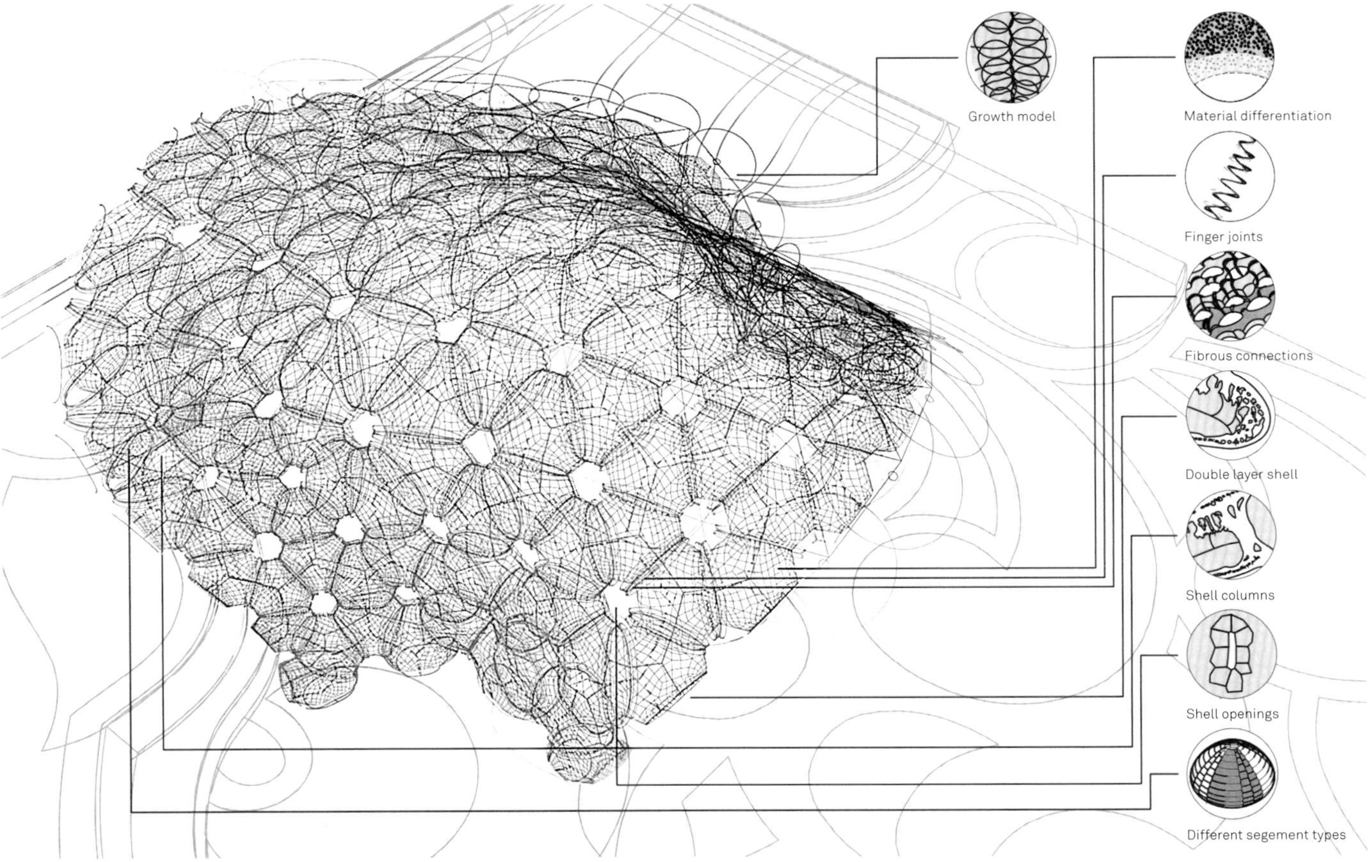

3] Integration of biological principles into computational design

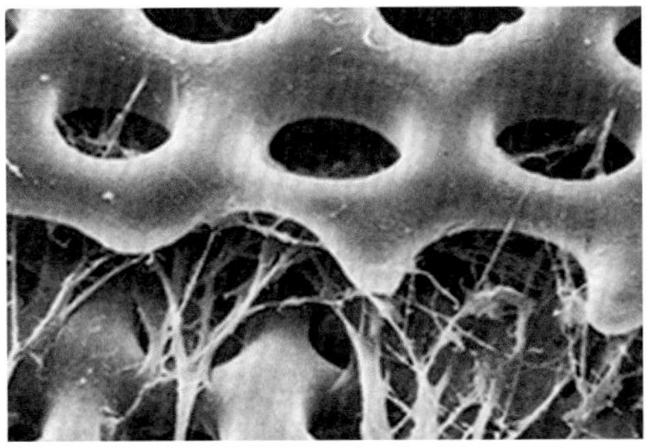

4] Natural connections with fibers: The plates of the sea urchin species *Diadema antillarum* are connected with collagen fibers.[98]

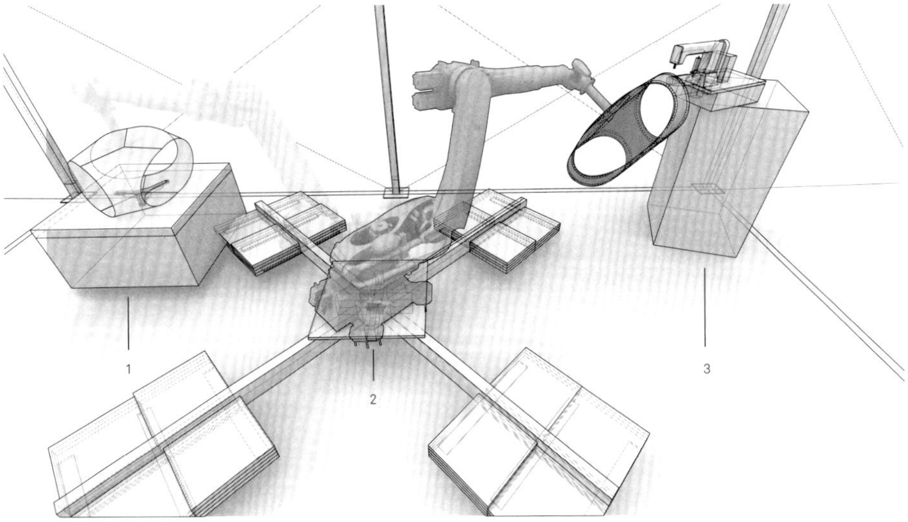

1 Workpiece assembly station mounting position
2 KUKA KR 120 R3900 industrial robot
3 HIGHTEX CB4500 industrial sewing machine

5] Fabrication setup: The initially planar components were positioned by the robot in their complex three-dimensional form and sewn fully automatically for their fixing.

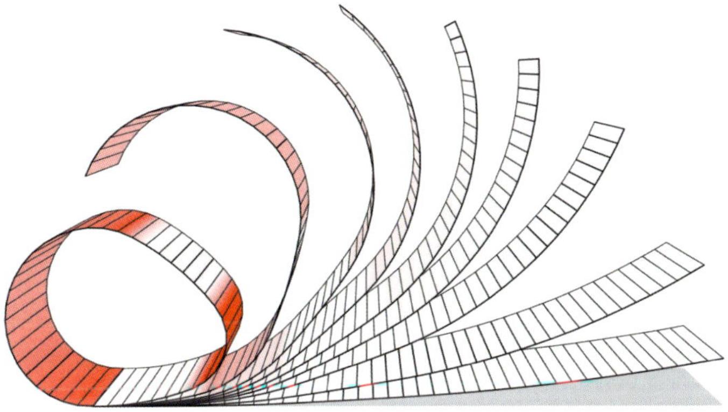

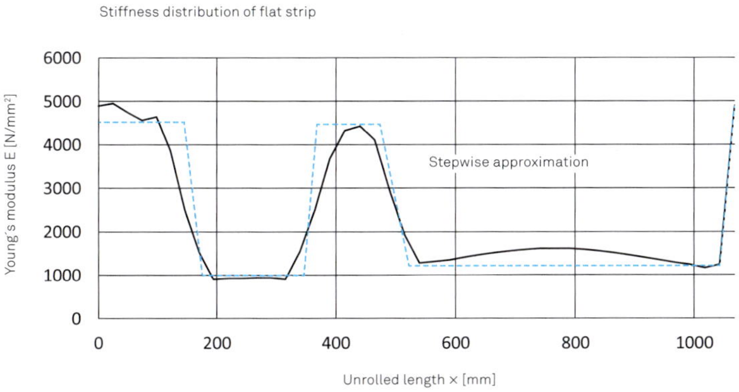

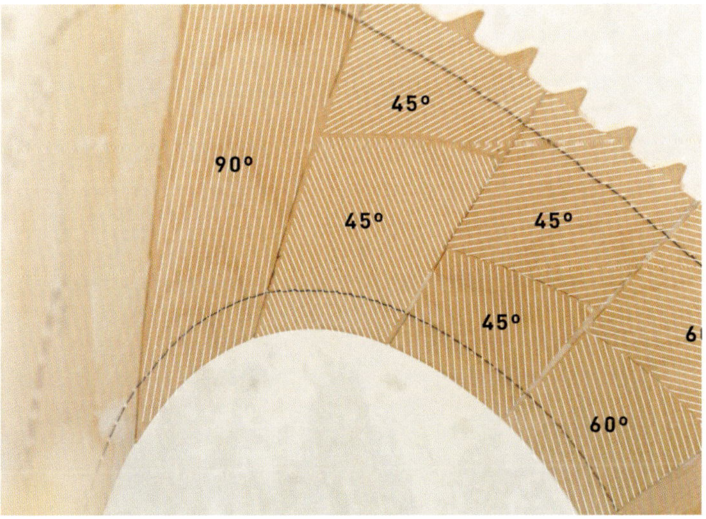

6, 7, 8] Laminate with stiffness gradients: The fiber orientations of the laminate layers were determined in such a way that the pre-calculated geometry of the component was precisely met in a bent state.

ICD/ITKE RESEARCH PAVILION 2015/16

University of Stuttgart, Campus City Center

Realization: Design studio with students, scientists and researchers

PROJECT INFORMATION

Completion: April 2016

Floor area: 85 m²

Shell surface: 105 m²

Dimensions: 11.5 × 9.5 m

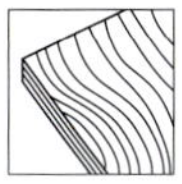

MATERIAL

Individualized veneer plywood beech

CONSTRUCTION

Segmented shell made of triangular, laced hollow segments

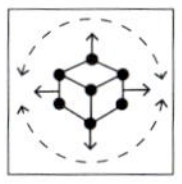

DESIGN

Inverse equilibrium modeling of bending-active components

FABRICATION

Robotic sewing

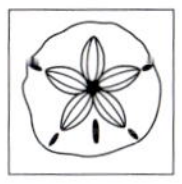

BIOLOGICAL ROLE MODEL

Plate skeleton of the sand dollar

→ **PROJECT PARTICIPANTS**

___ 212

→ **REFERENCES**

[93], [94], [95], [96], [97], [98]:
___ 226

9] Robotic sewing: Sewing permitted permanent fixing of the elastically formed segments as a pressed laminate as well as the application of the edge strips for lacing.

veneer components and the material thickness. This allows the stiffness of the initially flat components to be adjusted so that a specific segment geometry with different radii of curvature is created through elastic deformation, controlled solely by the laminate structure.

ROBOT-CONTROLLED SEWING TECHNOLOGY FOR WOOD

The use of the thin-walled and curved wood segments also required the development of a new joining technique. On the one hand, it was necessary to dispense with the metallic fasteners used in conventional point-to-point connections in order to prevent the drill holes in the thin-walled laminates from being torn out. On the other hand, the target geometry would usually require contact pressure maintained during lamination and shape retention that could only be achieved using complex forming tools. This led to the idea of testing the potential of textile production techniques and their transferability to thin veneer boards.

A robot-controlled production process was developed for the experimental structure, which enables the joining, form closure and press laminate of the individually bent plywood plates by sewing the wood layers using an industrial sewing machine. The curved plywood strips were temporarily fixed in the desired geometric configuration by an industrial robot. During the subsequent sewing process, the robot guided the curved strips through the sewing machine and joined them together in the desired segment shape. Each segment consisted of three single, individually laminated veneer beech wood strips. These individual segments with bending radii between 0.3 and 0.75 m were adapted in shape and fiber orientation to the local structural and geometrical requirements. In addition, membrane strips were sewn on as connecting elements between the segments, and later, during construction, laced together by Kevlar cords to transfer the tensile forces between the individual segments. The robot and sewing machine controls were integrated via custom-programmed software. This interface enables the robot to always know both the current position of the part and the status of the sewing machine, and to synchronize the movement.

For the pavilion, which covered an area of 85 m^2 and spanned 9.3 m, a total of 151 different, robotically prefabricated segments were joined together. The two-layer segments transferred external loads mainly through normal forces and shear forces in the plane parts at top and bottom of the segments. While the latter were mainly transmitted in the segments connected by finger joints, tensile forces were transferred by the lacing. The result was an efficient and complexly shaped shell structure made of simple, flat veneer strips, whose construction weight of 7.85 kg/m^2 in relation to the shell surface was extremely light.

10] The 151 geometrically different segments had individual seam patterns.

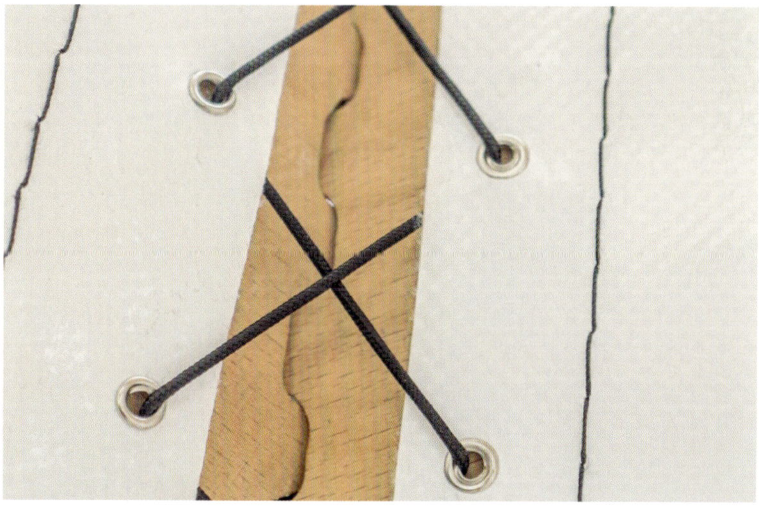

12] Lacing to the segments: The thin-walled segments could not be connected with screws so a new type of connection was developed using sewn textile strips and lacing.

11] Sewing of plywood laminate: An industrial sewing machine is integrated into the robotic system in terms of control technology, enabling the fully automated sewing of plywood.

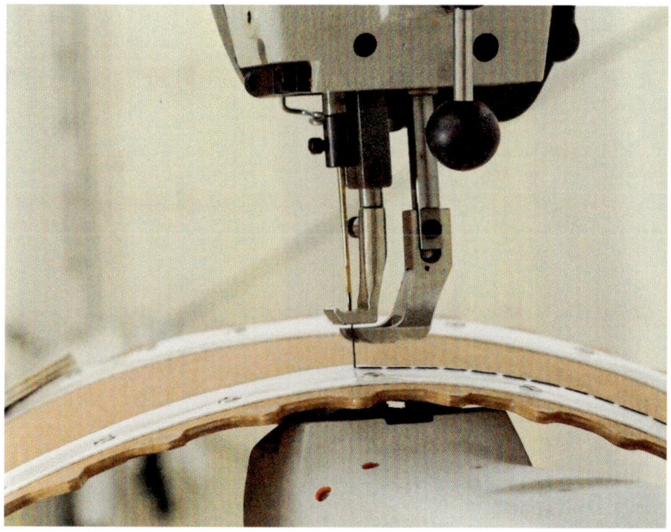

13, 14] Interior view (left) and rear elevation (top): Like the biological model – the sand dollar – the pavilion was neither a pure compression-stressed shell nor a pure bending plate, but instead combined both structural typologies.

15] Front elevation: The form and texture of the novel wooden structure of sewn and laced elements gave the pavilion its special shape. It achieved a free span of more than 9 m with a material thickness of just 3–5 mm.

POSITION: JANE BURRY ON COMPUTATIONAL DESIGN

Digital computation has not changed the fundamentals of architectural thought but it has presented architects and engineers with a cerebral annex.

It has allowed them to hold a great many more dimensions in play and more easily explore many more options at key points in design. Contemporary computational design has arguably enfranchised many people to work closer to a way that was only accessible to a notable few before digital computing. At a stroke it has moved architecture from the Greek tradition of three-dimensional geometry constructed from two dimensions, to post-Descartian, highly diverse and variable models of geometry and space, including topology, complexity, optimization, and space-filling packings, latter-day mathematical models borrowed from biology, chemistry or mineralogy.

Predating digital computing, the notable few, unconstrained by Euclidean, Projective and Descriptive Geometry, were those who most closely observed natural processes and found analog and mathematical (graphic static) ways to abstract natural behaviors in empirical architectural models – their own methods of computational design. Antoni Gaudí's live funicular model for the Colonia Güell church and his observation of the variability of hyperbolic geometries approximating natural form are well-known examples from a lifetime of observations of the underlying processes of plant and cell growth and mineralogy translated into architecture through physical modeling. Structural artists such as Robert Maillart, Félix Candela, Eduardo Torreja, Heinz Isler and Eladio Dieste were similarly leaders, as was Frei Otto in opening our eyes to the translation of physical behaviors and systems in the world into computational models for optimal and differentiated performance in architecture. As the magnitude of computing power and data grow, the digitally computed world can move closer to our physical and sensory experience. Computer code, an abstract language potentially alienating to the constructivist reality of architecture, encounters the concrete physicality of digital fabrication and materials. Similarly, real-time feedback, the basis of all embodied human learning, is now the corollary of rapidly computed simulation, sometimes brought to the designer coupled with sensory experience in augmented reality. The integration of simulation and optimization into automated form-finding to create highly differentiated but resolved solutions mirrors natural processes of growth and form.

The ICD and IKTE pavilion projects of the last decade have provided beacons for the global architectural community by building on the successful tradition of the few, examining natural processes and extrapolating in surprising and awe-inducing ways. Building on a body of earlier work on morphogenetic design and emergence in architecture, and working with experts in the biological sciences, this highly integrated architecture-engineering partnership has been able to perfect the level of abstraction at which to extract and use biomimetic information.

In each case they have found a computational design twist and novel construction processes. Whether borrowed from the locally differentiated material variances in the elytra beetle wing shell, the diving bell spider creating and spinning reinforcement onto its underwater air bubble, or the collective strength of the thin jointed plates of the sand dollar sea urchin, these inventive new construction processes serve to both elucidate the optimal material economy and elegance of the highly evolved natural case study, and to demonstrate extensible real-world applications in construction.

There is a consistent underlying message about a lighter, stronger, more materially conservative built future, one less in conflict with the health of the planet. It is powerfully couched in a language of natural evolution that produces wonder. These are exquisitely executed proofs of concept that an extended team has subjected to a rigorous iterative design process at many levels of architecture, structural and mechanical engineering. Moreover, they are realized as prototypes at industrial scale.

These projects have shown us how to invite the material or material system itself to partner in computation, to see computational design not as an exclusively digital domain but as a continuous dialogue between the material, analog and digital, returning the digital to its vital but contextualized status as a cerebral annex.

This broader, more embodied understanding of computational design, once the preserve of the few, now disseminated by this fascinating collection of projects over a decade, is one of the greatest contributions of this work.

JANE BURRY
Prof. PhD /
Dean of the School of Design, Swinburne University of Technology / Melbourne, Australia
—— 221

>> ICD/ITKE RESEARCH PAVILION 2016/17

University of Stuttgart

The 2016 research pavilion demonstrates an alternative, novel concept for the production of long-span fiber composite construction. Fiber-based composite materials have tremendous potential for architectural applications. Thanks to their high performance, they are already used in many areas of engineering. Unlike in aviation or the automotive industry, however, there are no suitable architectural-scale fabrication methods that could economically produce small series of geometrically unique elements. For this reason, the production of large-scale fiber composite structures without the use of complex mold construction was explored in previous pavilions in 2012, 2013/14 and 2014/15. Although these experiments were no longer restricted by conventional production methods, their size was still limited by the working space of the industrial robots deployed. With the ICD/ITKE Research Pavilion 2016/17, it was possible to overcome these technical and economic limitations to produce long-span prototypes.

BIOMIMETICS AS A DESIGN STRATEGY

The naturally occurring structural formation processes of the cocoons of leaf miner moths (*Lyonetia clerkella* and *Leucoptera erythrinella*) were identified as a suitable template in interdisciplinary cooperation with the Eberhard Karls University of Tübingen. The larvae of this species spin silk hammocks between anchor points on bent leaves. The morphology of the cocoon and the process of its formation served as the basis for the technological transfer. The imitation of the biological structure can be used on three levels. The combination of coreless wound fiber reinforcement and a bending-active substructure provides the necessary flexibility, while the hierarchical fiber arrangement over a long span ensures the load-bearing capacity. The multistage process of volumetric fiber deposition enables the creation of complex three-dimensional shapes.

1, 2] The ICD/ITKE Research Pavilion 2016/17 opens up new possibilities for wide-span fiber composite structures in architecture through an innovative manufacturing process that combines the advantages of unmanned aircraft and precise industrial robots.

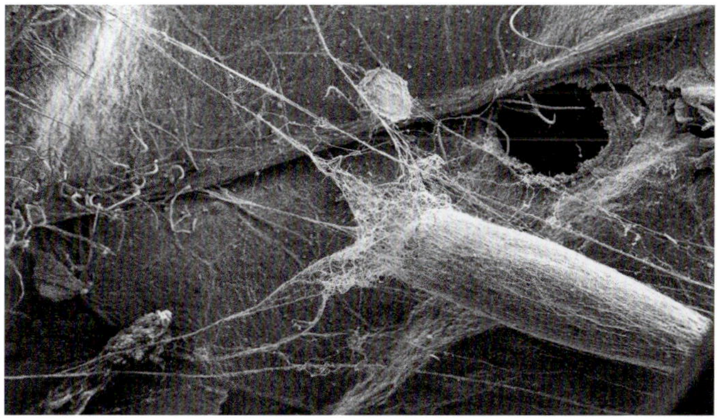

3] Microscopic image of the cocoon construction of the leaf miner moth (*Leucoptera erythrinella*)

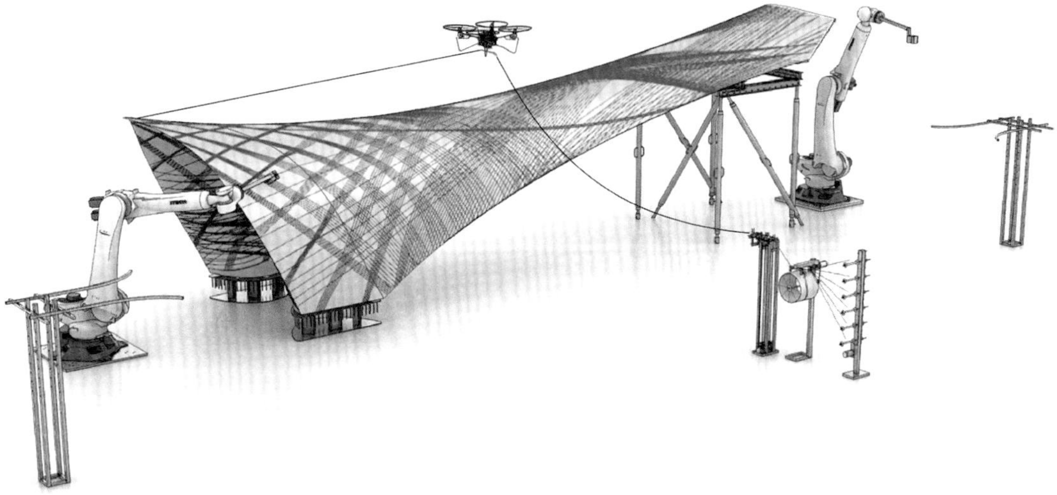

4] Fabrication concept for large-scale fiber composite components: A combination of stationary, precise robots with a limited range but high tensioning forces and mobile flying robots with a high range but low precision and load capacity.

NETWORKED MACHINES

Two technological principles are combined to implement a large-scale cyber-physical production system of networked machines to build the structure. The fabrication process is based on the collaboration of strong and precise yet stationary robots with limited reach but high tensioning forces, and robots with a long range due to their mobility but with limited precision and tensioning forces. As glass and carbon fibers are extremely light compared to other construction materials, machines with a low payload but long range, such as drones, can be used. For the construction of the ICD/ITKE Research Pavilion 2016/17, two industrial robots with the necessary power and accuracy for fiber winding were positioned at both ends of the structure. In between, the fibers could be passed back and forth by an autonomously operating transport system – a drone specially developed for this task. The combination of freedom of movement and precision provides a wide range of possibilities for depositing the fibers on, over and through the supporting structure. The result is a structure with load-bearing behavior that would not have been possible with only one of the two production machines. To ensure that the different machine types can communicate and interact with each other during the fiber-laying process, an adaptive control and communications system was developed. An integrated sensor interface allows the industrial robots and the drone to adapt to changing fabrication conditions in real time. The drone can fly and land autonomously, without the assistance of a pilot. The tension of the fibers is computationally controlled and adjusted jointly by the industrial robots and the drone. For the digital and physical "handshake," a localization system has been developed to control the

5] Simulation model: The 12 m-long cantilever had to be subjected to a very careful structural analysis to determine the orientation and density of the load-bearing carbon fibers.

6] Networking of the machines: Data integration and communications protocols had been developed for the different machines working autonomously together in one fabrication setup.

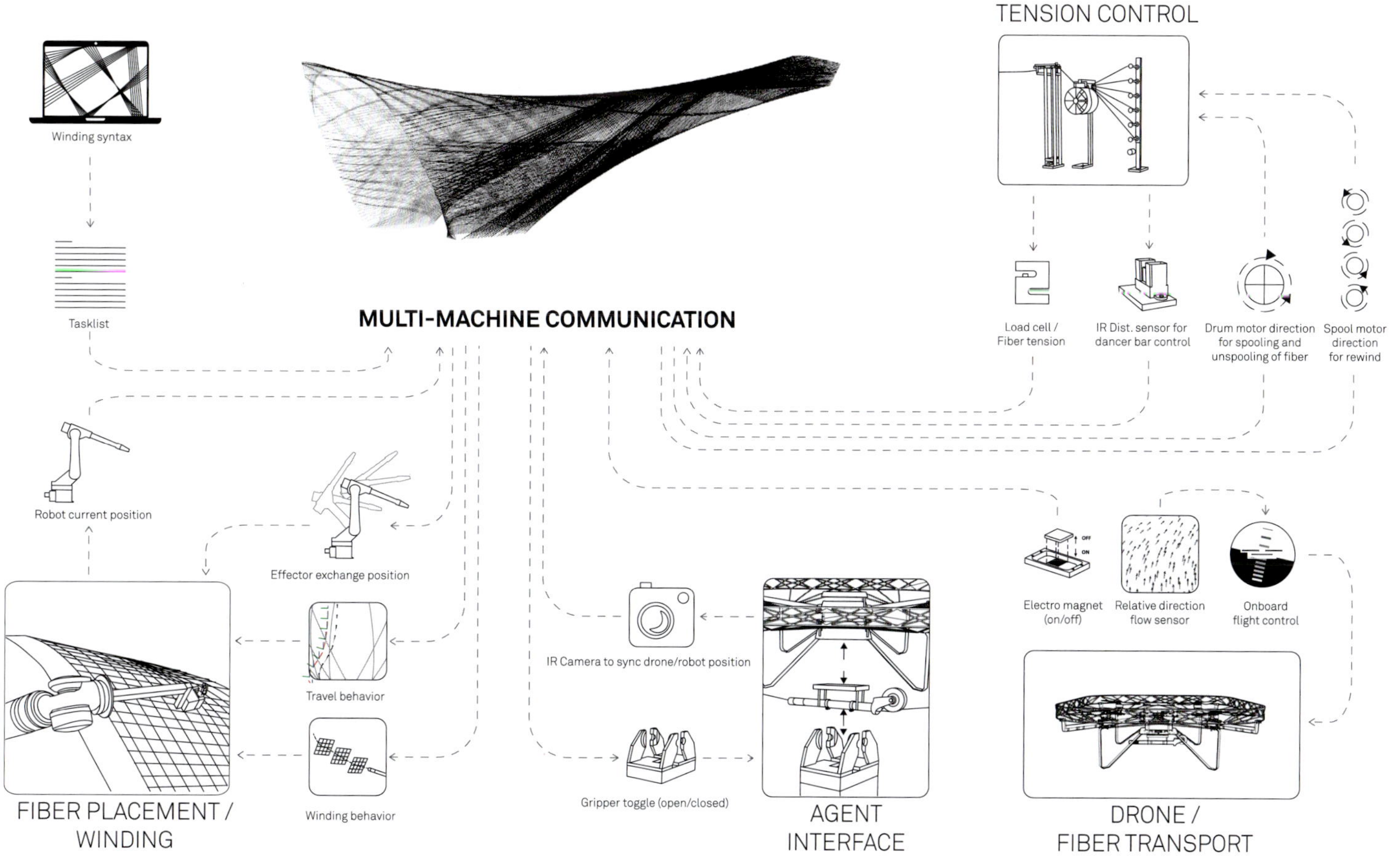

7] Fabrication setup: Fiber-winding robot arms and autonomous drone

exchange of fibers between the fabrication machines. This precise working method is necessary to minimize the use of materials and at the same time to ensure the performance of the areas subject to particular loading.

INTEGRATIVE DEMONSTRATOR

The pavilion was made of resin-impregnated carbon and glass fibers with a total length of 184 km. The lightweight material system formed a 12 m-long cantilever, which demonstrated the structural potential of this material combination. The surface covered an area of about 40 m^2 and weighed roughly 1,000 kg. The one-piece cantilever was prefabricated and therefore could not exceed an allowable transport volume. On-site production would permit even larger spans.

Despite this limitation, the prototypical building successfully demonstrates the scalability of the fabrication processes for long-span fiber composite structural elements in architecture.

8] Transport of long-span fiber composite structure to site

9] A drone transported glass and carbon fibers between the robots to form the 12 m-long cantilever.

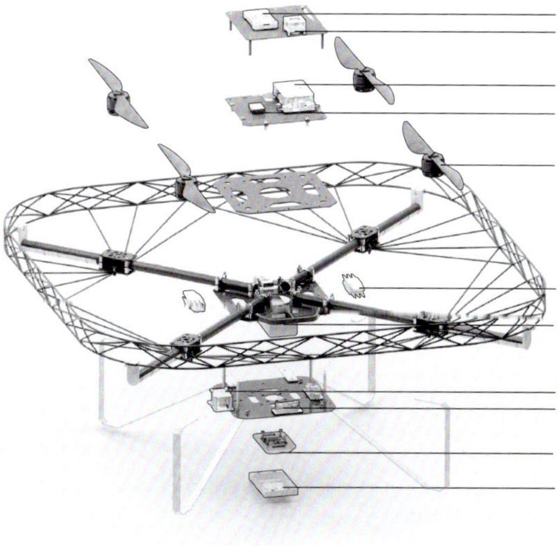

10] Build-up of a custom-made autonomous drone, developed specifically for this project

11, 12, 13] Side and rear elevation: The entire 12 m-long structure consisted exclusively of glass and carbon fibers. Under its own weight and the wind, the large cantilever leads to considerable structural loads, which are carried by the carbon fibers and transferred to the foundation.

ICD/ITKE RESEARCH PAVILION 2016/17
University of Stuttgart, Campus City Center
Realization: Design studio with students, scientists, and researchers

PROJECT INFORMATION
Completion: March 2017
Floor area: 26.5 m^2
Volume: 58 m^3
Fiber length: 184 km
Weight: 1,000 kg
Dimensions: 12 m x 2.6 m x 3.1 m

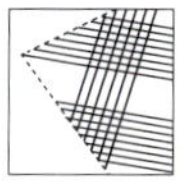

MATERIAL
Carbon fiber rovings and glass fiber rovings with epoxy resin

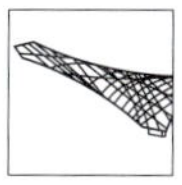

CONSTRUCTION
One-piece cantilever arm made of fiber composite lattice

DESIGN
Agent-based modeling in feedback with cyber-physical production system

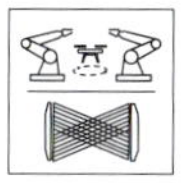

FABRICATION
Coreless robotic 12-axis winding with integrated UAV

BIOLOGICAL ROLE MODEL
Cocoon construction of the larva of the leaf miner moth

→ **PROJECT PARTICIPANTS**
—— 213

→ **REFERENCES**
[99], [100], [101], [102]:
—— 226

>> ELYTRA FILAMENT PAVILION

Victoria and Albert Museum, London

The profound impact of new technologies on conceptions of design, construction and production of architecture was brought to life for visitors in 2016 in the inner courtyard of the Victoria and Albert Museum. Instead of a static installation, the ICD and ITKE, in cooperation with Thomas Auer (TU Munich/ Transsolar Climate Engineering), created a dynamic structure that had the ability to develop independently. Sensors were integrated into the modular lightweight construction canopy, which continuously sensed the microclimatic conditions and the movements of visitors. In combination with a robotic winding unit installed on-site, a concept of a growing and changing structure of individually load-adapted modules became possible.

A highly differentiated sloping roof construction made of fiber composite modules awaited interested visitors in the John Madejski Garden, surrounded by Victorian facades. The column-supported canopy area had a clearance height of 4.75 m at the highest point and sloped down to 2.45 m.

ADAPTIVE AND GROWING ROOF STRUCTURE FOR PUBLIC SPACE

The special exhibition *V&A Engineering Season 2016* focused on the power and beauty of engineering and its impact on everyday life. For the realization of an installation in the museum's garden courtyard, an interdisciplinary team was sought that could demonstrate the innovative potential of integrative design, fabrication and construction strategies in a future-oriented way. The ICD/ITKE/Transsolar project team prevailed with this pavilion that was not only an architectural installation but also part of ongoing research activities due to its high degree of novelty and innovation.

As a dynamic and adaptable exhibition object, the canopy structure made of 40 robotically wound carbon and glass fiber modules demonstrated the unique spatial and aesthetic qualities that can be created from the synthesis of construction and climate engineering, as well as innovative fabrication methods.

1, 2] Growing, learning and adaptive structures – the Elytra Filament Pavilion overcomes previous characteristics of static architecture.

138

139

3, 4] Micro-computer tomography of an elytron (above) of an airworthy beetle (right)

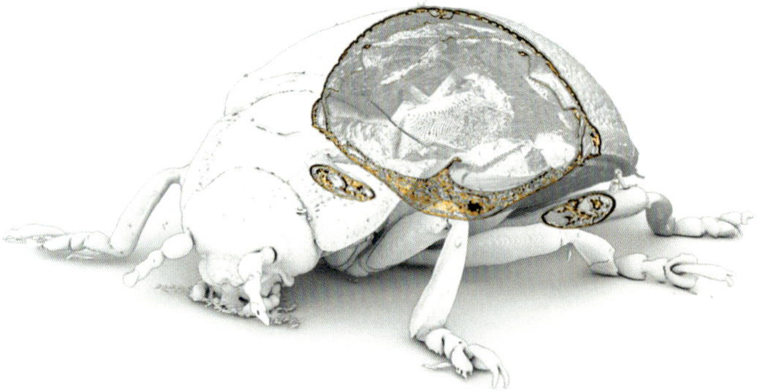

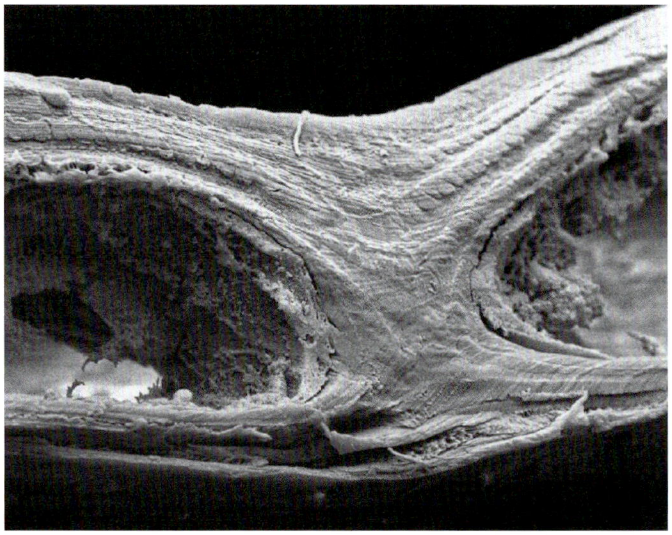

5] Scanning electron microscope photograph of a section through the elytron shell: The two sides of the double-layered, natural fiber composite shell are connected by continuous fibers along trabeculae. This principle was transferred to technical fiber composite components.

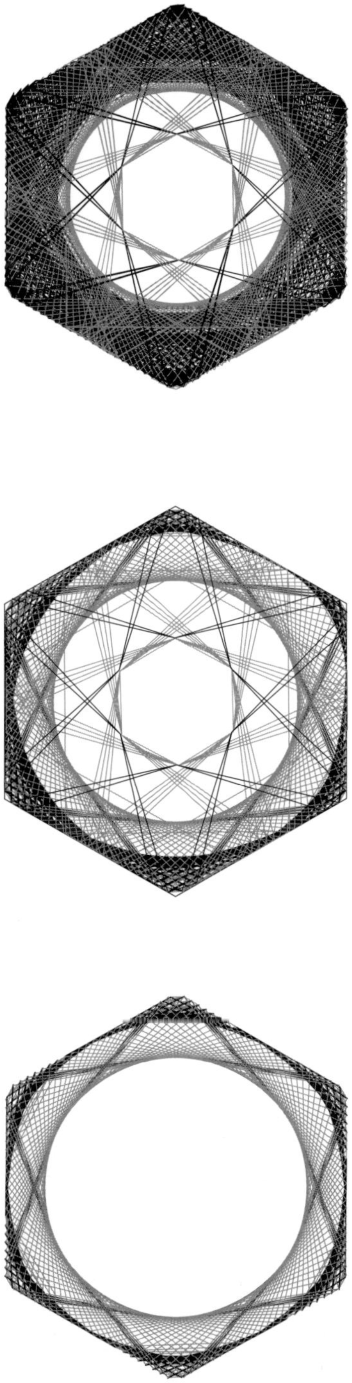

6] Differentiated fiber structure of the roof elements: All components had the same outer geometry, but an inner fiber structure and density adapted to the respective loading condition.

ELYTRA FILAMENT PAVILION

Victoria and Albert Museum, London
Realization: University of Stuttgart commissioned by the Victoria and Albert Museum

PROJECT INFORMATION

Completion: March 2016
Floor area: 200 m²*
Weight fiber composite structure: 9 kg/m²
Total weight of canopy structure: 2.5 t*
Number of fiber composite components: 40*
Building component size: 2.77 × 2.4 × 0.4 m
Average weight per component: 45 kg
Differentiated material usage: 35–70 kg per component

* At the beginning of the exhibition period – the roof grew over the course of time

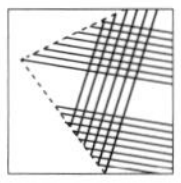

MATERIAL
Carbon fiber rovings and glass fiber rovings with epoxy resin

CONSTRUCTION
Segmented roof slab made of hexagonal fiber composite lattice segments

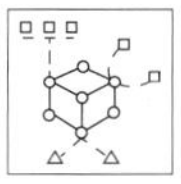

DESIGN
Parametric modeling in feedback with local and global material simulation

FABRICATION
Coreless robotic 8-axis winding, robot-guided fiber winding head, rotating winding scaffold

BIOLOGICAL ROLE MODEL
Forewing of airworthy beetle

→ **PROJECT PARTICIPANTS**
—— 214

→ **REFERENCES**
[103], [104], [105], [106]:
—— 227

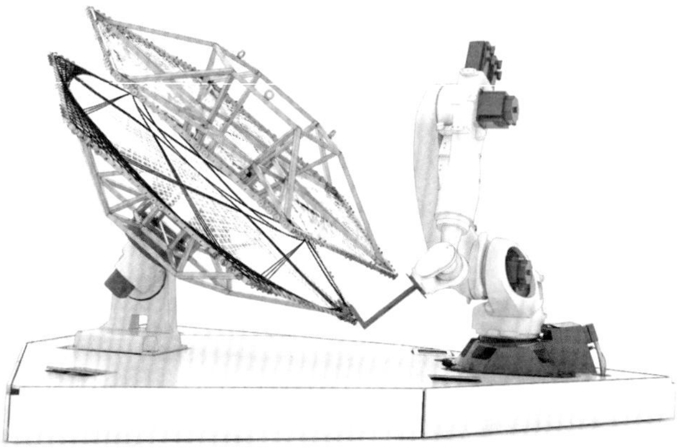

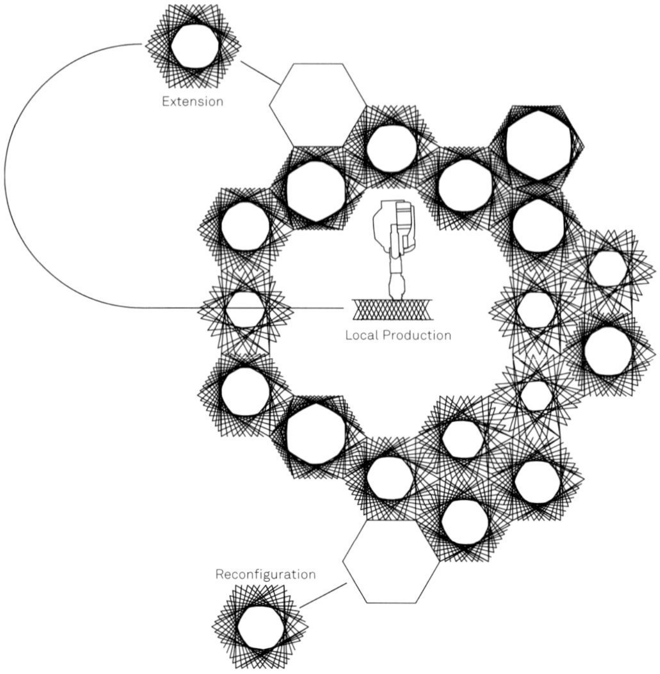

7, 8] Fabrication concept: The combination of the compact fabrication unit (left), the extremely light construction materials and their small quantity allowed for on-site production, which enabled the continuous extension and conversion of the pavilion.

Drawing on historical references to Victorian greenhouses – also built as experimental structures in an early phase of iron construction during the first Industrial Revolution, the installation provided a glimpse of how the so-called fourth Industrial Revolution of robotics and cyber-physical production systems has enabled the emergence of new structural and material systems. In the Victorian greenhouse, the convergence of construction and environmental aspects resulted in a unique experience of covered public green spaces. The transparent installation ties in with this and extends the concept toward adaptable and growing structures.

RECONFIGURATION USING REAL-TIME SENSOR TECHNOLOGY

The sensor systems integrated into the fiber structure make it possible to correlate visitor behavior, climatic parameters and the stress conditions in the load-bearing structure. Based on this information, a growth algorithm determines the reconfiguration of the structure and informs the local robot about the resulting requirements for the components to be produced for further expansion. This enabled visitors to experience in real time the development of this fascinating lightweight construction system as a dynamic process. To demonstrate this idea, several components were manufactured on-site and attached to the roof, so that it grew over the course of the exhibition and adapted its form to local use.

DEVELOPMENT OF BIOMIMETIC FIBER COMPOSITE STRUCTURES

The Elytra Filament Pavilion is in the line of development of its predecessor pavilions made of composite materials and is thus the result of four years of research into the integration of architecture, engineering and biomimetic principles. The structure, which measures over 200 m^2, is based on the lightweight construction principles of the natural fiber composite structure in the forewing shells of airworthy beetles known as elytra – hence the name.

The ICD/ITKE Research Pavilion 2012 was the first prototype to investigate the robotic winding process also underlying the Elytra Filament Pavilion. It consisted of a monocoque shell with a diameter of 8 m wound with continuous fibers. Its successor, the ICD/ITKE Research Pavilion 2013/14, was based on the design logic of the beetle shells, implemented in the form of a segmented, double-layered fiber composite structure. Thanks to their robustness and scalability, the potential for use as a construction system was recognized and pursued in the London project. The fiber composite structure of the Elytra Filament Pavilion consisted of two different

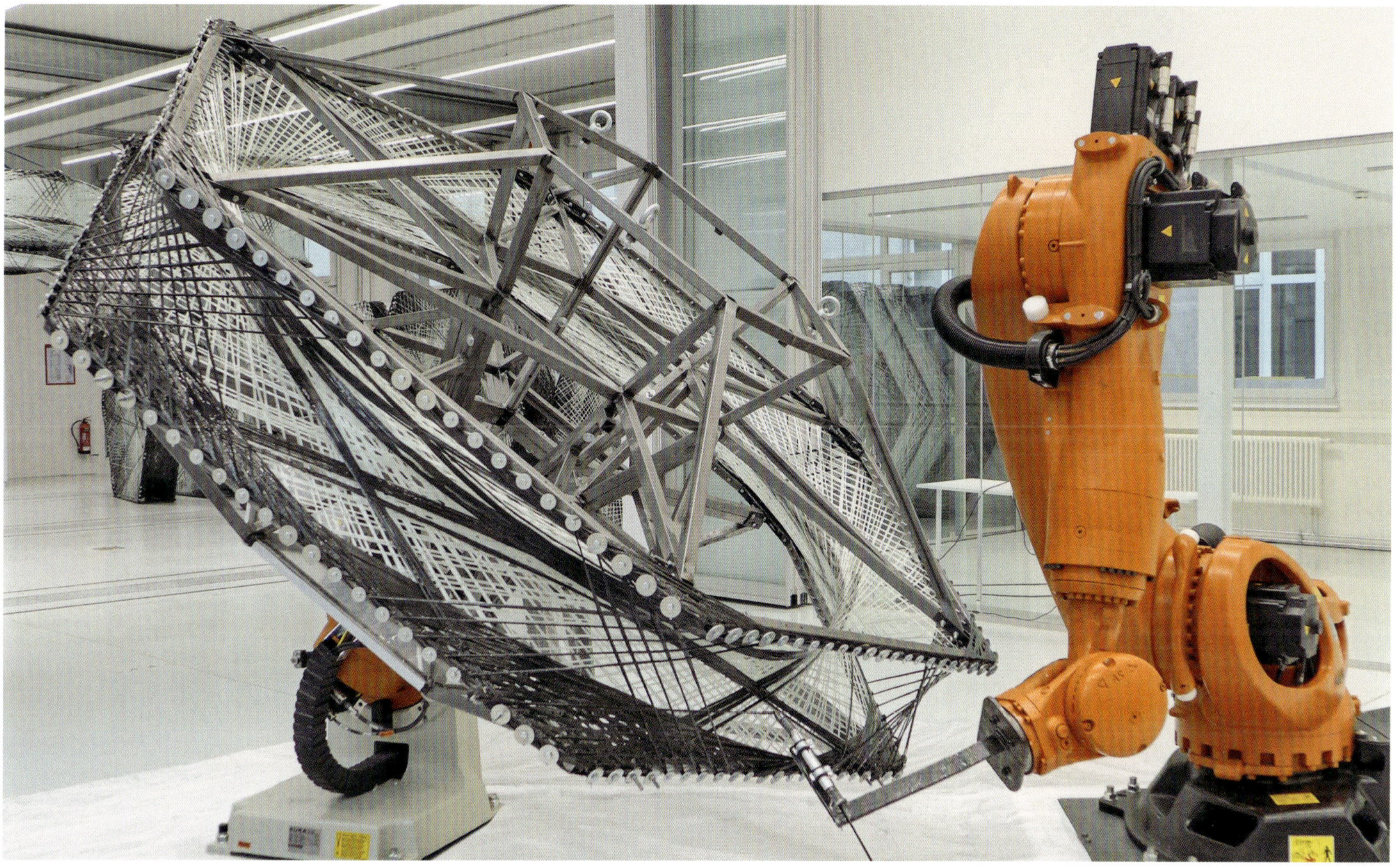

9] Fabrication setup: Eight-axis robot system with a reusable steel frame on which all of the different components were manufactured. In the course of the winding process, the form was created as a hyperbolic glass fiber body to which the load-bearing carbon fiber was applied in a load-adapted manner.

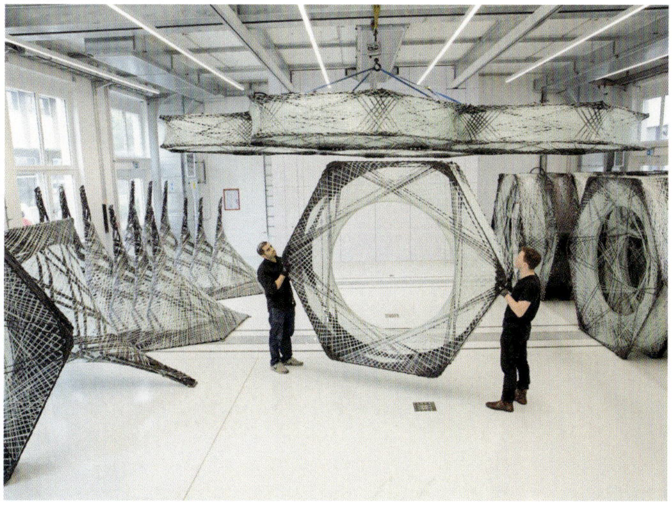

10, 11] Lightweight construction elements: The components were extremely light, with the structure weighing only 9 kg/m^2.

12, 13, 14] View of the pavilion in the central courtyard of the Victoria and Albert Museum in London: The canopy, which measured over 200 m², was covered with transparent polycarbonate sheets.

15] Evening view: As darkness fell, the glass fibers served to illuminate the inner courtyard.

basic modules: the canopy cells and the column heads. The latter represented the interface and connection of the canopy structure with the load-bearing columns. Both module types are based on a wound fiber structure of transparent glass fibers and black carbon fibers. The production is a result on a robotic winding process not requiring any mold, which has been continuously improved since the ICD/ITKE Research Pavilion 2012. A robot applies resin-saturated glass and carbon to a hexagonal winding tool. The transparent glass fibers create the spatial formwork on which the load-bearing structure of carbon fibers is placed. These have much greater stiffness and strength than glass fibers. Once the composite material is cured, the winding frame can be removed and reused.

The result was a structure entirely built from fiber composite. Only the screws between the components and the support feet were made of steel. Each module was adapted to its specific loading condition by differentiating the order, density and orientation of the fibers, resulting in a material-efficient and lightweight structure with a structural weight of only 9 kg/m^2. The majority of the fiber composite components were prefabricated in the ICD's manufacturing laboratory in Stuttgart.

OMETH FROM THE LORD AND IS WITH HIM FOR

17] Adaptable structure: The on-site winding robot permitted the production of additional elements, allowing the pavilion to grow and adapt in response to its use.

16, 18] Fibrous tectonics: The entire load-bearing structure of the pavilion consisted of fiber composite material. The high degree of integration of form, material, structure and fabrication resulted in a new kind of fibrous tectonics.

POSITION:
METTE RAMSGAARD-THOMSEN
ON

INTERDISCIPLINARITY: A NECESSARY MEANS FOR INNOVATION IN A NEW GLOBAL CONTEXT

Architecture is in the process of expanding its methodologies. As the new global contexts of the sustainability crisis challenge the way we think and build our societies, we come to the deep realization that the forming of architecture and the built environment is a local undertaking with global effect. In order to steer and change the way we build and thus form a more sustainable future for our societies, we need to expand our thinking and engage in broader discussions that impact the way we use resources, the way we adapt to a changing climate, the way we live in our cities, the way we understand health and the way we empower equality. Interdisciplinary dialogue is a necessary means for innovation. We need to create synergy between expertises, share our conceptual and practical tools and interface our methodologies.

Where this call for interdisciplinary collaboration has resonated over the last 50 years, the new urgency challenges our tendency to retreat into the traditionally siloed institutions that shape both research and practice.

We can understand this call from two different perspectives. A first, more introverted perspective challenges us to reconceive our practice and develop holistic methods that engage the breadth of the design chain. The formation of a shared digital platform and the ubiquity of the practice of modeling in design, analysis, specification and fabrication allows us to interface design information and create new feedback loops between processes and fundamentally rethink how we use materials and what building systems can be.

The new sciences of computational design, with their interdisciplinary links to the bourgeoning fields of data science and artificial intelligence, allow us to rethink the representational paradigms of architecture and create more resilient models of engagement.

By expanding our modeling boundaries – boundaries shaped by the proprietary conventions of disciplinary concern, methodology and perceptions of resolution – we come to perceive the interrelatedness of disciplines and their potential for creating new interdisciplinary, interscalar and intertemporal practices.

A second, more extroverted perspective asks for whom these innovations are intended. Situating research concerns within a global and socially rooted enquiry challenges our sense of grounding and aims for impact.

Interdisciplinary thinking also means considering the communities that receive these innovations. What systems of production and consumption do they become part of, what social and cultural frameworks of workmanship, citizenship and globalization do they affect? To truly innovate the way we build, we must develop partnerships with the communities through which these impacts can be articulated and understood.

Interdisciplinary collaboration is a condition of contemporary design practice. In the work of the ICD/ITKE and their collaborations on biomimetics as a model for architecture, they demonstrate how interdisciplinary collaboration can rethink not only existing building systems and the methods of design that enable them, but also our fundamental thinking about the foundational material systems of architecture. And this is of fundamental importance. Where the demonstrators presented in this volume can seem like formal studies exploring the shape and form of architecture, this belies the fundamental impact they embody. What is discovered here is not only a rethinking of the structural morphologies or the technologies of production – although these are serious contributions – but also the actual connective tissue of the digital chain that allows us to rethink the relationships between design, analysis, registration, specification, fabrication, assembly and operation of buildings. They help us consider how interdisciplinary thinking allows us to continue to reformulate and rethink the way we work in support of creating a new building future.

METTE RAMSGAARD-THOMSEN
Prof. PhD / Architecture and Digital Technology, Royal Danish Academy of Fine Arts (KADK) / Director, Centre for Information Technology in Architecture (CITA), KADK / Copenhagen, Denmark
—— 222

>> BUGA WOOD PAVILION

Bundesgartenschau Heilbronn, 2019

Using a minimum amount of material, the stunning wood roof spanned 30 meters above one of the BUGA's main concert and event venues, creating a special space. The transportable BUGA Wood Pavilion celebrated a completely new approach to digital timber construction. The project involved the development of a robotic manufacturing platform for the automated assembly and milling of the pavilion's 376 bespoke hollow segments. This fabrication process ensured that all the wooden segments fit together like a big, three-dimensional puzzle with a precision of three-tenths of a millimeter.

BIOMIMETIC LIGHTWEIGHT CONSTRUCTION: SEGMENTED WOOD SHELLS

The pavilion was one of the architectural attractions of the so-called Sommerinsel (summer island) – a core area of the Bundesgartenschau 2019 (the Federal Horticultural Show) in Heilbronn. Based on the research for the ICD/ITKE Research Pavilion 2011 and the Exhibition Hall at the Landesgartenschau 2014 in Schwäbisch Gmünd, the research team's goal was to raise the structural performance of biomimetically segmented wood shells to a new level and thus open up new fields of application for timber construction. The structure had to be designed to be completely reusable so that it could be dismantled after the BUGA and rebuilt at another location with no loss of performance.

The segmented shell construction is based on the biological principles of the plate skeleton of the sea urchin, researched by ICD and ITKE for almost a decade. To minimize material consumption and weight, each shell segment of the BUGA Wood Pavilion consisted of a large-scale hollow wooden cassette with a polygonal form. Each of these cassettes was composed of two thin plates connected by a ring of edge beams, all glued together to form a load-bearing component. The lower plate contained a large opening that allowed access to the concealed bolt connections during assembly, while at the same time creating a special architectural appearance. It also significantly improved the acoustic properties of the shell. The lightweight segments were connected by finger joints following the morphological principles of anatomic features found on the edge of sea urchins' plates. When assembled, the wooden shell,

1, 2] The roof made of wooden segments of the BUGA Wood Pavilion spans 30 m, creating a unique architectural space.

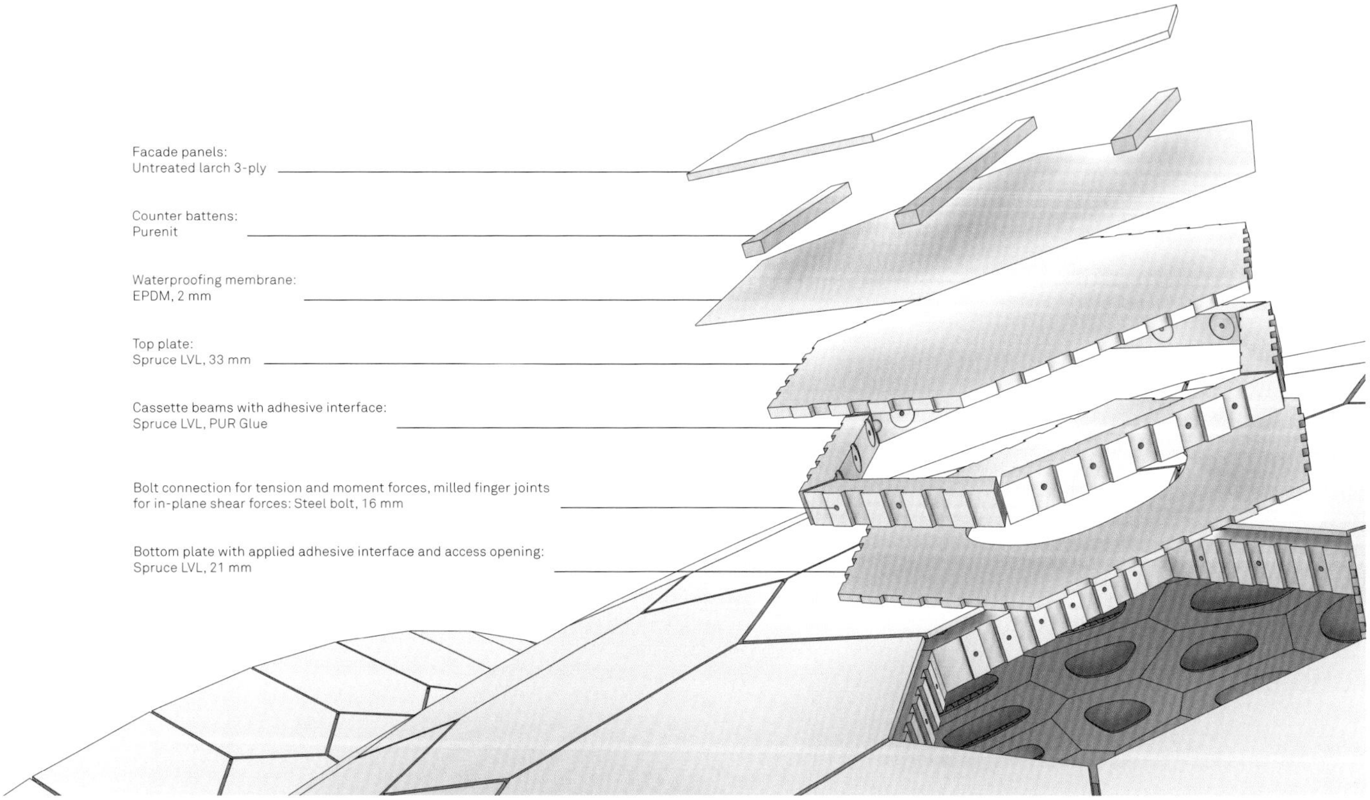

3] Buildup of the shell segments: The construction of the hollow cassettes was structurally very efficient and at the same time gave rise to very good acoustics.

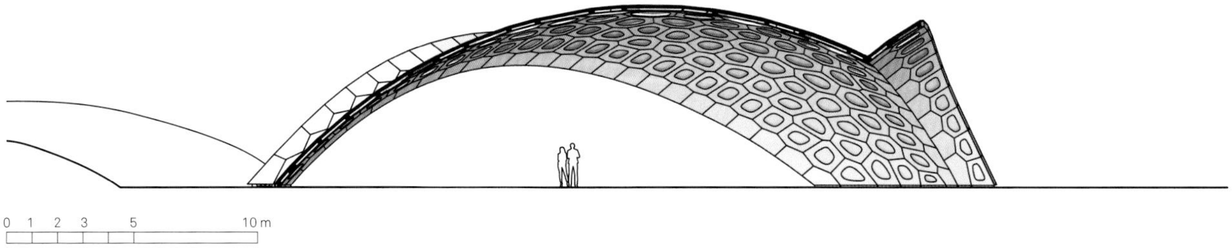

4] Section M 1:300: The span of the pavilion was almost three times the size of the Exhibition Hall in Schwäbisch Gmünd. Nevertheless, the weight per unit area is even lower at 36 kg/m² due to the transition to hollow segments.

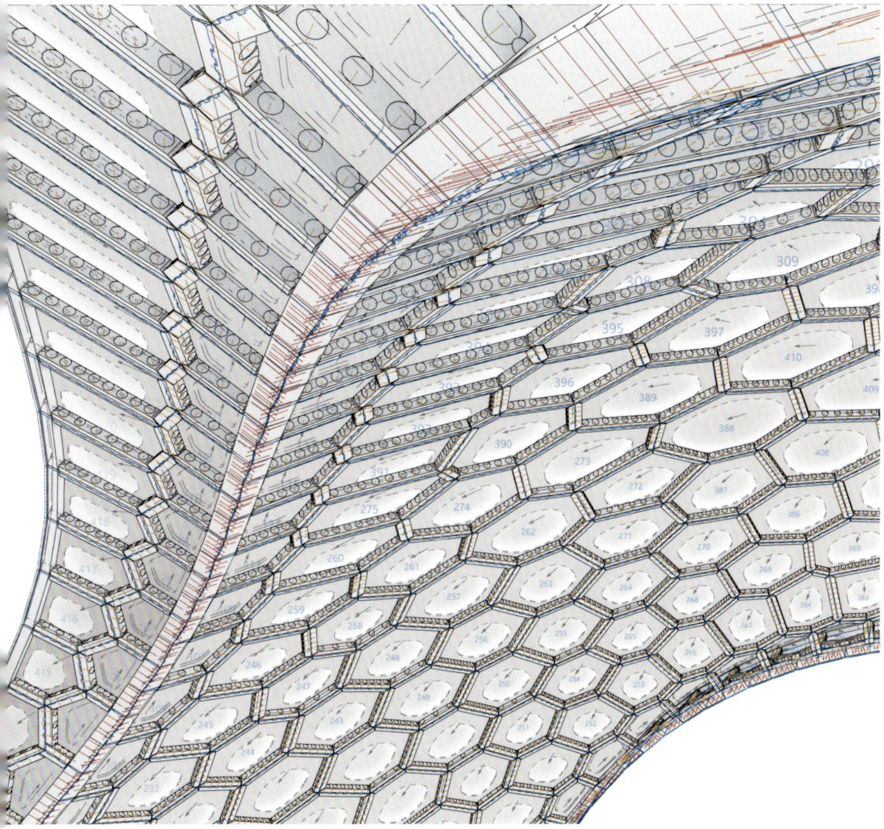

5] Integrative codesign: The segmented shell was generated by agent-based modeling in feedback with the development of the robotic manufacturing unit.

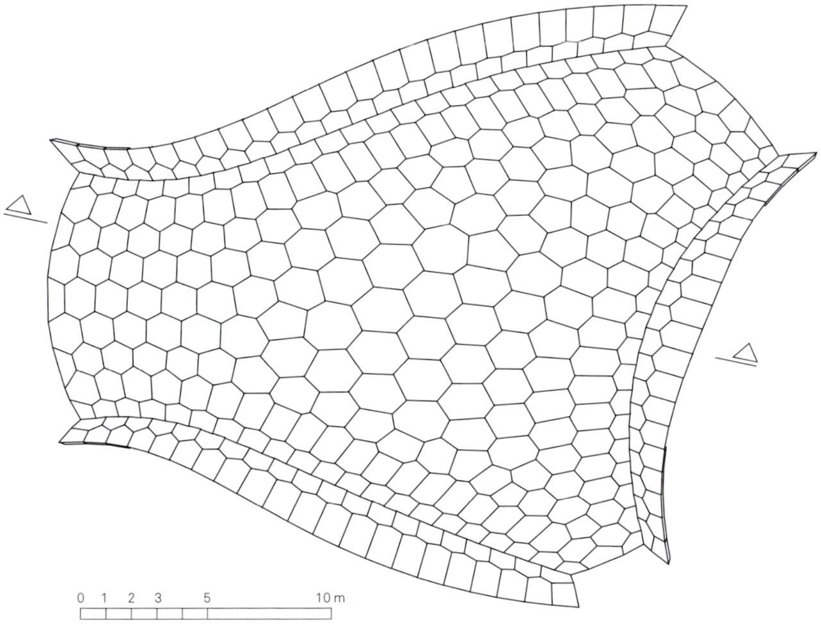

6] Plan view of the pavilion, M 1:300

BUGA WOOD PAVILION

Bundesgartenschau Heilbronn, 2019

Realization: Cooperation project of the Bundesgartenschau Heilbronn, the University of Stuttgart, and the implementing company müllerblaustein Bauwerke GmbH

PROJECT INFORMATION

Completion: April 2019

Floor area: approx. 500 m²

Shell area: 600 m²

Weight of load-bearing timber construction: 36.8 kg/m²

Dimensions: approx. 32 × 25 × 7 m

Structural load-bearing shell: Robot-manufactured hollow cassette segments made of veneered spruce plywood with UV protection

Cladding: EPDM sealing, 3-axis CNC-cut untreated larch triple-layer plates

MATERIAL

Laminated veneered lumber spruce/fir

CONSTRUCTION

Segmented shell made of polygonal hollow cassette segments

DESIGN

Multi-agent-based modeling

FABRICATION

Robotic 13-axis positioning, gluing, milling

BIOLOGICAL ROLE MODEL

Plate skeleton of the sand dollar

→ **PROJECT PARTICIPANTS**

— 215

→ **REFERENCES**

[107], [108], [109], [110], [111], [112]: — 227

with its expressive, doubly curved geometry, worked as a form-active structure.

INTEGRATIVE CO-DESIGN: FEEDBACK-DRIVEN DESIGN, ENGINEERING AND FABRICATION DEVELOPMENT

New construction methods require new forms of design and fabrication. The BUGA Wood Pavilion is an excellent example of codesign. The term describes the simultaneous and mutually informing development of design methods and production processes by an interdisciplinary team. The codesign method created for this project generated the shape of each component of the pavilion according to the architectural design intent and structural load. The concept and development of the transportable robotic manufacturing unit used was also an integral part of the codesign. This highly integrative process was the only possible way to produce 376 unique plate segments with 17,000 different finger joints in response to multifaceted design criteria for the overall structure and its details with an accuracy of three-tenths of a millimeter.

ROBOTIC PREFABRICATION: COMBINING AUTOMATED ASSEMBLY WITH HIGH-PRECISION MACHINING

Compared to solid wood elements, as for example those used for the Landesgartenschau Exhibition Hall, the hollow wood cassettes significantly reduce weight and material, but also increase the number of building parts eightfold, leading to more complex fabrication. The pursuit of greater resource efficiency therefore needed to go hand in hand with automated robotic production of the shell segments. For this purpose, ICD and the company BEC GmbH developed a novel, transportable, 14-axis robotic timber-manufacturing platform, which was used by the industrial partner müllerblaustein Bauwerke GmbH. The platform included two high-payload industrial robots mounted on a 20-foot standard container base. The flexibility of the industrial robots enabled the integration of all prefabrication steps of the pavilion's segments within one compact manufacturing unit. During production, each shell segment was first robotically assembled. This entailed the placement of preformatted timber plates and beams, controlled

7] Transport state of manufacturing unit: Within the context of the project, a location-independent robotic fabrication platform was developed.

8] Multifunction effectors: Two robots equipped with project-specific effectors cooperate in automated fabrication.

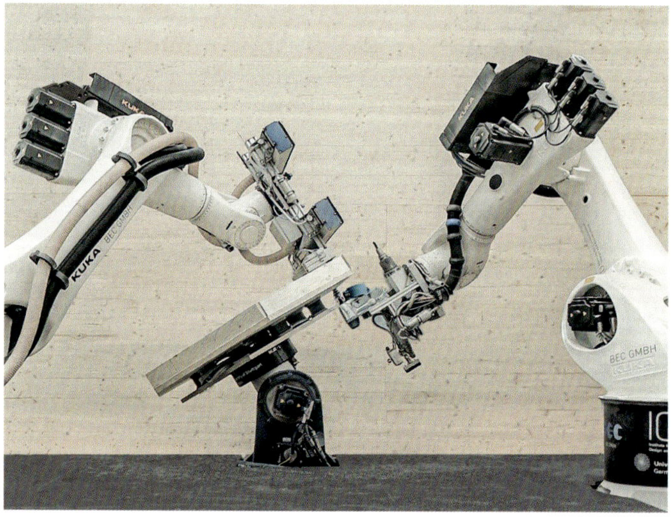

9] All 376 geometrically different hollow cassette segments were assembled and machined fully automatically.

10] High-precision, form- and force-fitting connection: The milling of the finger joints had a precision of 300 μm. This high accuracy is required so that the forces are transmitted from cassette to cassette via contact.

11] On-site assembly: Due to the high stiffness in combination with the low weight, the shell could be assembled almost entirely without the usually required scaffolding or formwork.

application for the structural glue joint between plate and beams, and temporary fixation with beech nails while the adhesive was setting. In a second step, the tailor-made finger joints and openings were machined with 300 µm accuracy into the assembled segments. From the assembly of beams and plates to the multitool machining and sensorial process- and image-based quality control, everything happened in a fully automated workflow, controlled by two million lines of robotic code directly exported from the computational design framework. On average, the assembly time per segment was eight minutes, with the high-precision milling taking another 30 minutes.

AN INNOVATIVE STRUCTURE AND AN EXCITING ARCHITECTURAL SPACE

The completely prefabricated wooden cassettes were assembled on-site by two craftsmen in just ten workdays. Due to the high rigidity of the hollow cassettes in conjunction with their low weight, the assembly was carried out without the extensive scaffolding or formwork usually required. Only the edge beams were supported locally in the middle. This simple assembly is essential for the economic efficiency of the construction. After the segments were connected by reusable bolts, an EPDM foil was rolled over the pavilion in eight strips to provide waterproofing. Untreated larch facade plates were used for the visible external cladding. All construction elements were designed for easy disassembly and reuse at a different site. The pavilion's load-bearing wood shell achieved a column-free span of 30 m, but weighed only 36.8 kg/m². Despite a threefold increase in span and fivefold increase in size, this is less than the Landesgartenschau Exhibition Hall benchmark.

The BUGA Wood Pavilion was located at a central crossroads in the undulating landscape of the summer island on the grounds of the Bundesgartenschau. Three dynamic arches formed inviting openings to the main directions and guided visitors into the pavilion's interior. The shell created a sinuous space for concerts and public events, characterized by excellent acoustics and a unique architectural atmosphere. This was especially true at night, when thousands of LED lights embedded in the shells' inner openings bathed the pavilion's interior in a subtle, warm, welcoming light.

12] View of the pavilion with illuminated hollow chambers of the structural cassette segments

13] Event space: The wood pavilion was used intensively for events during the BUGA. The good acoustic properties played a decisive role.

14, 15, 16] Landscape embedding: Within sight of the Fibre Pavilion, the Wood Pavilion stood at the intersection of two main axes of the Bundesgartenschau. The shape of the pavilion took up these spatial relationships (above) and embedded itself in the undulating landscape of the summer island (left and below).

>> BUGA FIBRE PAVILION

Bundesgartenschau Heilbronn, 2019

Embedded in the undulating landscape of the Bundesgartenschau 2019 in Heilbronn, the BUGA Fibre Pavilion offered an unusual architectural experience and a glimpse of future construction. The pavilion showed how the combination of cutting-edge computational technologies with constructional principles found in nature enables the development of a completely new type of building system. The pavilion's load-bearing structure consisted exclusively of fiber composites. Only a few years previously, it would have been impossible to design or build a pavilion of this kind. The globally unique structure was not only highly efficient and exceptionally light, but also provided a distinctive architectural expression.

Black carbon fibers, evoking tensed muscles, wrapped around a translucent fiberglass mesh. In combination with an outer ETFE membrane stretched over the supporting structure for weather protection the different materials create a rich contrast. The construction and design principles underlying the building remained comprehensible for the visitors. This was especially important given that most had probably never seen such a structure before. The unusual appearance exemplified new kinds of digital construction – no longer a vision of the future, but a tangible reality.

INTEGRATIVE COMPUTATIONAL DESIGN AND ROBOTIC FABRICATION

The pavilion consisted of over 150,000 m of spatially arranged glass and carbon fibers. The individual orientation of the fibers and the resulting laminates would have been almost impossible to realize with linear design processes and conventional production technologies. Instead, the density and alignment of the fibers in each component were realized with the help of a novel codesign approach – a parallel and feedback-oriented development of design methods and fabrication processes. Form, structure and architectural appearance could be calibrated taking into account the fabrication conditions.

In a coreless fiber winding process, a robot placed the

1, 2] The unique structure of the BUGA Fibre Pavilion is not only highly efficient and exceptionally light, but also creates an unmistakable, authentic architectural expression.

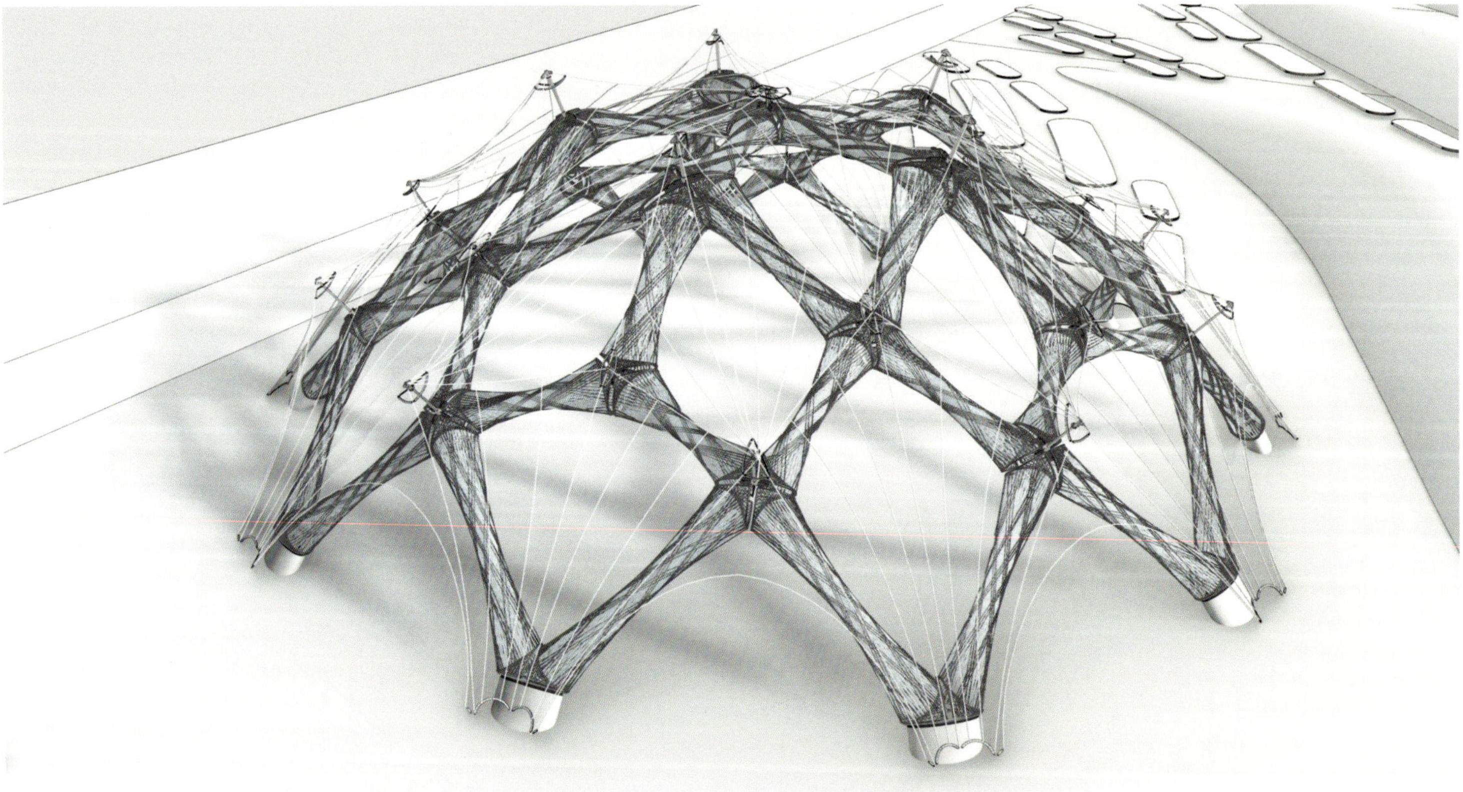

3] Integrative design model: The digital model was generated in feedback with the development of the structure and fabrication constraints. It contains all components and production data.

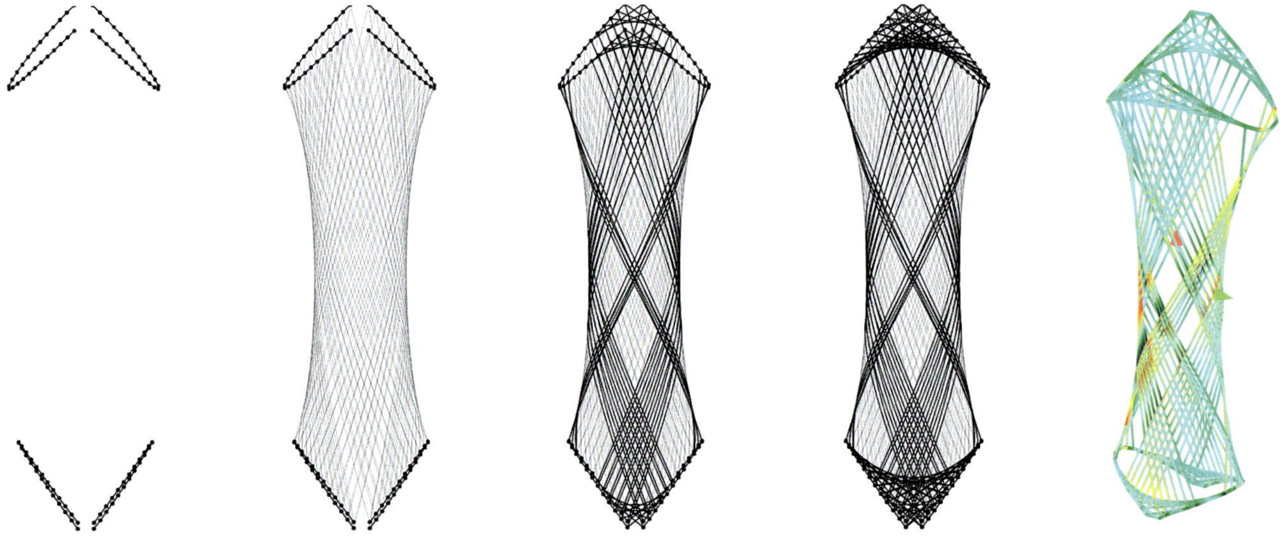

4] Fabrication and simulation model: As with the previous fiber pavilions, the hyperbolic glass fiber body was wound first, onto which the load-bearing carbon fibers were then laid. The stress on the individual carbon fiber filaments was structurally simulated.

5] Fabrication setup: The up to 5 m-long fiber composite components were fabricated by a winding robot on a rotating linear axis (top). First, the winding points were connected with glass fiber, whereby the shape emerged (middle). This was followed by the application of the load-bearing carbon fibers (bottom).

BUGA FIBRE PAVILION

Bundesgartenschau Heilbronn, 2019
Realization: Cooperation project Bundesgartenschau Heilbronn with the University of Stuttgart, and the implementing company FibR GmbH, Stuttgart

PROJECT INFORMATION

Completion: April 2019
Diameter: approx. 23 m
Floor area: approx. 400 m²
Weight of load-bearing fiber composite structure: approx. 7.6 kg per m² surface area
Construction system: 60 load-bearing, robotically fabricated glass and carbon fiber composite elements made of a total of 150,000 m of glass and carbon fibers; transparent, mechanically prestressed ETFE membrane

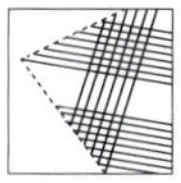

MATERIAL

Carbon fiber rovings and glass fiber rovings with epoxy resin

CONSTRUCTION

Rod dome made of fiber composite lattice tubes with mechanically prestressed ETFE membrane

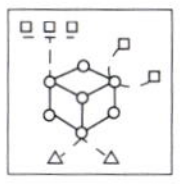

DESIGN

Parametric modeling in feedback with local and global material simulation

FABRICATION

Coreless robotic 7-axis winding, robot-guided fiber winding head, rotating winding frame

→ **PROJECT PARTICIPANTS**

—— 216

→ **REFERENCES**

[113], [114], [115], [116], [117]:
—— 227

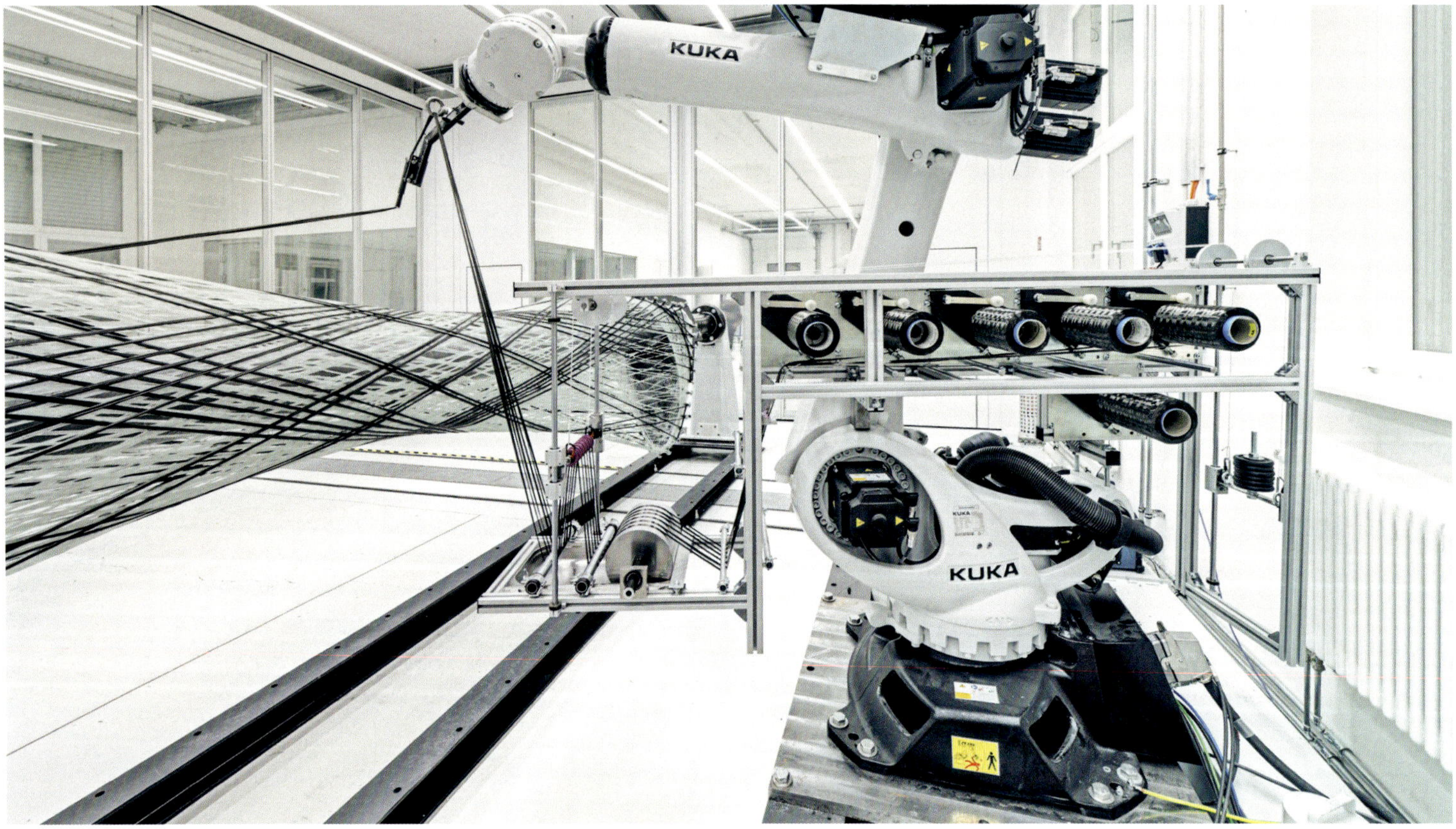

6, 7] Fabrication setup for research and development (top) and test setup for building approval (bottom)

8] On-site assembly: The low weight of the components enabled assembly without heavy scaffolding or lifting gear.

fibrous filaments freely between two rotating winding scaffolds to produce the components. As with the ICD/ITKE Research Pavilion 2016/17, for example, the shape of the components resulted from the interactions of the fibers, eliminating the need for any mold or mandrel. This process enables a bespoke form and individual fiber layup for each component without any economic disadvantages compared to series production of identical components. Neither production waste nor material waste is generated. During production, a lattice of translucent glass fibers is created first, onto which the black carbon fibers are placed exactly where structurally needed. This produces highly load-adapted components with a distinctive architectural appearance. The elements were produced by the industrial partner FibR GmbH. Each component took between four to six hours to make from around 1,000 m of glass fiber and 1,600 m of carbon fiber.

UNIQUE LIGHTWEIGHT STRUCTURE AND EXPRESSIVE ARCHITECTURAL SPACE

The pavilion covered a floor area of around 400 m^2 and achieved a free span of more than 23 m. The primary load-bearing structure consisted of 60 bespoke fiber composite components. With 7.6 kg/m^2, the fiber structure was about five times lighter than a conventional

9, 10] Close-up of the fiber composite structure

steel structure of comparable span. Elaborate testing procedures required for full approval showed that a single fibrous composite component can absorb up to 250 kN of compressive force – equivalent to about 25 t or the weight of more than 15 cars – with a net weight of the individual components of only about 70–80 kg.

The pavilion is the result of years of biomimetic research and combined the knowledge gained from all previous ICD/ITKE research pavilions made of fiber composite materials. It shows how an interdisciplinary exploration of biological principles in combination with digital technologies can lead to a novel and genuinely digital fiber composite building system. And it demonstrates how a novel construction system can be realized even under the conditions of strict German building regulations.

11] Unique lightweight construction: Pavilion with load-bearing fiber composite construction and transparent ETFE membrane as weather protection

12] Membrane detail

13, 14, 15] Genuinely digital construction: The extremely material-efficient dome, with a 23 m span and a structural weight of 7.6 kg/m², was a product of the profound integration of form, material, structure and fabrication made possible by digital technologies. It allowed this process to be experienced spatially and become architecturally effective.

POSITION: **PHILIPPE BLOCK** ON INNOVATIVE STRUCTURES

Innovation in structures, and in the materials used to realize them, offers an important opportunity to address one of the most pressing challenges humankind has ever had to face: the environmental crisis. As a major negative contributor, the building industry urgently needs to propose solutions to reduce pollution, especially greenhouse-gas emissions, resource depletion and waste. We desperately need a disruptive change, a paradigm shift!

Due to decades of research in more efficient heating and cooling strategies and increased ability to use clean or green energy, one could argue that the problem of operational energy and emissions could have straightforward solutions. In contrast, embodied energy and emissions (of greenhouse gases) remain the primary bottlenecks of construction. They result from the sourcing, producing, forming, transporting, demolishing and disposing of building materials and components, which can not be replaced in immediately obvious ways. Considering that, particularly for long-span and high-rise construction, the structure is a dominant component and major contributor to embodied energy and emissions, innovation in this field can provide the key to solving the "wicked problem" of our changing climate.

Two extreme strategies could be imagined to reduce the damaging impact of building structures and materials on the environment. One could build for longevity, for future adaptability in use (and thus loading cases), so that buildings do not grow obsolete. Alternatively, one could build with the least impact, which means reducing the volume and the negative/polluting impact, for example, the embodied carbon coefficient of the materials used. Ideally, one achieves both, developing strategies to keep materials in a circular construction in a respectively circular economy.

Significant improvements can be obtained by a) achieving strength through the structure's geometry rather than through material quantities, but also by b) using materials in the way they want to work. The former refers to material efficiency that optimized shapes, such as a doubly-curved shell, offer to carry loads. The latter, conversely, refers to material effectiveness, since lighter is not necessarily better if it demands high-strength, heavily polluting materials such as brick or concrete, both without real tensile capacity, that want to be used in compression only – as an arch or vault, for example, while cables or thin strands of fiber without buckling capacity want to be kept in tension – for example, as a prestressed net.

To use a material effectively, the structure's geometry thus needs to be aligned with the material's strengths and weaknesses.

Indeed, many clues for efficient and effective structural form might be found in nature, whose forms have evolved over time to align with the specificities of the materials they are made of. It is here that the impressive ICD/ITKE collaboration excels: in showing how to discover principles in nature that can be meaningfully translated and scaled up to offer innovative solutions for architectural construction. But to achieve the efficiencies that these structural geometries offer, one needs to find, develop and integrate novel fabrication and construction strategies in the design process in order to realize those nonstandard forms in an economically viable way without producing excessive waste.

Passing on responsibilities and liabilities from the designers to the engineers to the fabricators to the contractors leads to inefficiencies in communication, planning, redundancy and so on, and ultimately to the grand challenges of sustainability facing our industry. As a result, these sequential steps in current practice are producing an immensely nefast pressure on our planet. Furthermore, this does not leave any margin for profits and ultimately hinders innovation.

This outdated, restraining model needs to be entirely rethought. A fully integrated design-engineering-construction practice is needed in which computation is the glue, balancing all the requirements and interdependencies of form, performance, fabrication and assembly. Classical roles should be abandoned and authorship redefined.

Last, but not least, our industry's slow adoption of digitization, in all phases from design to construction, has led to a problematic stagnation of labor productivity in the sector. This is not an innocent observation, as the stagnation of design and construction methods in the last century is one of the direct causes of the many challenges we now face. We are expected to double the building stock in the next 40 years. This is not possible with outdated practices that have barely evolved in the last decade.

Achim Menges and Jan Knippers are leading the way in rethinking preconceptions and breaking with antiquated models. They have introduced the effective mode of the real-scale pavilion to challenge concepts of education, practices of engineering, notions of aesthetics, methods of design, compartmentalization of professions and processes for fabrication and construction. These pavilions and demonstrators, the main topic of this book, not only provoke; they inspire an entire generation of students, stir discussion and debate, allow a discourse with industry, and most importantly, give hope that the needed, disruptive change is possible.

By pushing the boundaries of construction, the ICD/ITKE partnership is a trailblazing pioneer in bridging the gap between academia and practice.

PHILIPPE BLOCK
Prof. Dr. / Block Research Group BRG, Institute of Technology in Architecture, ETH Zurich / Director NCCR Digital Fabrication / Zurich, Switzerland
___ 221

>> URBACH TOWER

Remstal Gartenschau 2019, Urbach

Until now, the production of curved wood has been an elaborate and energy-intensive, mechanical forming process requiring heavy machinery. A novel research approach now represents a change: without mechanical influence, flat wood components bent into their predefined shape by themselves in a controlled, industrial drying process. The 14 m-high Urbach Tower is the world's first building made of self-shaped, large-format components. Not only does it demonstrate an innovative fabrication approach resulting in novel timber construction, but it also architecturally intensifies the experience of space and landscape as a striking landmark that was the municipality of Urbach's contribution to the Remstal Gartenschau 2019 (Remstal Garden Show).

MATERIAL PROGRAMMING AND SELF-SHAPING OF WOOD

Changes in humidity normally cause undesirable deformations and cracks in timber construction, which are minimized as far as possible. In this project, however, this moisture-induced swelling and shrinkage is used in a novel manufacturing process to actively control the change in shape based on a digital simulation model. Just as machines can be programmed to perform different movements, wood can be programmed to transform into predetermined shapes when dried. During drying, wood shrinks more strongly perpendicular to the grain direction than lengthwise. If two layers of wood are glued together to form a bilayer, in which the layers are arranged in 0°- and 90°-orientation of the grain direction, the bilayer will bend due to shrinkage across the grain direction. This curving bilayer is the basic element of the new process. The curvature can be defined in advance by the thickness of the element, its layer structure, the fiber orientation and the varying moisture content of the wood. The development of large-scale self-shaping constitutes a paradigm shift in timber manufacturing. Instead of employing laborious mechanical forming processes, the material shapes entirely by itself.

The components are initially manufactured as flat panels using computer-aided models. The 5 × 1.2 m bilayers made of spruce wood, which initially have a high wood moisture content, are dried in a standard industrial process. The curvature changes in proportion to the

1, 2] The striking shape of the Urbach Tower is created in a novel process of self-forming the complex curved components.

3] Self-shaping of wood: Wood components can be manufactured in such a way that they bend into a previously defined and calculated shape by themselves when the moisture content is reduced during the drying process. No forming or pressing tools are required.

4, 5] Recording and sorting: In the sawmill, the existing equipment is used to record the fiber angle and moisture content of the lumber (left) and sort it accordingly (right).

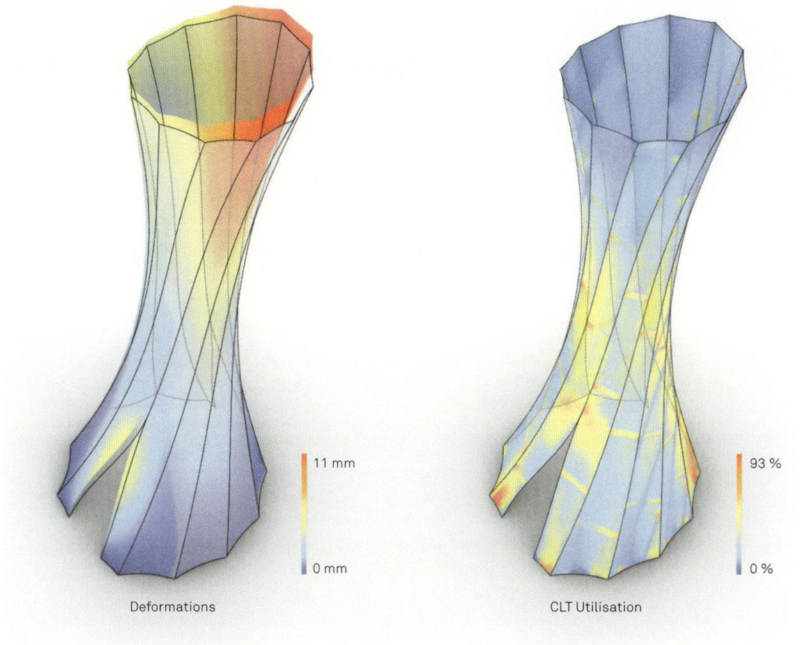

6] High-performance structure: The geometry enables a 14.2 m-high tower made of only 90 mm-thick wooden elements without any further stiffening measures.

7] Drying for self-shaping: The two-layer wooden components are dried industrially in a kiln. The self-shaping process occurs in a precalculated form.

URBACH TOWER

Location: Urbach, Germany

Realization: University of Stuttgart commissioned by the municipality of Urbach, research partner for self-shaping wooden components ETH Zurich/ EMPA, industry partner Blumer-Lehmann AG

PROJECT INFORMATION

Completion: May 2019

Height: 14.2 m

Dimensions: radius 4.0 m bottom, 3.0 m top, 1.6 m center

Material: spruce wood CLT with 10-30-10-30-10 mm buildup, larch wood facade with titanium oxide surface treatment

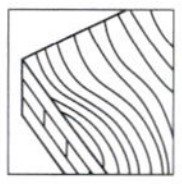

MATERIAL

Cross-laminated spruce wood

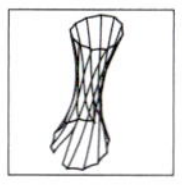

CONSTRUCTION

Tower made of curved cross-laminated timber strips

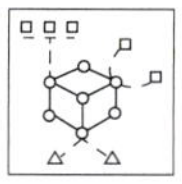

DESIGN

Parametric modeling in feedback with local and global material simulation

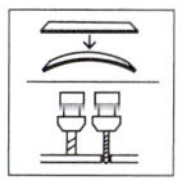

FERTIGUNG

Self-shaping,
5-axis CNC milling and drilling

BIOLOGICAL ROLE MODEL

Self-shaping conifer cones

→ **PROJECT PARTICIPANTS**

—— 217

→ **REFERENCES**

[118], [119], [120], [121], [122]:
—— 227

8, 9] Self-shaped components: The components of the tower consist of two layers of self-shaped wood and an additional locking layer.

decrease in moisture content. When removed from the drying chamber – which takes a few days in the standard industrial drying process – the elements are precisely curved according to the specifications. In order to lock the geometry in place, they are then laminated together. In this way, dimensionally stable cross-laminated timber components are produced which, in contrast to conventional curved elements fabricated using the elastic cold-bending process, no longer change their shape because there were hardly any residual forces and related springback. The entire process of self-shaping manufacturing, from the cutting of the logs in the sawmill to the production of the self-shaping panels, the drying process, and the final machining and pre-assembly, can be easily integrated into existing industrial wood processing and manufacturing workflow.

EXPRESSIVE AND EFFECTIVE WOOD CONSTRUCTION

The Urbach Tower consists of 12 curved components made from cross-laminated timber. The tower's load-bearing structure exhibits a thickness of 90 mm while cantilevering over 14 m, resulting in a span-to-thickness ratio of approximately 160:1. The curvature enhances stiffness, and thus enables a slender structure of only 38 kg/m^2 surface area. With precisely pre-calculated curvature and optimal fiber alignment from the manufacturing process, each component could be cut and processed in only 90 minutes machine time. The components were five-axis CNC-cut from half-cylinder blanks, which were then pre-assembled into building groups of three components for transport, including water barrier and external wood cladding. Crossing screws, whose placement and angle are optimized in relation to their structural utilization, connect the lightweight building elements. A continuous connection along the seam ensures a homogeneous load transfer. Apart from the screws, no other steel components are required to stiffen the structure. On the outside, a custom-made facade of cut glulam beams made of larch was applied. A transparent, durable, inorganic coating protects the wood from UV radiation and fungal attack. Instead of the usual cracking and turning silver-gray under the influence of the weather, the larch wood whitens over time.

The prefabricated assembly groups of the tower, each consisting of three curved components, were erected in a single working day by a team of four craftsmen with no need for elaborate scaffolding or formwork, and topped off by a transparent roof. The structure showcases the possibilities for efficient, economical, ecological and expressive wood architecture arising at the interface of master craftsmanship, digital innovation and scientific research.

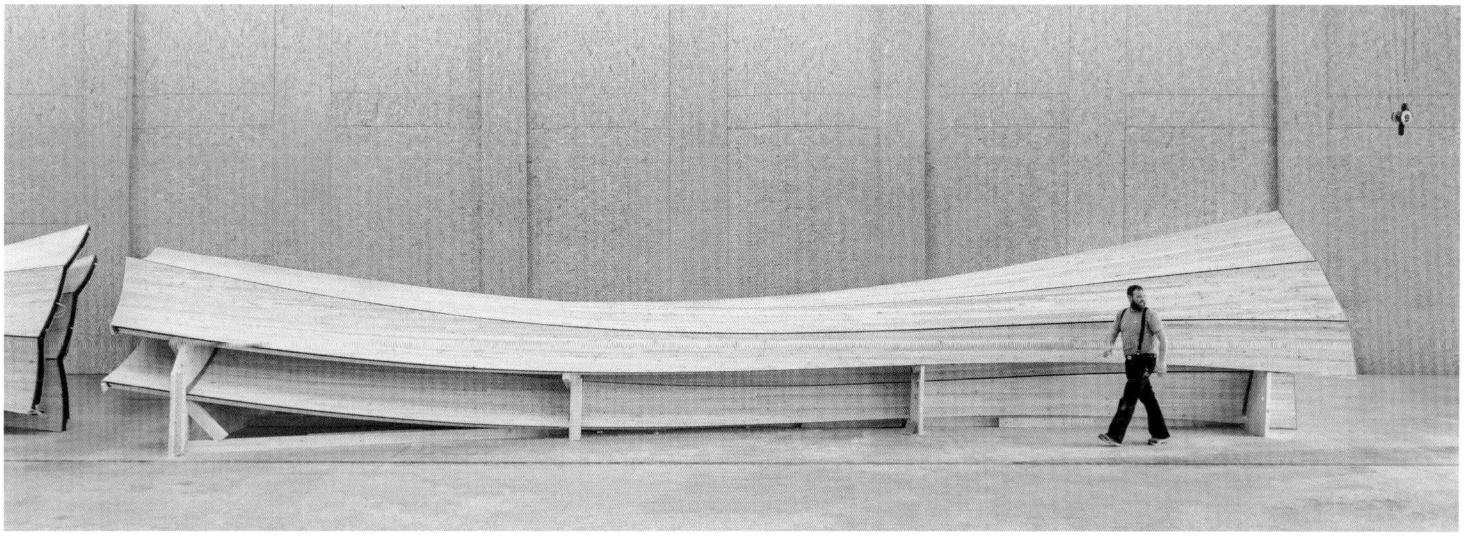

10, 11] Prefabrication: The curved, load-bearing cross-laminated timber parts are protected with larch wood cladding (top). The tower was completely prefabricated in four assembly groups (below).

ARCHITECTURAL LANDMARK FOR THE REMS VALLEY

During the Remstal Garden Show 2019, the Urbach Tower was one of 16 stations designed by some of the most renowned German architects. The tower now continues to stand as a striking landmark on a slope in the center of the valley, visible from afar. A place of shelter that caters to inner reflection, it also commands an impressive view of the landscape. Its distinctive form lends a contemporary architectural expression to the traditional construction material, wood. Its elegantly curved shape celebrates the natural properties of the material. The concave curvature of the elements results in sharp lines and crisp surfaces on the outside of the tower, accentuated by daylight and the whitening of the larch cladding over time. In contrast, in the interior the convex curvature creates an unexpected visual and tactile material experience, with the timber structure appearing to be almost soft and textile-like. The impression of gently curved surfaces is further intensified by the indirect light illuminating the interior from above through the transparent roof.

12] On-site construction: The 14 m-high tower was erected in one day. The wall thickness of the wooden construction is only 90 mm and, with the exception of the screws, does not require any steel stiffening or connection elements.

13, 14] Interior and exterior effect: The shape of the tower is accentuated by the concave, upright exterior surfaces (above). In contrast, the convex curvature of the structure in the interior has a soft, textile-like appearance (right).

15, 16, 17] View and scenic embedding: The gently curved opening frames a wide view over the Rems valley (left). A striking landmark, the tower dominates the surrounding landscape.

POSITION:
PETER CACHOLA SCHMAL
ON

LESS WEIGHT THROUGH MORE FORM

Underlying all the ICD/ITKE pavilions is the considerable interest in innovative material developments and manufacturing techniques.

Achim Menges and Jan Knippers are seeking to explore the limits of our profession and demonstrate their working hypotheses in small temporary structures – the traditional reason why pavilions have been made. (The word "pavilion" derives from the Latin "papilio" [butterfly], an old military term for mobile tents.)

The inspiration for the design approaches often lies in natural load-bearing structures, such as the shells of beetles or sea urchins. Their morphology is transferred, abstracted and processed with robotic methods into high-performance shell structures, often by interdisciplinary research communities including structural engineers and biologists.

In addition to new developments, these pavilions also impress with their beautiful poetry, which results from their arrangement of small, structural elements.

One of the most enchanting results is the hydroscopic works completed for the FRAC Centre in Orléans in 2014: a weather-sensitive pavilion whose wafer-thin wooden flaps can open independently as humidity increases – a new type of climate-responsive architecture developed further in the Urbach Tower for the Remstal Gartenschau 2019. Here the natural shrinking process has been exploited through controlled, industrial drying for independent form generation. The twisted leaves result in a 9 cm-high, thin but very powerful support structure for a tower with a height of 14 m, and the almost unimaginable slenderness of 160:1 – particularly striking considering that the new sensational pencil towers in Manhattan have a slenderness of just 25:1.

It is no coincidence that these pavilions recall the work of the great role model Frei Otto, who founded the legendary Collaborative Research Center SFB 230 Natural Constructions – Lightweight Construction in Architecture and Nature at the same university 30 years ago. After the DFG funded a new Collaborative Research Center at the University of Stuttgart in 2014 called SFB Transregio 141 Biological Design and Integrative Structures, founded by Achim Menges from the ICD and Jan Knippers from the ITKE, in 2019 the two partners went on to establish a DFG Cluster of Excellence called EXC 2120: Cluster of Excellence IntCDC – Integrative Computational Design and Construction for Architecture.

Research has once again reached the highest level in the Faculty of Architecture at the University of Stuttgart – congratulations!

PETER CACHOLA SCHMAL
Architect, Curator and Architectural Publicist / Executive Director of the German Architecture Museum (DAM) / DAM Curator / Frankfurt am Main, Germany
—— 221

PROS PECTS

FOR RESEARCH AND PRACTICE

It is in the nature of fundamental research projects that they open up two possible prospects: on the one hand, the transfer of results into practice; and on the other, that most of the findings will give rise to questions for subsequent research.

The same applies for the works presented in this book. During the course of the latter we have repeatedly tested what possibilities our research opens up for architectural practice. The aim of our work is to make a positive contribution to the development of built architecture. The first step in this direction has generally been participation in competitions via various collaborations and partnerships. However, new scientific questions and research directions have also frequently arisen in the interplay between the projects themselves, which have then been pursued in the context of research work by the institutes and master's theses of the ITECH degree program.

Both prospects – further exploration as well as application-oriented transfer – are important components and drivers of our work.

>> PROSPECT ACADEMIC RESEARCH: TIMBER CONSTRUCTION

Building with wood offers many possibilities for interlinked technical and architectural innovations. One exciting challenge is to develop an integrative approach for the use of simple and low-cost, semifinished wood products, as was the case with the presented projects. Another important aspect is striving for mono-material systems using neither additional fasteners nor adhesives.

MONO-MATERIAL SYSTEMS

The IBA Timber Prototype House embodies this approach to digitally simplified timber construction. The experimental building – a sideways-turned interpretation of a log house for the twenty-first century – combines the advantages of traditional, low-cost block construction with the possibilities of digital design and fabrication methods. The project investigates a new timber construction system for an environmentally friendly, economical and architecturally expressive mono-material building envelope. In contrast to the horizontal stacking of typical block construction methods, here the solid scantlings are lined up vertically. This means that the alignment of the wall components corresponds to the main load-bearing direction of the wood. At the same time, it is possible to make slits in the solid scantlings without impairing the load-bearing capacity. On the one hand, the slits act as relief cuts that prevent the solid wood from splitting. This ensures dimensional stability and airtightness, a considerable difficulty in conventional block construction. At the same time, the slits are also used as air chambers, which reduces thermal conductivity and increases the insulation values of the material. The digital fabrication process enables highly precise, airtight, mono-material joints between the wooden elements, thus eliminating the need for additional metal fasteners or adhesives. The resulting sustainable mono-material building system is a structure, skin and insulation in one. No additional insulation is required even to meet strict German energy-saving

1] IBA Prototype House, IBA Thüringen, 2019:
ICD Institute for Computational Design and Construction (Prof. A. Menges)
Jade University of Applied Sciences Oldenburg (Guest Prof. H. Drexler)
IBA (International Building Exhibition) Thüringen (Dr. M. Doehler-Behzadi, T. Haag)

2] Mono-Material Wood Wall: Highly insulating, mono-material timber construction system made of solid scantlings

standards. The airtightness has also been proven in a blower door test.

This new type of block construction makes it possible to overcome the strictly right-angled character of most wooden architecture. The integrative computational design and fabrication approach allows walls and ceilings to be gently curved. This not only enables the ratio of space to enveloping surface to be maximized, but also the architectural expression of this unique micro-building to be intensified. Beyond the specific case of this experimental prototype house, the developed building system offers various application possibilities for digital solid-wood construction.

HUMAN-ROBOT INTERACTION

The segmented wood shells shown in this book aim to test the architectural and constructive potential of robotic prefabrication for timber construction and demonstrate it as effectively as possible. With the mobile manufacturing unit for the BUGA Wood Pavilion, it was shown that fully automated prefabrication of complex components can also be implemented in a traditional, medium-sized, timber construction company, thus opening up new fields of activity to such companies. This platform-based approach to prefabrication in timber construction is currently being deepened and expanded in cooperation with partners from the production technology sector. Another field of research is the assembly of timber construction elements on the construction site, which in previous projects was largely carried out manually. The approaches to human-machine cooperation in timber construction prefabrication that have been investigated in various research projects – for example, the Collaborative Robotic Workbench – are a next step to be extended to on-site assembly, so that manual construction-site processes can be rendered more effective using digital assistance systems.

DISTRIBUTED ROBOTICS

Also, the relatively low weight of timber construction elements in relation to their structural performance opens up completely new approaches for construction. For example, the Distributed Robotic Assembly System for In-Situ Timber Construction project is investigating the possible effects of distributed robotics in timber construction. The developed system consists of networked single-axis robots that use standardized timber elements both as a building material and a component of the robot system. The wooden elements are therefore not only components of the structure to be built, but also an integral part of the robotic system that builds the structure. This simultaneous approach reduces and simplifies the complexity of the robot system. The lower costs, lightness and robustness of the overall system open up new possibilities for timber construction. A large number of robots can work together quickly and in parallel during prefabrication or on-site to create structures, which may even be reversible and adaptable. Thus, future construction work becomes conceivable in which distributed robotic systems call into question the hitherto strict demarcation between the design, construction, use and dismantling phases by merging them.

3] Collaborative Robotic Workbench:
KUKA Innovation Award 2018, Finalist
ICD, Prof. A. Menges

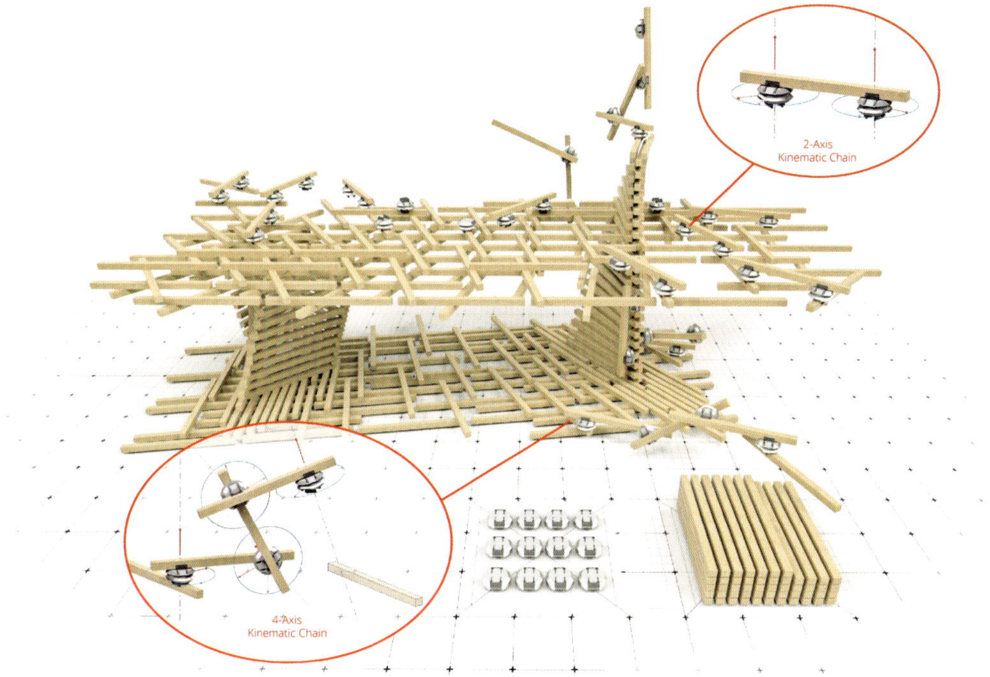

4] Distributed Robotic Assembly System for In-Situ Timber Construction:
ITECH MSc thesis project by S. Leder, R. Weber
Advisors: D. Wood, O. Bucklin
Supervisor: Prof. A. Menges, second supervisor: Prof. J. Knippers

TRANSFER INTO PRACTICE

A further goal is to transfer the digital methods and processes developed into general multistory construction tasks. Multistory buildings made of wood are currently primarily characterized by strict, regular grids and small spans. Digital manufacturing offers the possibility of varying the geometry of the construction elements individually and adapting them to the respective functional and constructional requirements. To this end, new building systems need to be developed that dispense with steel components as far as possible. Instead, they should use glued fitting connections that can be prefabricated in a systematic computational process. Further challenges are posed by the integration of building services, as well as other functional layers and finishes. Here, too, the building systems must be adapted in such a way that design, production and assembly can be integrated into computational processes.

The aim is to use adaptable, differentiable timber building systems to open up new types of structural typologies and building morphologies for timber construction that will enable more advanced, high-quality architecture.

5] The single-axis robot is part of a team of many small robots that create the construction as a decentralized robot system.

>> PROSPECT ACADEMIC RESEARCH: FIBER COMPOSITE CONSTRUCTION

One focus of the ICD and ITKE's research is the investigation of genuinely digital building approaches that result from the integration of design methods, fabrication and construction processes and the associated material and building systems. Examples include the fiber composite constructions presented in this book, created from continuous fibers in a robotic manufacturing process without the need for extensive mold making.

6] Specimens for material tests: Four test objects made of flax fibers and various petroleum and plant oil-based epoxy resins (left), one made of carbon fibers impregnated in epoxy resin (right)

ECOLOGICAL MATERIALS

The materiality of the fiber and the matrix plays only a minor role in the developed manufacturing process. For the fiber composite projects described, glass and carbon fibers and epoxy resin were used only due to their availability and performance. However, the use of alternative and ecologically more efficient starting materials for resins and fibers is an obvious and pressing question. Future projects will increasingly focus on the use of natural fibers made from flax, hemp and bio-based resin systems, some consisting of renewable raw materials. The use of mineral binders is also being investigated, as currently none of the organic resins meet the high fire-protection and durability requirements. Besides hemp, jute and kenaf, flax has the best mechanical properties and can also be grown in Europe. The mechanical properties almost reach the values of glass,

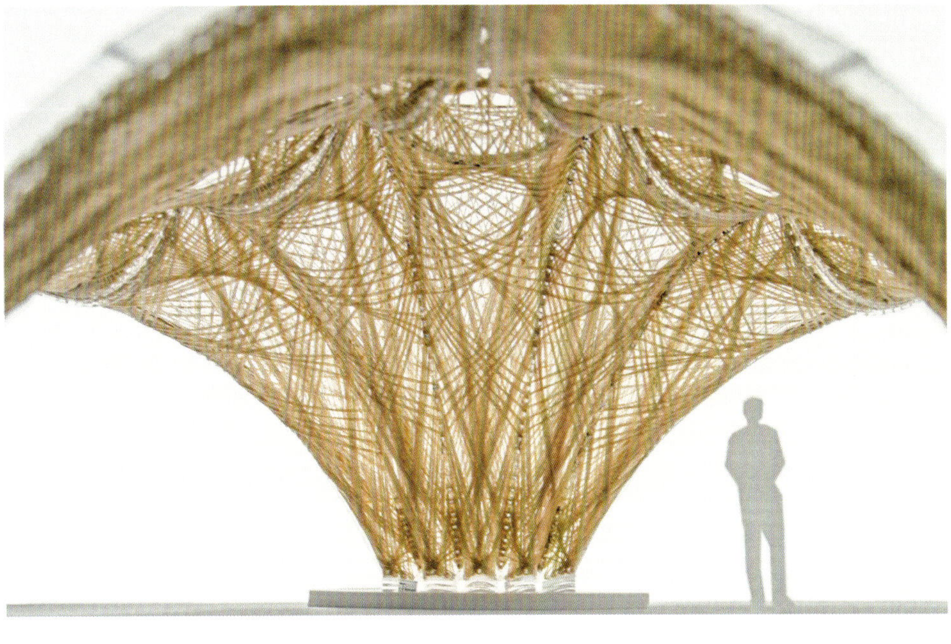

7] Physical model of the *liv*MatS Pavilion made of flax fibers for the Freiburg Botanical Garden

8] The component spans 2.7 m and carries a load of 560 kg with a dead weight of only 10.2 kg.

ITECH MSc thesis project by J. Christie
Advisors: J. Solly and S. Bodea
Supervisor: Prof. J. Knippers
Second supervisor: Prof. A. Menges

but show a greater deviation. Plant oil-based polyester or epoxy resins have been available for some time. Their widespread use is countered above all by their high cost.

ANALYSIS AND SIMULATION

The fiber orientation of the projects presented in this book has been adapted to the main load paths identified in a structural analysis. However, the load-bearing capacity of the components had to be determined primarily by experiment. These component tests involve considerable effort. For a broad application, though, the reliable computational prediction of the failure load is an indispensable prerequisite. In research, form finding and simulation methods must be developed for this purpose, which cover the multitude of material and system parameters and take into account the geometric restrictions of the winding process. Only in this way can the structures be statically optimized and the full lightweight potential of the building system be exploited. For this reason, smaller prototypes were repeatedly produced in parallel to the projects presented in the book, including in the context of master's theses, on the basis of which simulation methods were developed and evaluated step-by-step. However, the integration of these approaches into a robust and reliable structural analysis method is a task that will require many years of research and development.

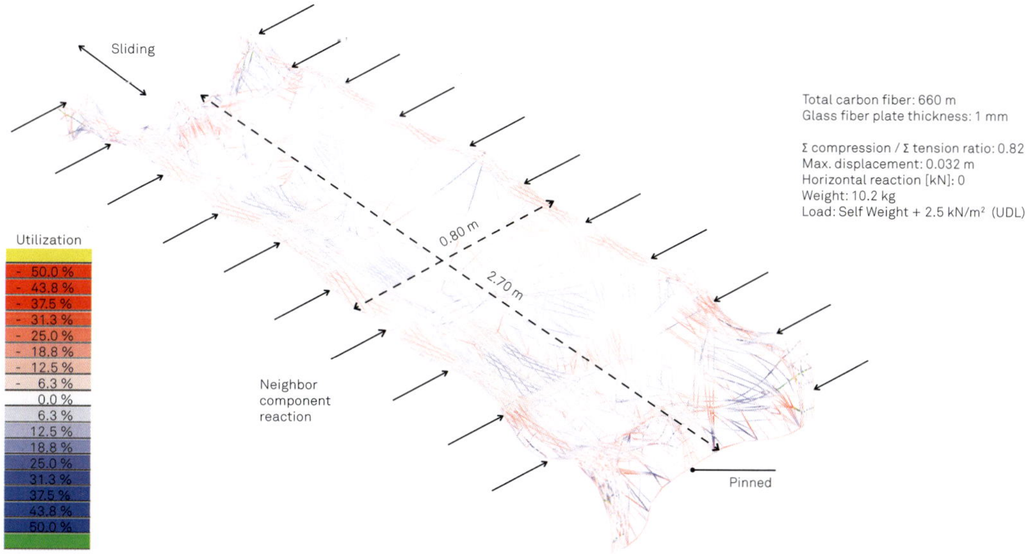

9] Development of a simulation method for form finding and structural analysis of a wound ceiling element

FUNCTIONAL INTEGRATION

Since the robotic winding process requires neither high temperatures nor high pressure, it allows the integration of additional functional components such as sensors and actuators. Of particular interest here are fiber-optic sensors, which in principle can be laid at the same time as the load-bearing structural fibers. This will in the future enable the creation of multifunctional building systems that monitor themselves and thus reduce the high safety factors for fiber composite constructions currently required by building authorities. In this way, the already astonishingly low material consumption could be reduced even further. These ideas have already been tested to some extent in the Elytra Filament Pavilion. There it became clear that the real challenge lies less in the physical integration of the sensors than in the evaluation and interpretation of the large amounts of data. Accordingly, new forms of cooperation for data management and data integration were established with partners from computer science.

MOBILE ROBOT SYSTEMS

The production approaches presented for the manufacture of the fiber composite construction systems were

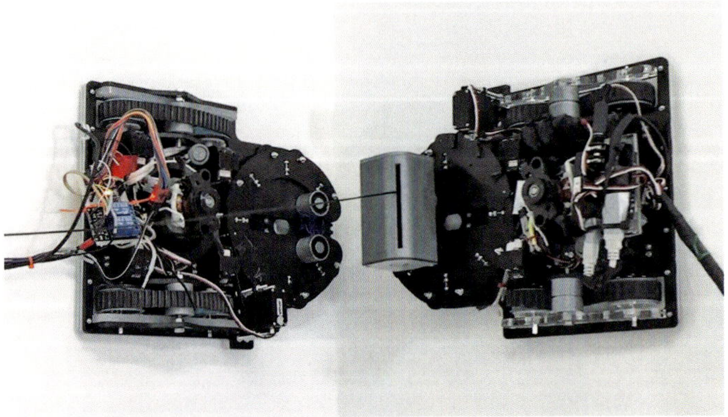

10, 11] Mobile Robotic Fabrication System for Filament Structures
ITECH MSc thesis project by M. Yablonina
Advisors: E. Baharlou, M. Prado, T. Schwinn
Supervisor: Prof. A. Menges, second supervisor: Prof. J. Knippers

12, 13] Cyber Physical Macro Material as a UAV [Re]configurable Architectural System:
ITECH MSc thesis project by M. Aflalo, J. Chen, B. Tahanzadeh
Advisors: D. Wood, M. Yablonina
Supervisor: Prof. A. Menges, second supervisor: Prof. J. Knippers

mostly based on industrial robots, which were used in various configurations in the workshop. At a relatively early stage, the question arose as to whether the machines for local on-site production of large structures would have to be much smaller and more agile. As the construction method places only moderate demands on the load capacity the processing machines, this is quite possible. In addition to the expansion of the working space of industrial robots by adding an unmanned flying machine investigated in the ICD/ITKE Research Pavilion 2016/17, there were a number of other projects dealing with distributed mobile robot systems for the production of fiber composite structures.

In the Mobile Robotic Fabrication System for Filament Structures project the foundations were laid for cooperating fiber-applying robots that can be navigated on both horizontal and vertical surfaces. These "wall climbers" have been supplemented in subsequent projects with more differentiated robots, for example, "thread walkers" using taut fibers to transport more filaments from one end of the structure to the other. In the future, distributed production systems of many semiautonomous robots will be able to create larger fiber structures on-site in highly parallel processes.

RECONFIGURABLE ARCHITECTURE

Furthermore, the construction method for fiber composite structures makes it possible to question the strict separation of the design, construction, use and dismantling phase emblematic of current building approaches. Due to the extremely small dimensions and very compact construction equipment of the fiber composite construction method, all these phases can be combined in a dynamic and adaptable architectural system.

This approach, first presented in connection with the Elytra Filament Pavilion, was taken up and further developed in the project entitled Cyber Physical Macro Material as a UAV [Re]configurable Architectural System. The agile roof system consists of a combination of cyber-physical components, a kind of large-scale macro material. This is based on a lightweight carbon fiber structure with integrated electronics for communications and sensor technology as well as autonomous flight devices that interact with the elements and can continuously assemble, reconfigure and disassemble them. Physical adaptivity through integrated sensor technology enables a new kind of architectural behavior in radical contradiction to traditional ideas of structural permanence, passive buildings and lethargic construction processes.

>> PROSPECT ARCHITECTURAL PRACTICE

14] Arena 2036, University of Stuttgart:
Allmann Sattler Wappner Architekten,
Achim Menges Architekt,
Knippers Helbig Advanced Engineering

The experimental and temporary buildings presented in this book aim to test the architectural and constructive potential and limits of the methods, processes and systems developed. They thus represent a decisive intermediate step on the path from fundamental academic research to architectural practice. Our aim is to promote this transfer and to shape it together with partners in the building sector.

PIONEERING TIMBER CONSTRUCTION

The application potential of segmented wooden shells points in various directions. They enable load-adapted shell geometries that can efficiently span large areas. Such a structure was developed, for example, for a competition entry for the laboratory hall of the Arena 2036 research building on the University of Stuttgart's Vaihingen campus. Here, a gently undulating roof made of cross-laminated timber segments spans an area of

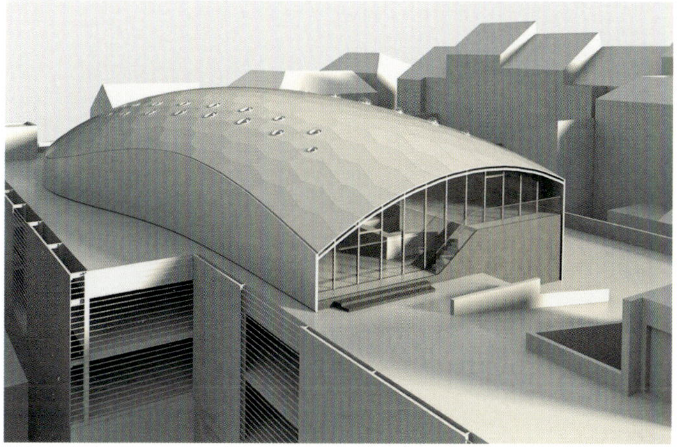

15] Extension of multistory car park:
Menges Scheffler Architekten,
Jan Knippers Ingenieure,
müllerblaustein Holzbauwerke

39 × 145 m and thereby unfolds a new architectural expression for industrial buildings.

The low weight and geometric adaptability of segmented wooden shells are particularly important for building on top of existing building stock. This is shown by our plan for a vertical extension to an existing inner-city parking garage. The design of a wide-span timber shell structure can respond both to the programmatic requirements and the geometry of the top parking level, the position of the existing load-bearing columns and the considerable geometric restrictions imposed by building regulations. This shows how the new timber construction method enables urban redensification, which creates additional inner-city space, something of considerable socioeconomic importance.

The segmented wooden shells with hollow cassettes, as developed for the BUGA Wooden Pavilion, are suitable for expressive temporary buildings and event spaces due to their lightweight design, very good spatial acoustics and the possibility of non-destructive dismantling. We took advantage of all this with our competition entry for the Baden-Württemberg-Haus, a temporary pavilion for Expo 2020 in Dubai that was awarded second prize. Here hollow cassettes span a multistory exhibition and event space. For the first time, inner edges in the form of slit-like skylights in the segment shell provide natural light. They prevent direct sunlight from entering but allow indirect illumination, which in combination with the materiality of the shell and the lighting in the cassette cavities creates a unique spatial atmosphere. The entire pavilion was designed in such a way that it could be completely dismantled and rebuilt elsewhere after the end of the Expo.

16, 17] Baden-Württemberg-Haus Pavilion, Expo 2020 in Dubai:
Lederer Ragnarsdóttir Oei with Menges Scheffler Architekten
and ICD University of Stuttgart, Jan Knippers Ingenieure, DS-plan
Ingenieurgesellschaft

18] Stage Envelope, Pier 17, New York City:
Menges Scheffler Architekten,
Knippers Helbig Advanced Engineering

FILIGREED FIBER COMPOSITE STRUCTURES

The fiber composite constructions developed by the ICD and ITKE have reached a development stage that enables their transfer into architectural practice. Their low weight in particular is of great importance for certain applications.

For a temporary, yet recurring, canopy on Pier 17 in New York City, a design for a modular fiber composite structure was proposed. This filigreed structure of fiber composite elements covers the stage of the event area on the roof of the existing building. The structure opens wide towards the auditorium and at the same time protects the stage area while offering maximum transparency and an uninterrupted view of the neighboring Brooklyn Bridge. The innovative lightweight construction of the Stage Envelope at Pier 17 thus celebrates this special location. Moreover, it not only reduces the load on the underlying multistory structure, but also facilitates assembly and dismantling, which is to be carried out every season.

19] Texoversum, Reutlingen University:
Allmann Sattler Wappner Architekten,
Menges Scheffler Architekten,
Jan Knippers Ingenieure

A special feature of the developed coreless robotic winding process is the ability to vary the fiber orientation individually for each component without significant additional effort. This not only allows adaptation to the respective structural loads – as shown in the projects presented in this book – but also to other design parameters, for example, the solar energy input. This was examined in our competition entry for the Texoversum – a building for teaching and research in the field of textile technologies at Reutlingen University. The design won first prize and is currently in the design stage. Using robotic winding, a facade design with a textile appearance was conceived which not only shapes the characteristic expression of the building envelope, but also integrates the shading. The fiber layout of the robotically wound shading elements is based on the direction of the sun in terms of depth, density and fiber orientation.

These current projects show that the ICD's and ITKE's collaborative developments in timber construction and fiber composite construction are at present on the threshold of application in general architectural practice. We are sure that many more projects will follow and open up new possibilities for architecture, and we strive to be part of this process proactively, not only as scientists, but also as architects and engineers.

ANNEX

>> PROJECT PARTICIPANTS ICD/ITKE BUILDINGS

>>ICD/ITKE RESEARCH PAVILION 2010

University of Stuttgart

PROJECT PARTNERS
ICD – Prof. Achim Menges
ITKE – Prof. Dr.-Ing. Jan Knippers

CONCEPT AND REALIZATION
Andreas Eisenhardt, Manuel Vollrath, Kristine Wächter, Thomas Irowetz, Oliver David Krieg, Admir Mahmutovic. Peter Meschendörfer, Leopold Möhler, Michael Pelzer, Konrad Zerbe

SCIENTIFIC DEVELOPMENT
Moritz Fleischmann (project management), Simon Schleicher (project management), Christopher Robeller (construction management), Julian Lienhard (structural design), Diana D'Souza (structural design), Karola Dierichs (documentation)

SUPPORTERS
OCHS GmbH / KUKA Roboter GmbH / Leitz GmbH & Co. KG / A. WÖLM BAU GmbH / ES CAD Systemtechnik GmbH / Ministerium für Ländlichen Raum, Ernährung und Verbraucherschutz Landesbetrieb Forst Baden-Württemberg (ForstBW)

PROJECT INFORMATION
Location: Keplerstr. 11–17, 70174 Stuttgart, Germany
Realization: Design studio with students, scientists and researchers
Completion: June 2010
Floor area: 70 m^2
Volume: 20 m^3

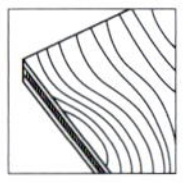

MATERIAL
Veneered birch plywood

CONSTRUCTION
Radially arranged 7-joint arch construction made of bending-active lamellae

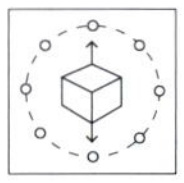

DESIGN
Global form-finding by local interaction of bending-active components

FABRICATION
Robotic 3-axis milling

>>ICD/ITKE RESEARCH PAVILION 2011

University of Stuttgart

PROJECT PARTNERS

ICD – Prof. Achim Menges

ITKE – Prof. Dr.-Ing. Jan Knippers

CONCEPT AND PROJECT DEVELOPMENT

Oliver David Krieg, Boyan Mihaylov

PLANNING AND REALIZATION

Peter Brachat, Benjamin Busch, Solmaz Fahimian, Christin Gegenheimer, Nicola Haberbosch, Elias Kästle, Oliver David Krieg, Yong Sung Kwon, Boyan Mihaylov, Hongmei Zhai

SCIENTIFIC DEVELOPMENT

Markus Gabler (project management), Riccardo La Magna (structural design), Steffen Reichert (detailing), Tobias Schwinn (project management), Frédéric Waimer (structural design)

SUPPORTERS

Main sponsors: KUKA Roboter GmbH / Ochs GmbH

Sponsors: KST2 Systemtechnik GmbH / Landesbetrieb Forst Baden-Württemberg (ForstBW) / Stiftungen LBBW / Leitz GmbH & Co. KG / müllerblaustein Holzbau GmbH / Hermann Rothfuss Bauunternehmung GmbH & Co. / Ullrich & Schön GmbH / Holzhandlung Wider GmbH & Co. KG

PROJECT INFORMATION

Location: Keplerstr. 11–17, 70174 Stuttgart, Germany

Realization: Design studio with students, scientists and researchers

Completion: August 2011

Floor area: 72 m²

Volume: 200 m³

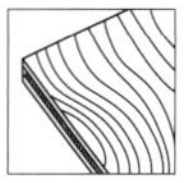

MATERIAL

Veneered birch plywood

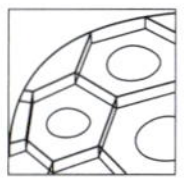

CONSTRUCTION

Segment shell from polygonal hollow cassette segments

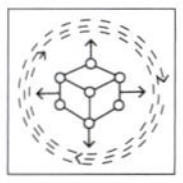

DESIGN

Dynamic equilibrium modeling with multicriteria form steering

FABRICATION

Robotic 7-axis milling and drilling

BIOLOGICAL ROLE MODEL

Plate skeleton of the sand dollar

>>ICD/ITKE RESEARCH PAVILION 2012

University of Stuttgart

PROJECT PARTNERS
ICD – Prof. Achim Menges
ITKE – Prof. Dr.-Ing. Jan Knippers

CONCEPT DEVELOPMENT
Manuel Schloz, Jakob Weigele

SYSTEM DEVELOPMENT AND REALIZATION
Sarah Haase, Markus Mittner, Josephine Ross, Manuel Schloz, Jonas Unger, Simone Vielhuber, Franziska Weidemann; Jakob Weigele, Natthida Wiwatwicha
With the support of Michael Preisack and Michael Tondera (Faculty of Architecture Workshop)

SCIENTIFIC DEVELOPMENT AND PROJECT MANAGEMENT
Riccardo La Magna (structural design), Steffen Reichert (detail design), Tobias Schwinn (robotic fabrication), Frédéric Waimer (fiber composite technology and structural design)

IN COLLABORATION WITH
Institute of Evolution and Ecology, Department of Evolutionary Biology of Invertebrates
University of Tübingen – Prof. Oliver Betz / Center for Applied Geoscience, Department of Invertebrates-Paleontology, University of Tübingen – Prof. James Nebelsick / Institute of Textile Technology and Process Engineering ITV, DITF Denkendorf – Dr.-Ing. Markus Milwich

SUPPORTERS
Main sponsors: KUKA Roboter GmbH / Competence Network Biomimetics / SGL Group / Momentive
Sponsors: AFBW – Allianz Faserbasierte Werkstoffe Baden-Württemberg / FBGS Technologies GmbH / MFTech SARL / Minda Schenk Plastic Solutions GmbH / Stiftungen LBBW / Südwestbank AG / Wayss & Freytag Ingenieurbau AG

PROJECT INFORMATION:
Location: Keplerstr. 11–17, 70174 Stuttgart, Germany
Realization: Design studio with students, scientists, and researchers
Completion: November 2012
Floor area: 29 m²
Volume: 78 m³
Construction weight: 5.6 kg/m²

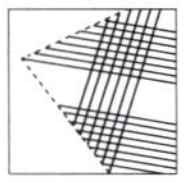

MATERIAL
Carbon fiber rovings and
glass fiber rovings with epoxy resin

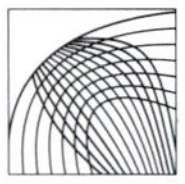

CONSTRUCTION
Monocoque shell made of
fiber composite lattice

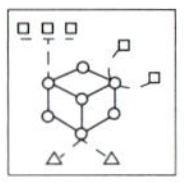

DESIGN
Parametric modeling in feedback
with local and global material simulation

FABRICATION
Coreless robotic 7-axis winding,
robot-guided fiber winding head,
rotating winding frame

BIOLOGICAL ROLE MODEL
Exoskeleton of the lobster

>>ICD/ITKE RESEARCH PAVILION 2013/14

University of Stuttgart

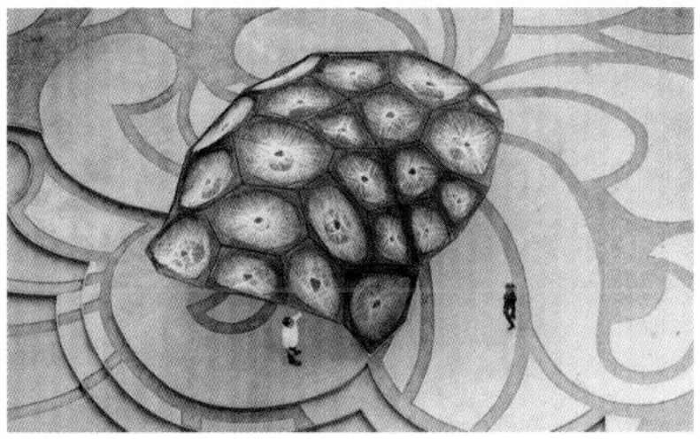

PROJECT PARTNERS
ICD – Prof. Achim Menges
ITKE – Prof. Dr.-Ing. Jan Knippers

RESEARCH DEVELOPMENT AND PROJECT MANAGEMENT
Moritz Dörstelmann, Vassilios Kirtzakis, Stefana Parascho, Marshall Prado, Tobias Schwinn

CONCEPT DEVELOPMENT
Leyla Yunis

SYSTEM DEVELOPMENT AND REALIZATION
WiSe 2012 – SoSe 2013: Desislava Angelova, Hans-Christian Bäcker, Maximilian Fichter, Eugen Grass, Michael Herrick, Nam Hoang, Alejandro Jaramillo, Norbert Jundt, Taichi Kuma, Ondrej Kyjánek, Sophia Leistner, Luca Menghini, Claire Milnes, Martin Nautrup, Gergana Rusenova, Petar Trassiev, Sascha Vallon, Shiyu Wie / WiSe 2013: Hassan Abbasi, Yassmin Al-Khasawneh, Desislava Angelova, Yuliya Baranovskaya, Marta Besalu, Giulio Brugnaro, Elena Chiridnik, Eva Espuny, Matthias Helmreich, Julian Höll, Shim Karmin, Georgi Kazlachev, Sebastian Kröner, Vangel Kukov, David Leon, Stephen Maher, Amanda Moore, Paul Poinet, Roland Sandoval, Emily Scoones, Djordje Stanojevic, Andrei Stoiculescu, Kenryo Takahashi, Maria Yablonina. With support of Michael Preisack

IN COOPERATION WITH
Institute of Evolution and Ecology, Evolutionary Biology of Invertebrates, University of Tübingen – Prof. Oliver Betz / Department of Geosciences, Paleontology of Invertebrates and Paleoclimatology, University of Tübingen – Prof. James H. Nebelsick / Module Bionics of Animal Constructions, WiSe 2012: Gerald Buck, Michael Münster, Valentin Grau, Anne Buhl, Markus Maisch, Matthias Loose, Irene Viola Baumann, Carina Meiser / ANKA Institute for Photon Science and Synchrotron Radiation, Karlsruher Institute of Technology KIT – Dr. Thomas van de Kamp, Tomy dos Santos Rolo, Prof. Dr. Tilo Baumbach / Institute for Machine Tools, University of Stuttgart – Dr.-Ing. Thomas Stehle, Rolf Bauer, Michael Reichersdörfer / Institute of Textile Technology and Process Engineering ITV, DITF Denkendorf – Dr. Markus Milwich

SUPPORTERS
Competence Network Biomimetics / KUKA Roboter GmbH / SGL Group / Sika / AFBW – Allianz Faserbasierte Werkstoffe Baden-Württemberg

PROJECT INFORMATION
Location: Keplerstr. 11–17, 70174 Stuttgart, Germany
Realization: Design studio with students, scientists and researchers
Completion: March 2014
Floor area: 50 m²
Volume: 122 m³

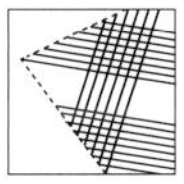

MATERIAL
Carbon fiber rovings and glass fiber rovings with epoxy resin

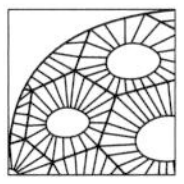

CONSTRUCTION
Segmented shell made of polygonal fiber composite lattice segments

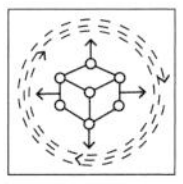

DESIGN
Dynamic equilibrium modeling with multicriteria form steering

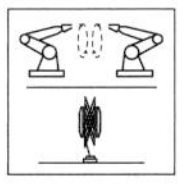

FABRICATION
Coreless robotic 12-axis winding, stationary fiber winding head, robot-guided winding frames

BIOLOGICAL ROLE MODEL
Forewing of airworthy beetle

>>LANDESGARTENSCHAU EXHIBITION HALL

Landesgartenschau Schwäbisch Gmünd, 2014

PROJECT TEAM
ICD – Prof. Achim Menges, Tobias Schwinn, Oliver David Krieg
ITKE – Prof. Dr.-Ing. Jan Knippers, Jian-Min Li
IIGS Institut für Ingenieurgeodäsie – Prof. Volker Schwieger, Annette Schmitt
müllerblaustein Holzbau GmbH – Reinhold Müller, Benjamin Eisele
KUKA Roboter GmbH – Alois Buchstab, Frank Zimmermann
Landesbetrieb Forst Baden-Württemberg (ForstBW) – Sebastian Schreiber, Frauke Brieger
Landesgartenschau Schwäbisch Gmünd 2014 GmbH – Karl-Eugen Ebertshäuser, Sabine Rieger

FUNDING
EFRE European Union / Clusterinitiative Forst und Holz Baden-Württemberg / Landesgartenschau Schwäbisch Gmünd 2014 GmbH / müllerblaustein Holzbau GmbH / KUKA Roboter GmbH / Landesbetrieb Forst Baden-Württemberg (ForstBW)

SUPPORTERS
Autodesk GmbH / Adler Deutschland GmbH / Carlisle Construction Materials GmbH / Fagus Stiftung / Gutex H. Henselmann GmbH & Co. KG / Hess & Co. AG / MPA – Materialprüfanstalt der Universität Stuttgart / Leitz GmbH & Co. KG / Spax International GmbH & Co. KG

PROJECT INFORMATION
Location: Landesgartenschau Schwäbisch Gmünd 2014
Realization: Cooperation project Landesgartenschau Schwäbisch Gmünd with the University of Stuttgart, implementing company müllerblaustein Holzbau
Completion: 2014
Floor area: 125 m²
Shell surface: 245 m²
Weight of load-bearing structure per surface area: 37.5 kg/m²

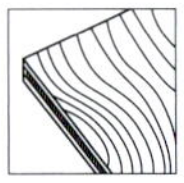

MATERIAL
Veneered beech plywood

CONSTRUCTION
Segment shell made of polygonal plate segments

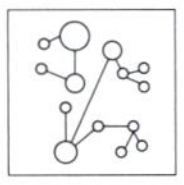

DESIGN
Multi-agent-based modeling

FABRICATION
Robotic 7-axis milling and drilling

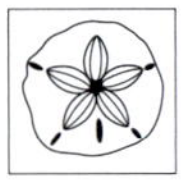

BIOLOGICAL ROLE MODEL
Plate skeleton of the sand dollar

>>ICD/ITKE RESEARCH PAVILION 2014/15

University of Stuttgart

PROJECT PARTNERS
ICD – Prof. Achim Menges
ITKE – Prof. Dr.-Ing. Jan Knippers

SCIENTIFIC DEVELOPMENT AND PROJECT MANAGEMENT
Moritz Dörstelmann, Valentin Koslowski, Marshall Prado, Gundula Schieber, Lauren Vasey

SYSTEM DEVELOPMENT AND REALIZATION
WiSe13/14 – WiSe14/15: Hassan Abbasi, Yassmin Al-Khasawneh, Yuliya Baranovskaya, Marta Besalu, Giulio Brugnaro, Elena Chiridnik, Tobias Grun, Mark Hageman, Matthias Helmreich, Julian Höll, Jessica Jorge, Yohei Kanzaki, Shim Karmin, Georgi Kazlachev, Vangel Kukov, David Leon, Kantaro Makanae, Amanda Moore, Paul Poinet, Emily Scoones, Djordje Stanojevic, Andrei Stoiculescu, Kenryo Takahashi und Maria Yablonina / WiSe14/15: Rebecca Jaroszewski, Yavar Khonsari, Ondrej Kyjanek, Alberto Lago, Kuan-Ting Lai, Luigi Olivieri, Guiseppe Pultrone, Annie Scherer, Raquel Silva, Shota Tsikoliya
With the support of: Ehsan Baharlou, Benjamin Felbrich, Manfred Richard Hammer, Axel Körner, Anja Mader, Michael Preisack, Seiichi Suzuki, Michael Tondera

IN COOPERATION WITH
Department of Evolutionary Biology of Invertebrates, University of Tübingen – Prof. Oliver Betz / Department of Paleontology of Invertebrates, University of Tübingen – Prof. H. James Nebelsick / Institute for Machine Tools, University of Stuttgart – Dr. Thomas Stehle, Rolf Bauer, Michael Reichersdörfer / Institute of Aircraft Design, University of Stuttgart – Stefan Carosella, Prof. Dr.-Ing. Peter Middendorf

SUPPORTERS
KUKA Roboter GmbH / GettyLab / tat aiRstructures / SGL Carbon SE / Sika Deutschland GmbH / Daimler AG / Walther Spritz- und Lackiersysteme GmbH / Lange+Ritter GmbH / Gibbons Fan Products Ltd / igus® GmbH / Peri GmbH / HERZOG Maschinenfabrik GmbH & Co. KG / AFBW – Allianz Faserbasierter Werkstoffe Baden-Württemberg e. V. / Reinhausen Plasma GmbH / Reka Klebetechnik GmbH / HECO-Schrauben GmbH & Co. KG / Airtech Europe S.A. / Mack Gerüsttechnik GmbH / RentES / Stahlbau Wendeler GmbH + Co. KG / CARU Containers GmbH / EmmeShop Electronics / STILL GmbH / SH-Elektrotechnik / GEMCO / Zeppelin Rental GmbH & Co. KG

PROJECT INFORMATION
Location: Keplerstr. 11–17, 70174 Stuttgart
Realization: Design studio with students, scientists and researchers
Completion: June 2015
Floor area: 40 m²
Volume: 130 m³
Span: 7.5 m
Construction weight: 260 kg

MATERIAL
Carbon fiber rovings pre-impregnated with epoxy resin on ETFE membrane

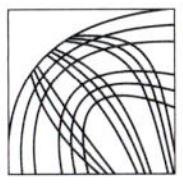

CONSTRUCTION
Monocoque shell made of ETFE foil with glued-in resin-impregnated fibers

DESIGN
Agent-based modeling in feedback with cyber-physical production system

FABRICATION
Robotic 6-axis fiber placement

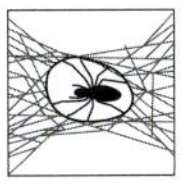

BIOLOGICAL MODEL
Water spider web building

>>ICD/ITKE RESEARCH PAVILION 2015/16

University of Stuttgart

PROJECT PARTNERS

ICD – Prof. Achim Menges
ITKE – Prof. Dr.-Ing. Jan Knippers

SCIENTIFIC DEVELOPMENT AND PROJECT MANAGEMENT

Simon Bechert, Oliver David Krieg, Tobias Schwinn, Daniel Sonntag

CONCEPT DEVELOPMENT, SYSTEM DEVELOPMENT AND REALIZATION

Martin Alvarez, Jan Brütting, Sean Campbell, Mariia Chumak, Hojoong Chung, Joshua Few, Eliane Herter, Rebecca Jaroszewski, Ting-Chun Kao, Dongil Kim, Kuan-Ting Lai, Seojoo Lee, Riccardo Manitta, Erik Martinez, Artyom Maxim, Masih Imani Nia, Andres Obregon, Luigi Olivieri, Thu Nguyen Phuoc, Giuseppe Pultrone, Jasmin Sadegh, Jenny Shen, Michael Sveiven, Julian Wengzinek, Alexander Wolkow. With the support of: Long Nguyen, Michael Preisack and Lauren Vasey.

IN COOPERATION WITH

Institute of Evolution and Ecology, Evolutionary Biology of Invertebrates, University of Tübingen – Prof. Oliver Betz / Department of Geosciences, Paleontology of Invertebrates and Paleoclimatology, University of Tübingen – Prof. James H. Nebelsick

SUPPORTERS

German Research Foundation DFG as part of subproject A07 of the Collaborative Research Centre SFB-TRR 141 / GettyLab / BW-Bank / Edelrid / Frank Brunnet GmbH / Forst BW /Groz-Beckert KG / Guetermann GmbH / Hess & Co. / KUKA Roboter GmbH / Mehler Texnologies GmbH

PROJECT INFORMATION

Location: Keplerstr. 11–17, 70174 Stuttgart, Germany
Realization: Design studio with students, scientists and researchers
Completion: April 2016
Floor area: 85 m²
Shell surface: 105 m²
Dimensions: 11.5 x 9.5 m

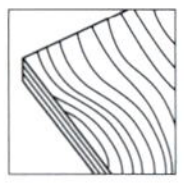

MATERIAL

Individualized veneer plywood beech

CONSTRUCTION

Segmented shell made of triangular, laced hollow segments

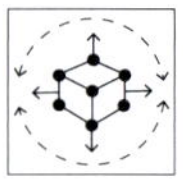

DESIGN

Inverse equilibrium modeling of bending-active components

FABRICATION

Robotic sewing

BIOLOGICAL ROLE MODEL

Plate skeleton of the sand dollar

>>ICD/ITKE RESEARCH PAVILION 2016/17

University of Stuttgart

PROJECT PARTNERS

ICD – Prof. Achim Menges
ITKE – Prof. Dr.-Ing. Jan Knippers

SCIENTIFIC DEVELOPMENT

Benjamin Felbrich, Nikolas Früh, Marshall Prado, Daniel Reist, Sam Saffarian, James Solly, Lauren Vasey

SYSTEM DEVELOPMENT, FABRICATION AND CONSTRUCTION

Miguel Aflalo, Bahar Al Bahar, Lotte Aldinger, Chris Arias, Léonard Balas, Jingcheng Chen, Federico Forestiero, Dominga Garufi, Pedro Giachini, Kyriaki Goti, Sachin Gupta, Olga Kalina, Shir Katz, Bruno Knychalla, Shamil Lallani, Patricio Lara, Ayoub Lharchi, Dongyuan Liu, Yencheng Lu, Georgia Margariti, Alexandre Mballa, Behrooz Tahanzadeh, Hans Jakob Wagner, Benedikt Wannemacher, Nikolaos Xenos, Andre Zolnerkevic, Paula Baptista, Kevin Croneigh, Tatsunori Shibuya, Nicoló Temperi, Manon Uhlen, Li Wenhan. With the support of Artyom Maxim and Michael Preisack

IN COOPERATION WITH

IFB Institute of Aircraft Design – Prof. Dr.-Ing. P. Middendorf, Markus Blandl, Florian Gnädinger / IIGS Institute of Engineering Geodesy – Prof. Dr.-Ing. habil. Volker Schwieger, Otto Lerke / Institute of Evolution and Ecology, Evolutionary Biology of Invertebrates, University of Tübingen – Prof. Oliver Betz / Department of Geosciences, Paleontology of Invertebrates and Paleoclimatology, University of Tübingen – Prof. James H. Nebelsick

SUPPORTERS

Volkswagen Stiftung / GettyLab / KUKA Roboter GmbH / Peri GmbH / SGL Technologies GmbH / Hexion Stuttgart GmbH / Ed. Züblin AG / Lange Ritter GmbH / Stahlbau Wendeler GmbH / Leica Geosystems GmbH / KOFI GmbH

Researchers on this project received funding from the European Union's Horizon 2020 research and innovation program under Marie Sklodoska-Curie grant agreement No 642877, from the Collaborative Research Center CRC 141 of the German Research Foundation, and from the Volkswagen Stiftung's Experiment! funding program.

PROJECT INFORMATION

Location: Keplerstr. 11–17, 70174 Stuttgart, Germany
Realization: Design studio with students, scientists and researchers
Completion: March 2017
Floor area: 26.5 m²
Volume: 58 m³
Fiber length: 184 km
Weight: 1,000 kg
Dimensions: 12 × 2.6 × 3.1 m

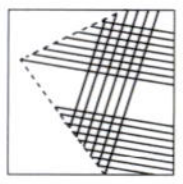

MATERIAL

Carbon fiber rovings and
glass fiber rovings with epoxy resin

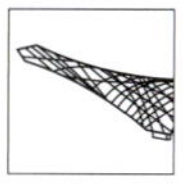

CONSTRUCTION

One-piece cantilever arm made
of fiber composite lattice

DESIGN

Agent-based modeling in feedback
with cyber-physical production system

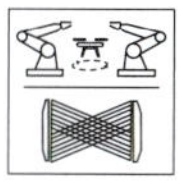

FABRICATION

Coreless robotic 12-axis winding
with integrated UAV

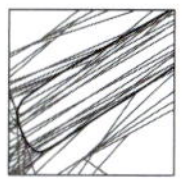

BIOLOGICAL ROLE MODEL

Cocoon construction of the larva
of the leaf miner moth

>>ELYTRA FILAMENT PAVILION

Victoria and Albert Museum London, 2016

DESIGN, ENGINEERING AND FABRICATION TEAM

ICD – Prof. Achim Menges mit Moritz Dörstelmann / Achim Menges Architekt, Frankfurt am Main / Team also includes: Marshall Prado (fabrication development), Aikaterini Papadimitriou, Niccolo Dambrosio, Roberto Naboni. With support by Dylan Wood, Daniel Reist

ITKE – Prof. Dr.-Ing. Jan Knippers / Knippers Helbig Advanced Engineering, Stuttgart, New York / Team also includes: Valentin Koslowski and James Solly (structure development), Thiemo Fildhuth (structural sensors)

Prof. Thomas Auer / Transsolar Climate Engineering, Stuttgart / Building Technology and Climate Responsive Design, TU München / Team also includes: Elmira Reisi, Boris Plotnikov

With the support of: Michael Preisack, Christian Arias, Pedro Giachini, Andre Kauffman, Thu Nguyen, Nikolaos Xenos, Giulio Brugnaro, Alberto Lago, Yuliya Baranovskaya, Belen Torres, IFB Universität Stuttgart – Prof. P. Middendorf

FUNDING

Victoria and Albert Museum, London / University of Stuttgart

GettyLab / KUKA Roboter GmbH + KUKA Robotics UK Ltd / SGL Carbon SE / Hexion / Covestro AG / FBGS International NV / Arnold AG / PFEIFER Seil- und Hebetechnik GmbH / Stahlbau Wendeler GmbH + Co. KG / Lange+Ritter GmbH / STILL GmbH

PROJECT INFORMATION

Location: Victoria and Albert Museum, London, UK
Realization: University of Stuttgart commissioned by the Victoria and Albert Museum
Completion: March 2016
Floor area: 200 m²*
Weight fiber composite structure: 9 kg/m²
Total weight of canopy structure: 2.5 t*
Number of fiber composite components: 40*
Building component size: 2.77 × 2.4 × 0.4 m
Average weight per component: 45 kg
Differentiated material usage: 35–70 kg per component

* At the beginning of the exhibition period – over the course of time the roof has grown.

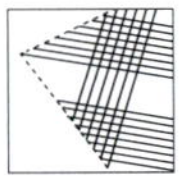

MATERIAL
Carbon fiber rovings and glass fiber rovings with epoxy resin

CONSTRUCTION
Segmented roof slab made of hexagonal fiber composite lattice segments

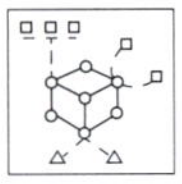

DESIGN
Parametric modeling in feedback with local and global material simulation

FABRICATION
Coreless robotic 8-axis winding, robot-guided fiber-winding head, rotating winding scaffold

BIOLOGICAL ROLE MODEL
Forewing of airworthy beetle

>>BUGA WOOD PAVILION

Bundesgartenschau Heilbronn, 2019

PROJECT PARTNERS

ICD – Prof. Achim Menges, Martin Alvarez, Monika Göbel, Abel Groenewolt, Oliver David Krieg, Ondrej Kyjanek, Hans Jakob Wagner

ITKE – Prof. Dr.-Ing. Jan Knippers, Lotte Aldinger, Simon Bechert, Daniel Sonntag

müllerblaustein Bauwerke GmbH, Blaustein – Reinhold Müller, Daniel Müller, Bernd Schmid

BEC GmbH, Reutlingen – Matthias Buck, Zied Bhiri

Bundesgartenschau Heilbronn 2019 GmbH – Hanspeter Faas, Oliver Toellner

PROJECT BUILDING PERMIT PROCESS

Landesstelle für Bautechnik – Dr. Stefan Brendler, Willy Weidner / Proof Engineer – Prof. Dr.-Ing. Hugo Rieger / Materialprüfungsanstalt, University of Stuttgart – Dr. Simon Aicher

SUPPORTERS

State of Baden-Württemberg / University of Stuttgart / EFRE European Union / GettyLab / DFG German Research Foundation

Carlisle Construction Materials GmbH / Puren GmbH / Hera GmbH & Co.KG / Beck Fastener Group / J. Schmalz GmbH / Niemes Dosiertechnik GmbH & Co. KG / Jowat Adhesives SE / Raithle Werkzeugtechnik / Leuze electronic GmbH & Co. KG / Metsä Wood Deutschland GmbH

PROJECT INFORMATION

Location: Bundesgartenschau Heilbronn 2019
Realization: Cooperation project Bundesgartenschau Heilbronn with the University of Stuttgart, implementing company müllerblaustein Bauwerke GmbH
Completion: April 2019
Floor area: approx. 500 m²
Shell area: 600 m²
Weight of load-bearing timber construction: 36 kg/m²
Dimensions: approx. 32 × 25 × 7 m
Structural load-bearing shell: robot-manufactured hollow cassette segments made of veneered spruce plywood with UV protection
Cladding: EPDM sealing, 3-axis CNC-cut untreated larch triple-layer plates

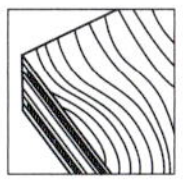

MATERIAL

Laminated veneered lumber spruce/fir

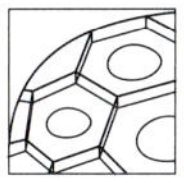

CONSTRUCTION

Segmented shell made of polygonal hollow cassette segments

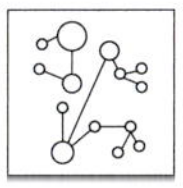

DESIGN

Multi-agent-based modeling

FABRICATION

Robotic 13-axis positioning, gluing, milling

BIOLOGICAL ROLE MODEL

Plate skeleton of the sand dollar

>>BUGA FIBRE PAVILION

Bundesgartenschau Heilbronn, 2019

PROJECT PARTNERS
ICD – Prof. Achim Menges, Serban Bodea, Niccolo Dambrosio, Monika Göbel, Christoph Zechmeister
ITKE – Prof. Dr.-Ing. Jan Knippers, Valentin Koslowski, Marta Gil Pérez, Bas Rongen
FibR GmbH, Stuttgart – Moritz Dörstelmann, Ondrej Kyjanek, Philipp Essers, Philipp Gülke
Bundesgartenschau Heilbronn 2019 GmbH – Hanspeter Faas, Oliver Toellner

PROJECT BUILDING PERMIT PROCESS
Landesstelle für Bautechnik – Dr. Stefan Brendler, Dipl.-Ing. Steffen Schneider / Proof Engineer – Dipl.-Ing. Achim Bechert, Dipl.-Ing. Florian Roos / DITF German Institutes of Textile and Fiber Research – Prof. Dr.-Ing. Götz T. Gresser, Pascal Mindermann

SUPPORTERS
State of Baden-Württemberg / University of Stuttgart / Baden-Württemberg Stiftung / GettyLab / Forschungsinitiative Zukunft Bau

Pfeifer GmbH / Ewo GmbH / Fischer Group

PROJECT INFORMATION
Location: Bundesgartenschau Heilbronn 2019
Realization: Cooperation project Bundesgartenschau with the University of Stuttgart, implementing company FibR GmbH, Stuttgart
Completion: April 2019
Diameter: approx. 23 m
Floor area: approx. 400 m²
Weight of load-bearing fiber composite structure: approx. 7.6 kg/m²
Construction system: 60 load-bearing, robotically fabricated glass and carbon fiber composite elements made of a total of 150,000 m of glass and carbon fibers; transparent, mechanically prestressed ETFE membrane

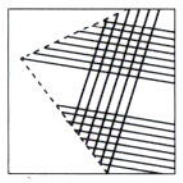

MATERIAL
Carbon fiber rovings and glass fiber rovings with epoxy resin

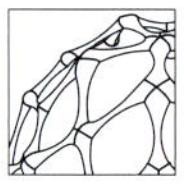

CONSTRUCTION
Rod dome made of fiber composite lattice tubes with mechanically prestressed ETFE membrane

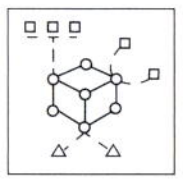

DESIGN
Parametric modeling in feedback with local and global material simulation

FABRICATION:
Coreless robotic 7-axis winding, robot-guided fiber-winding head, rotating winding frame

>>URBACH TOWER

Remstal Gartenschau 2019, Urbach

PROJECT PARTNERS:
ICD – Prof. Achim Menges, Dylan Wood
ITKE – Prof. Dr.-Ing. Jan Knippers, Lotte Aldinger, Simon Bechert

Scientific Collaboration:
Laboratory of Cellulose and Wood Materials, Empa (Swiss Federal Laboratories for Materials Science and Technology), Switzerland / Wood Materials Science, ETH Zurich (Swiss Federal Institute of Technology Zurich), Switzerland – Dr. Markus Rüggeberg, Philippe Grönquist, Prof. Ingo Burgert

Industry Collaboration:
Blumer-Lehmann AG, Gossau, Switzerland – Katharina Lehmann, David Riggenbach

SUPPORTERS
Gemeinde Urbach / Remstal Gartenschau 2019 GmbH / German Federal Environmental Foundation / Innosuisse – Swiss Innovation Agency / Carlisle Construction Materials GmbH / Scanntronik Mugrauer GmbH

PROJECT INFORMATION
Location: Urbach, Germany
Realization: University of Stuttgart commissioned by the municipality of Urbach
Completion: May 2019
Height: 14.2 m
Dimensions: radius 4.0 m bottom, 3.0 m top, 1.6 m center
Material: spruce wood CLT with 10-30-10-30-10 mm buildup, larch wood facade with titanium oxide surface treatment

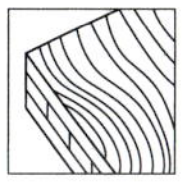

MATERIAL
Cross-laminated spruce wood

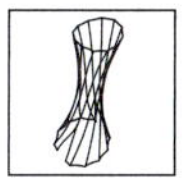

CONSTRUCTION
Tower made of curved cross-laminated timber strips

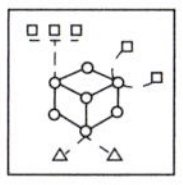

DESIGN
Parametric modeling in feedback with local and global material simulation

FABRICATION
Self-shaping,
5-axis CNC milling and drilling

BIOLOGICAL ROLE MODEL
Self-shaping conifer cones

ILPÖ

Our special thanks for the work presented in this book are due to the ITECH students, the research associates at ICD and ITKE, the University of Stuttgart and our cooperation partners. A moment of this special community can be seen here on the occasion of the ITECH Final Review 2018.

>> BIOGRAPHIES

>> ACHIM MENGES

... completed his pre-diploma in architecture at the TU Darmstadt and graduated with honors from the Architectural Association (AA) School of Architecture in London in 2002. Immediately thereafter he took up teaching and research work at the AA, initially from 2002 to 2009 at the AA Graduate School as Studio Master of the Emergent Technologies and Design Program, then from 2003 to 2005 also at the AA Diploma School as Unit Master. From 2005 to 2008 he was likewise Professor for Form Generation and Materialization at the Academy of Art and Design in Offenbach. In 2008 Achim Menges was appointed Professor at the University of Stuttgart. There he heads the Institute for Computational Design and Construction (ICD), which he founded. From 2009 to 2015 he was also a guest professor at the Graduate School of Design (GSD) at Harvard University and at various other universities in the USA and Europe. Achim Menges is the author of more than 175 scientific publications and 15 books. Since 2019 he has also been director of the DFG Cluster of Excellence Integrative Computational Design and Construction for Architecture (IntCDC).

In addition to research and teaching, he has also been active in architectural practice since 2002, for example, as a partner in OCEAN from 2004 to 2009 and as a partner in Menges Scheffler Architekten since 2017. His research work and construction projects have been awarded various international prizes and exhibited and published worldwide. They also form part of the permanent collection of several renowned museums, including the Centre Pompidou in Paris and the Victoria and Albert Museum in London.

>> JAN KNIPPERS

... studied civil engineering at the TU Berlin and in 1992 earned his doctorate there with a theoretical thesis on the numerical simulation of metals at high temperatures. He then worked for several years at the internationally renowned engineering office Schlaich Bergermann und Partner in Stuttgart. Key projects from this period include the bascule bridge in Kiel (with gmp Architekten) and several steel and glass roofs, including the courtyard roofing of the German Historical Museum in Berlin (with I. M. Pei). From 2001 to 2017 he was a partner at Knippers Helbig Advanced Engineering. Key projects from this period included the central entrance axis for the Expo 2010 in Shanghai (with SBA Architects), the Thematic Pavilion for the Expo 2012 in Yeosu, South Korea (with Soma Architects), the Soft House in Hamburg (with KVA Architects) and the Reverberation Gallery for the Deutsche Oper Berlin (with HG Merz).

In 2000, Jan Knippers was appointed head of the Institute of Building Structures and Structural Design (ITKE) at the University of Stuttgart, where he established research activities on resource-efficient and long-span structures. The focal areas are biomimetics, segmented wooden shells and fiber composite structures. In 2018 he founded Jan Knippers Ingenieure at the interface of research, development and practice. From 2014 to 2019 Jan Knippers was director of the DFG Collaborative Research Center TRR141 Biological Design and Integrative Structures. Since 2019 he has been Vice-Rector for Research at the University of Stuttgart and deputy director of the DFG Cluster of Excellence Integrative Computational Design and Construction for Architecture. He is also the German representative in the CEN/TS 250 Design of Fibre-Polymer Composite (FPC) Structures European standards committee.

>> PHILIPPE BLOCK

... is a professor at the Institute for Technology in Architecture (ITA) at ETH Zurich, where he heads the Block Research Group (BRG) together with Dr. Tom Van Mele. He is also director of the Swiss National Centre of Competence in Research (NCCR) Digital Fabrication. He studied architecture and civil engineering at the Vrije Universiteit Brussel (VUB) in Belgium and MIT in the USA. Dr. Philippe Block transfers his research work into the practical design and construction of new shell structures. He has received several awards, including the Berlin Art Prize 2018 in the field of architecture. His team's work was exhibited at the Architecture Biennale 2016 in Venice.

>> JANE BURRY

... is an architect and Dean of the School of Design at Swinburne University of Technology, Melbourne. Since 2017, Professor Jane Burry, PhD, has been leading the establishment of new programs in the fields of architecture, engineering and urban planning. Previously, she was Professor and Director of the Spatial Information Architecture Laboratory (SIAL) and Master of Design Innovation and Technology (MDIT) at RMIT University, Melbourne. Jane Burry's work focuses on two main strands: the use of digital technologies (computation) to creatively integrate mathematical computation into contemporary architecture, and the ability to combine data acquisition, mixed reality simulation, visualization and digital fabrication to create greener and more sensory environments.

>> PETER CACHOLA SCHMAL

...is an architect, curator and publicist. Since 2006 he has been the director of the Deutsches Architekturmuseum (DAM) in Frankfurt am Main, and the curator since 2000. He completed his studies of architecture at the Technical University of Darmstadt. Subsequently, he worked for Behnisch & Partner, Stuttgart, and ABE Architekten, Zeppelinheim/Neu-Isenburg, among others, and was a research assistant at the Technical University of Darmstadt in the field of building construction. In 2000 he received the Design II teaching assignment at the University of Applied Sciences in Frankfurt. Peter Cachola Schmal was Commissioner General of the German contribution to the 7th International Architecture Biennale São Paulo 2007, and Commissioner General of the German Pavilion at the 15th International Architecture Biennale in Venice in 2016. His publications include over 90 books and book contributions as well as around 250 specialist articles.

>> ANTOINE PICON

... is G. Ware Travelstead Professor of the History of Architecture and Technology and was Head of Research at the Harvard Graduate School of Design (GSD), Cambridge (MA) until 2019. Trained as an engineer, architect and historian, he is concerned with the technological development of architecture and urban planning from the eighteenth century to the present. Dr. Antoine Picon has received a number of awards for his writings. In 2010 he was elected a member of the French Académie des Technologies. Since 2014 he has been Chevalier des Arts et Lettres and Chairman of the Fondation Le Corbusier. He holds a degree in natural and engineering sciences from the École polytechnique and the École nationale des ponts et chaussées, a degree in architecture from the École d'architecture de Paris-Villemin, and a doctorate in history from the École des hautes études en sciences sociales.

>> METTE RAMSGAARD-THOMSEN

... is an architect and works in the field of interactive technologies. She is Professor of Architecture and Digital Technologies at the Royal Danish Academy of Fine Arts (KADK) and researches at the School of Architecture and Design at the University of Brighton. Mette Ramsgaard-Thomsen, PhD, also heads the CITA – Centre for Information Technology and Architecture at KADK. She previously researched and taught at the Bartlett School of Architecture at UCL and the School of Architecture and Design at the University of Brighton. She has taught in Calcutta, Ahmedabad, Amsterdam, Sydney, Perth, Halifax, Barcelona, Seoul, Copenhagen, Aarhus, Bonn and Braunschweig. Her research focuses on the interface between architecture and computer science, and the design of spaces defined by both physical and digital dimensions.

>> JENNY SABIN

... is Arthur L. and Isabel B. Wiesenberger Professor of Architecture and Associate Dean of Design at Cornell College of Architecture, Art and Planning, Ithaca (NY), where she established the research course Matter Design Computation. She is head of the experimental Jenny Sabin Studio for architectural design in Ithaca and director of the Sabin Lab at Cornell AAP. She focuses on the interfaces between architecture and science, applying findings and theories from biology and mathematics to the design of reactive material structures and adaptive architecture. Jenny Sabin holds a degree in ceramics and interdisciplinary visual arts from the University of Washington and a Master of Architecture from the University of Pennsylvania. She has been the recipient of the Pew Fellowship in the Arts 2010 and USA Knight Fellow in Architecture awards. In 2014 she was awarded the renowned Architectural League Prize.

>> BOB SHEIL

... is Professor of Architecture and Design through Production at the Bartlett School of Architecture UCL in London and has been its director since 2014. He is fascinated by the interfaces of design, production, craft and construction in architectural design practice. Bob Sheil is cofounder of the renowned international FABRICATE conference, for which he was co-chair and co-editor in 2011 (London) and 2017 (Zurich). For the 2020 event in London he is once again co-editor of the publication, together with conference leaders Jenny Sabin and Jane Burry. As director of the Bartlett School of Architecture, he has overseen an unprecedented period of growth for the 178-year-old institution, including the introduction of nine new teaching programs, such as MEng Engineering and Architectural Design, MArch Design for Manufacture and MArch Design for Performance and Interaction.

>> THOMAS SPECK

... has been Professor of Botany: Functional Morphology and Bionics and Director of the Botanical Garden of the University of Freiburg since 2001. He is the spokesman of the Biomimetics Competence Network, Vice President of BIOKON international and Vice Chairman of the Society for Technical Biology and Bionics. Dr. Thomas Speck is also deputy director of the Freiburg Center for Interactive Materials and Bioinspired Technologies (FIT), a scientific member of the Freiburg Materials Research Center (FMF) and a member of the team of spokespersons of the DFG Cluster of Excellence livMatS Living, Adaptive and Energy-autonomous Material Systems. He has received several scientific awards, is (co-)editor of several scientific books and journals and has published more than 280 scientific articles in peer-reviewed journals and books in the fields of functional morphology, biomechanics, biomimetics, evolutionary biology and paleobotany.

>> GEORG VRACHLIOTIS

... is Professor of Architectural Theory and Director of the Architectural Collection (saai | Southwest German Archive for Architecture and Engineering) at the Karlsruhe Institute of Technology (KIT). In 2016 he was appointed Dean of the Faculty of Architecture at KIT. Previously, Dr. Georg Vrachliotis taught and researched at the Institute for History and Theory of Architecture (gta) at ETH Zurich. He studied architecture at the Berlin University of the Arts and received his doctorate from ETH Zurich in 2009. He was a visiting researcher at the Center for Cognitive Science at the University of Freiburg, the Spatial Cognition Center at the University of Bremen and the UC Berkeley Department of Architecture in California. From 2006 to 2010 he was a guest lecturer in architectural theory at the TU Vienna. Georg Vrachliotis is a member of the advisory board of the journal ARCH+ and an external examiner at the Bartlett School of Architecture, UCL, in London.

>> REFERENCES

>>RETHINKING ARCHITECTURE

P. 16–21: EXPERIMENTAL ARCHITECTURE FOR THE TWENTY-FIRST CENTURY

[1] von Weizsäcker, C. F.: 1971, *Die Einheit der Natur,* Hanser Verlag, Munich, p. 23.

[2] See Vrachliotis, G.: 2011, *Geregelte Verhältnisse. Architektur und technisches Denken in der Epoche der Kybernetik*, Springer Verlag, Vienna/New York.

[3] An example of a conceptual debate in architecture is given here: Buckminster Fuller, R.: 1968, *Operating Manual for Spaceship Earth,* Southern Illinois University Press, Carbondale. On the initial use of the metaphor of the spaceship, see Boulding, K. E.: "The Economics of the Coming Spaceship Earth," in: Jarrett, H. (eds.): 1966, *Environmental Quality in a Growing Economy: Essays from the Sixth RFF Forum on Environmental Quality*, Johns Hopkins Press, Baltimore, MD, pp. 3–14.

[4] Meadows, D. et al.: 1972, *The Limits to Growth: Report of the Club of Rome on the Predicament of Mankind*, Universe Books.

[5] See "Das Individuum und sein Milieu. Über die kritische Situation in der wachsenden Sozietät. Tierbauten, Städtebau und biologische Erkenntnis", in: *Biologie und Bauen*, 1, IL Issue 3: 1971. And also: "Praktische Anwendung der Analogieforschung. Vom Hydroskelett zum Skelettmuskelsystem, Sandwichstrukturen bei Vogelschädeln. Zum Leichtbauprinzip der Organismen, Extremitätenstatik", in: *Biologie und Bauen*, 2, IL Issue 4: 1972, Institute for Lightweight Structures (IL), University of Stuttgart.

[6] One of Frei Otto's first and closest collaborators was Berthold Burkhardt. At the University of Stuttgart's Institute for Lightweight Structures (IL) he was involved in several building and research projects and responsible editor for numerous IL publications.

[7] See *Bauwelt, 20: 2015, Frei nach Otto. Sieben Betrachtungen zu seinem Erbe*. In particular, Sobek, W.: "„IL wird zu ILEK," pp. 14–18, and Menges, A: "Form und Findung," pp. 30–33. The symposium "Architektur als vermutete Zukunft" organized by the author in January 2017 at the ZKM Center for Art and Media Karlsruhe also dealt with Frei Otto's legacy.

[8] Concept for the foundation of a new collaborative research center with the working title "Natürliche Konstruktionen. Leichtbau in Architektur und Natur (Natural Constructions. Lightweight Construction in Architecture and Nature)" at the University of Stuttgart in conjunction with the University of Tübingen, Stuttgart (unpublished manuscript, July 15, 1982), saai | Archive for Architecture and Civil Engineering, Karlsruhe Institute of Technology, Frei Otto Archive.

[9] Hensel, M., Menges, A., Weinstock, M.: 2004, *Frei Otto in Conversation with the Emergence + Design Group,* 74 (3), pp. 18–25.

[10] See Schlaich, J.: "Das Olympiadach in München. Wie war das damals? Was hat es gebracht?", in: Schmidt, J.-K. (ed.): 1992, *Behnisch & Partner. Bauten 1952–1992*, exhibition catalog, Galerie der Stadt Stuttgart, Stuttgart, pp. 47–53.

P. 24–25: COMPUTATION INSTEAD OF COMPUTERIZATION

[11] A detailed explanation of the interrelation between digitization and standardization can be found in: Menges, A.: 2018, "Digitalisierung und Normierung," in: *ARCH+*, 233: Norm-Architektur, Berlin, pp. 110–111.

[12] The meaning of the two terms is based on one of the best texts for their delimitation in the context of digital design and planning methods: Terzidis, K.: 2006, *Algorithmic Architecture*, Elsevier Architectural Press, Oxford, p. XI.

[13] A historical derivation and differentiated presentation of computation in connection with architectural design thinking can be found in the following collection of writings: Menges, A., Ahlquist, S. (eds.): 2011, *Computational Design Thinking*, John Wiley and Sons, London.

[14] The conceptual framework underlying many of the projects in this book has been introduced here: Menges, A.: 2010, "Form Generation and Materialization at the Transition from Computer-Aided to Computational Design," in: *Detail* (English Edition), 2010(04), pp. 330–335.

[15] How a data-based approach enables a whole new approach to design is described in: Carpo, M.: 2017, *The Second Digital Turn: Design Beyond Intelligence*, MIT Press, Cambridge, MA.

P. 26-27: RESEARCH-BASED BUILDING AND BUILDING-BASED RESEARCH

[16] Barry Bergdoll has described the innovation of pavilions in detail and states: "Lack of permanence has often been a trampoline for invention. It might thus be possible to trace a history of architecture's leaps into new tasks, new experiences, and new formal, spatial and structural experiements by following the meandering path of pavilions." Bergdoll, B.: 2009, "The Pavilion and the Expanded Possibilities of Architecture," in: Schmal, P. C., *The Pavilion*, Hatje Cantz, Ostfildern, pp. 12-33.

[17] The reference to our pavilion buildings and the associated research into a "material culture," a term more commonly used in the social sciences, history, technology and the arts, is explained in more detail in Menges, A.: 2016, "Computational Material Culture," in: *Architectural Design*, 86(2), Wiley Academy, London, pp. 76-83.

>>INTEGRATIVE RESEARCH

P. 32–33: THE INTEGRATION OF FORM, MATERIAL, STRUCTURE AND SPACE

[18] Alberti, L. B.: 1987, *The Ten Books of Architecture*, Dover Publications, Mineola, New York.

[19] Nelson Goodman differentiates between arts that rely on a system of notation and others where this is not the case: Goodman, N.: 1968, *Languages of Art: An Approach to a Theory of Symbols*, Hackett Publishing, Indianapolis, IN, p. 121.

[20] Sanford Kwinter compares "computation" with other significant technological developments, such as the telescope or microscope, which have significantly altered our view of the world and thus brought about epochal changes: Kwinter, S.: 2011, "The Computational Fallacy," in: Menges, A., Ahlquist, S (eds.): *Computational Design Thinking*, Wiley, London, pp. 211-215.

[21] We have introduced our concept of Material Computation in the *AD* issue named alike: Menges, A. (ed.): 2012, "Material Computation – Higher Integration in Morphogenetic Design," in: *Architectural Design*, 82(2), Wiley Academy, London.

[22] Otto, F., Rasch B.: 1995, *Finding Form: Towards an Architecture of the Minimal*, Edition Axel Menges, Stuttgart.

[23] Our approach of deep integration of digital design generation and physical materialization is comprehensively presented in: Menges, A. (ed.): 2015, "Material Synthesis – Fusing the Physical and the Computational," in: *Architectural Design*, 85(5), Wiley Academy, London.

[24] A more comprehensive representation of the changes made possible by cyber-physical production systems can be found in: Menges, A.: 2015, "The New Cyber-Physical Making in Architecture – Computational Construction," in: *Architectural Design*, 85(5), Wiley Academy, London, pp. 28–33.

P. 34–35: BIOMIMETICS AS SCIENTIFIC LATERAL THINKING

[25] An overview of interesting and relevant properties can be found in: Jeronimidis, G.: 2004, "Biodynamics," in: Hensel, M., Menges, A., Weinstock, M. (eds.): "Emergence: Morphogenetic Design Strategies," in: *Architectural Design*, 74(3), Wiley Academy, London, pp. 90–96.

[26] An overview is given, for example in: Vincent, J.: 2012, *Structural Biomaterials*, Princeton University Press, Princeton, NJ.

[27] The possibilities and limits of bionics for structural engineering are described in: Knippers, J.: 2020, "The Use of Biological Models for Building Engineering Design," in: Addis, B. (ed.): *Physical Models: Their Historical and Current Use in Civil and Building Engineering Design*, Wiley/Ernst und Sohn, Berlin.

[28] A more detailed discussion of construction principles in nature and technology can be found in: Knippers, J., Speck, T.: 2012, "Design and Construction Principles in Nature and Architecture," in: *Bioinspiration and Biomimetics*, 7(1), 015002.

[29] The possibility of transferring morphogenetic building and process principles into architectural design is explained in more detail in: Menges, A.: 2012, "Biomimetic Design Processes in Architecture: Morphogenetic and Evolutionary Computational Design," in: *Bioinspiration and Biomimetics*, 7(1), 015003.

[30] An overview of the basic research in the field of bionics carried out between 2014 and 2019 at the Universities of Stuttgart, Freiburg and Tübingen within the Collaborative Research Center SFB-TRR 141 can be found in: Knippers, J., Schmid, U., Speck, T. (eds.): 2019, *Biomimetics for Architecture: Learning from Nature,* Birkhäuser, Basel, p. 208.

P. 36–37: STRUCTURES BEYOND TYPOLOGIES

[31] Knippers, J., Menges, A.: 2019, "Computer-Based Processes for Biomimetic Structures," in: Lang, W., Hellstern, C. (eds.): *Visionaries and Unsung Heroes: Engineers – Design – Tomorrow*, Detail Business Information GmbH, Munich, pp. 51–57.

[32] The constitution of the occupational profile of the civil engineer in the nineteenth century is described using the example of Schwedler in: Knippers, J.: 2000, "Johann Wilhelm Schwedler: Vom Experiment zur Berechnung", in: *Deutsche Bauzeitung*, 04/00, pp. 105–112.

[33] Polonyi describes the influence of fundamental models of thought on engineering very vividly in: Polonyi, S.: 1987: "Einfluss der Wissenschaft auf das Bauwesen", in: *... mit zaghafter Konsequenz. Aufsätze und Vorträge zum Tragwerksentwurf 1961-1987*, Vieweg, Braunschweig (Bauwelt Fundamente 81).

[34] The classification of load-bearing systems as known today took place in the mid-twentieth century. A frequently quoted example is: Engels, H.: 1967, *Tragsysteme / Structure Systems*, Deutsche Verlagsanstalt DVA, Stuttgart.

[35] The possibility of overcoming established structural typologies with digital planning methods is discussed in more detail in: Knippers, J.: 2013, "From Model Thinking to Process Design," in: *AD Architectural Design*, 2, pp. 74–81.

[36] Knippers, J.: 2012, "Von der Konstruktion des Bauwerks zur Gestaltung der Prozesse" (From the Construction of the Building to the Design of the Processes), in: *Detail*, 10, pp. 1142–1148.

[37] The traditional understanding of lightweight construction is discussed and critically reflected upon in: Knippers, J., Helbig, T: 2014, "Das Prinzip Leichtbau und seine Bedeutung für das konstruktive Entwerfen" (The Principle of Lightweight Construction and its Significance for Structural Design), in: *Stahlbau*, 83(11), pp. 777–783.

[38] Lightweight construction was the core theme for late twentieth century engineers, as described here for example: Schlaich, J: 2013, "Leichtbau – wieso und wie?" (Lightweight Construction – Why and How?), in: Bögle, A., Schmal, P. C., Flagge, I. (eds.): *Leicht weit / Light Structures: Jörg Schlaich – Rudolf Bergermann*, Prestel, Munich.

[39] The challenges of additive fabrication for structural analysis are discussed in: Knippers, J.: 2017, "The Limits of Simulation: Towards a New Culture of Architectural Engineering," in: *Technology, Architecture + Design*, 1(2), pp. 155–162.

P. 38–39: INNOVATION WOOD

[40] A detailed overview of the possibilities for timber construction arising from digital technologies is provided by: Menges, A.: 2016, "Integrative Design Computation for Advancing Wood Architecture," in: Menges, A., Schwinn, T., Krieg, O. (eds.): *Advancing Wood Architecture – A Computational Approach*, Routledge, Oxford, pp. 97–110.

P. 40–41: INNOVATION FIBER COMPOSITES

[41] The historical development and the state of the art of fiber-composite technology in architecture are described in: Knippers, J., Gabler, M., Lienhard, J., Cremers, J: 2012, *Construction Manual for Polymers + Membranes: Materials, Semi-finished Products, Form Finding, Design*, Edition Detail, Birkhäuser, Basel.

[42] A detailed derivation of the architectural possibilities and requirements can be found in: Menges, A., Knippers, J: 2015, "Fibrous Tectonics," in: *Architectural Design*, 85(5), Wiley Academy, London, pp. 40–47.

[43] The architectural potential of fiber-composite structures is explained in more detail here: Menges, A., Knippers, J: 2017, "Architektonisches Potential tragender Faserverbundstrukturen" (Architectural Potential of Load-bearing Composite Fiber Structures), in: *DBZ Deutsche BauZeitschrift*, 12, p. 61–66.

[44] We have described the emergence of a new construction language in more detail in the following article: Knippers, J., Menges, A: 2015, "Fasern neu gedacht – auf dem Weg zu einer Konstruktionssprache" (Fibers Rethought –Towards Novel Constructional Articulation), in: *Detail*, 12, pp. 1238–1242.

[45] A further comprehensive study of architectural morphologies related to this approach can be found in: Menges, A: 2016, *Material Performance – Fibrous Tectonics & Architectural Morphology*, Harvard University GSD, Cambridge, MA.

>>EXTERNAL POSITIONS

P. 66–67: ARCHITECTURE AND BIOMIMETICS

[46] Speck, T., Speck, O.: 2008, "Process Sequences in Biomimetic Research," in: Brebbia, C. A. (ed.): *Design and Nature*, IV, WIT Press, Southampton, pp. 3–11.

[47] Knippers, J., Nickel, K. G., Speck, T. (eds.): 2016, "Biomimetic Research for Architecture and Building Construction: Biological Design and Integrative Structures," in: *Biologically-Inspired Systems*, 8, Springer International Publishing, Cham (DOI: 10.1007/978-3-319-46374-2).

[48] Lienhard, J., Schleicher, S., Poppinga, S., Masselter, T., Milwich, M., Speck, T., Knippers, J.; 2011, "Flectofin: A Nature Based Hinge-less Flapping Mechanism," in: *Bioinspiration and Biomimetics*, 6(4), 045001.

[49] Körner, A., Born, L., Mader, A., Sachse, R., Saffarian, S., Westermeier, A. S., Poppinga, S., Bischoff, M., Gresser, G. T., Milwich, M., Speck, T., Knippers, J.: 2018, "Flectofold – A Biomimetic Compliant Shading Device for Complex Free Form Facades," in: *Smart Materials and Structures*, 27(1), 017001.

[50] Correa, D., Poppinga, S., Mylo, M., Westermeier, A. S., Bruchmann, B., Menges, A., Speck, T.: 2019, "Biomimetic 4D Printed Autonomous Scale and Flap Structures Capable of Multi-Phase Movement," in: *Philosophical Transactions of the Royal Society London A*.

[51] Speck, T.: 2015, "Approaches to Bio-inspiration in Novel Architecture," in: Imhof, B., Gruber, P. (eds.): *Built to Grow – Blending Architecture and Biology*, Birkhäuser, Basel, pp. 145–149.

[52] Speck, T., Speck, O.: 2019, "Emergence in Biomimetic Materials Systems," in: Wegner, L. H., Lüttge, U. (eds.): *Emergence and Modularity in Life Sciences*, Springer Nature, Basel, pp. 97–115.

P. 88–89. MATERIAL CULTURE

[53] Sabin, J. et al: 2020, *Embedded Architecture: Ada, Driven by Humans, Powered by AI*, in prep for Fabricate 2020, UCL, Bartlett, London.

[54] Lovelace, A.: 1843, "Notes" to a "Sketch of the Analytical Engine Invented by Charles Babbage, by L.F. Menabrea," in: *Scientific Memoirs*, 3, Richard and John E. Taylor, London.

[55] Freely quoted after Le Ricolais, 1973.

[56] Sabin, J., Jones, P. L.: 2017, *LabStudio: Design Research Between Architecture and Biology*, Routledge Taylor and Francis, London/New York.

[57] Sabin, J.: 2015, "Transformative Research Practice: Architectural Affordances and Crisis," in: *Journal of Architectural Education*, 69(1), pp. 63–71.

P. 112–113: COMPLEXITY AND CONTRADICTION IN MATERIAL COMPUTATION

[58] Quote after: Novalis: *Poems / The Disciples at Sais*, Chapter 1 (Original: Gedichte / Die Lehrlinge zu Sais, Kap. 1: Der Lehrling).

>>EXPERIMENTAL BUILDING

P. 46–55: ICD/ITKE RESEARCH PAVILION 2010

[59] Fleischmann, M., Knippers, J., Lienhard, J., Menges, A., Schleicher, S.: 2012, "Material Behaviour: Embedding Physical Properties in Computational Design Processes," in: *Architectural Design*, 82(2), Wiley Academy, London, pp. 44–51.

[60] Menges, A.: 2011, "Integrative Design Computation: Integrating Material Behaviour and Robotic Manufacturing Processes in Computational Design for Performative Wood Constructions," in: *Proceedings of the 31th Conference of the Association for Computer Aided Design in Architecture (ACADIA)*, Banff (Canada) October 13–16, 2011, pp. 72–81.

[61] Fleischmann, M., Menges, A.: 2011, "ICD/ITKE Research Pavilion: A Case Study of Multi-Disciplinary Computational Design," in: Gengnagel, C., Kilian, A., Palz, N., Scheurer, F. (eds.): *Computational Design Modeling* [Proceedings of the Design Modeling Symposium Berlin], Springer, Berlin/Heidelberg, pp. 239–248 (DOI: 10.1007/978-3-642-23435-4_27).

62] Menges, A., Schleicher, S., Fleischmann, M.: 2011, "Research Pavilion ICD/ITKE," in: Glynn, R., Sheil, B., *Proceedings of the Fabricate: Making Digital Architecture Conference*, University College London, April 15-16, 2011, Riverside Architectural Press, Waterloo, pp. 22-27.

[63] Knippers, J., Menges, A.: 2011, "ICD/ITKE Research Pavilion 2010," in: *A+U: Timber Innovation*, 7(490), pp. 10–15.

P. 56–65: ICD/ITKE RESEARCH PAVILION 2011

[64] La Magna, R., Gabler, M., Reichert, S., Schwinn, T., Waimer, F., Menges, A., Knippers, J.: 2013, "From Nature to Fabrication: Biomimetic Design Principles for the Production of Complex Spatial Structures," in: *International Journal of Spatial Structures*, 28(1), pp. 27–40 (DOI: 10.1260/0266-3511.28.1.27).

[65] Menges, A.: 2012, "Morphospaces of Robotic Fabrication – From Theoretical Morphology to Design Computation and Digital Fabrication in Architecture," in: Brell Cokcan, S., Braumann, J. (eds.): *Proceedings of the Robots in Architecture Conference 2012*, TU Wien, Springer, Vienna, pp. 28–47 (DOI: 10.1007/978-3-7091-1465-0_3).

[66] Schwinn, T., Krieg, O., Menges, A.: 2012, "Robotically Fabricated Wood Plate Morphologies – Robotic Prefabrication of a Biomimetic, Geometrically Differentiated Lightweight Finger Joint Timber Plate Structure," in: Brell Cokcan, S., Braumann, J. (eds.): *Proceedings of the Robots in Architecture Conference 2012*, TU Wien, Springer, Vienna, pp. 48–61.

[67] Knippers, J., Menges, A., Gabler, M., La Magna, R., Waimer, F., Reichert S., Schwinn, T.: 2012, "From Nature to Fabrication: Biomimetic Design Principles for the Production of Complex Spatial Structures," in: Hesselgren, L., Sharma, S., Wallner, J., Baldassini, N., Bompas, P., Raynaud, J. (eds.): 2012, *Advances in Architectural Geometry*, Springer, Vienna/New York, pp. 107–122.

[68] Schwinn, T., Krieg, O., Menges, A., Mihaylov, B., Reichert, S.: 2012, "Machinic Morphospaces: Biomimetic Design Strategies for the Computational Exploration of Robot Constraint Spaces for Wood Fabrication," in: Cabrinha, M., Johnson, J., Steinfeld, K. (eds.): *Proceedings of the 32nd Annual Conference of the Association for Computer Aided Design in Architecture*, San Francisco, pp. 157–168.

[69] Menges, A., Schwinn, T.: 2012, "Manufacturing Reciprocities," in: *Architectural Design*, 82(2), Wiley Academy, London, pp. 118–125.

P. 68–77: ICD/ITKE RESEARCH PAVILION 2012

[70] Knippers, J., La Magna, R., Menges, A., Reichert, S., Schwinn, T., Waimer, F.: 2015, "ICD/ITKE Research Pavilion 2012 – Coreless Filament Winding on the Morphological Principles of an Arthropod Exoskeleton," in: *Architectural Design*, 85(5), Wiley Academy, London, pp. 48–53 (DOI: 10.1002/ad.1953).

[71] Reichert S., Schwinn, T., La Magna, R., Waimer, F., Knippers, J., Menges, A.: 2014, "Fibrous Structures: An Integrative Approach to Design Computation, Simulation and Fabrication for Lightweight, Glass and Carbon Fibre Composite Structures in Architecture Based on Biomimetic Design Principles," in: *CAD Journal*, 52 (July), pp. 27–39 (DOI: 10.1016/j.cad.2014.02.005).

[72] Waimer, F., La Magna, R., Reichert S., Schwinn, T., Menges, A., Knippers, J.: 2013, "Bionisch-inspirierte Faserverbundstrukturen: Prinzipien für Fertigung und Auslegung", in: *Bautechnik*, 90(12), pp. 766–771 (DOI: 10.1002 / bate.201300079).

[73] La Magna, R.; Waimer, F.; Knippers, J.: 2016, "Coreless Winding and Assembled Core – Novel Fabrication Approaches for FRP Based Components in Building Construction", in: Building and Costruction Materials (127). pp. 1009-1016 (DOI: 10.1016/j.conbuildmat.2016.01.015).

[74] Waimer, F., La Magna, R., Reichert, S., Schwinn, T., Knippers, J., Menges, A.: 2013, "Integrated Design Methods for the Simulation of Fibre-Based Structures," in: Gengnagel, C., Kilian, A., Nembrini, J., Scheurer, F. (eds.): *Rethinking Prototyping* (Proceedings of the Design Modeling Symposium Berlin 2013), Verlag der Universität der Künste, Berlin, pp. 277–290.

[75] Menges, A., Knippers, J.: 2015, "Robotic Fabrication. ICD/ITKE Research Pavilion 2012," in: Andia, A., Spiegelhalter, L. (eds.): *Postparametric Automation in Design and Construction*, Artech House, Boston, MA, pp. 181–187.

[76] Waimer, F., La Magna, R.; Knippers, J.: 2013, "Integrative Numerical Techniques for Fibre Reinforced Polymers – Forming Process and Analysis of Differentiated Anisotropy," in: *Journal of the International Association for Shell and Spatial Structures*, 54, pp. 301–309.

P. 78–87: ICD/ITKE RESEARCH PAVILION 2013/14

[77] Dörstelmann, M., Knippers, J., Menges, A., Parascho, S., Prado, M., Schwinn, T.: 2015, "ICD/ITKE Research Pavilion 2013–14 – Modular Coreless Filament Winding Based on Beetle Elytra," in: *Architectural Design*, 85(5), Wiley Academy, London, pp. 54–59 (DOI: 10.1002/ad.1954).

[78] Parascho, S., Dörstelmann, M., Prado, M., Menges, A., Knippers, J.: 2015, "Modular Fibrous Morphologies: Computational Design, Simulation and Fabrication of Differentiated Fibre Composite Building Components," in: Block, P. Knippers J., Mitra, N., Wang, W. (eds.): *Advances in Architectural Geometry 2014*, Springer International Publishing, Cham, pp. 109–125 (DOI: 10.1007/978-3-319-11418-7_1).

[79] Dörstelmann, M., Parascho, S., Prado, M., Menges, A., Knippers, J.: 2014, "Integrative Computational Design Methodologies for Modular Architectural Fiber Composite Morphologies," in: *Design Agency* (Proceedings of the 34th Annual Conference of the Association for Computer Aided Design in Architecture), Los Angeles, pp. 219–228.

[80] Prado, M., Dörstelmann, M., Schwinn, T., Menges, A., Knippers, J.: 2014, "Coreless Filament Winding: Robotically Fabricated Fiber Composite Building Components," in: McGee, W., Ponce de Leon, M. (eds.): *Proceedings of the Robots in Architecture Conference 2014*, University of Michigan, pp. 275–289.

P. 90–99: LANDESGARTENSCHAU EXHIBITION HALL

[81] Horn, R., Groenewolt, A., Krieg, O., Gantner, J.: 2018, "Ökobilanzierung von Lebensende-Optionen, Szenarien im bauphysikalischen Kontext am Beispiel segmentierter Holzschalenkonstruktionen" , in: *Bauphysik*, 5, pp.298–306 (DOI: 10.1002/bapi.201800007).

[82] Grun, T. B., Koohi Fayegh Dehkordi, L., Schwinn, T., Sonntag, D., von Scheven, M., Bischoff, M., Knippers, J., Menges, A., Nebelsick, J. H.: 2016, "The Skeleton of the Sand Dollar as a Biological Role Model for Segmented Shells in Building Construction: A Research Review," in: Knippers, J., Nickel, K. G., Speck, T. (eds.), *Biomimetic Research for Architecture and Building Construction: Biological Design and Integrative Structures*, 8, Springer International Publishing, Cham, pp. 217–242 (DOI: 10.1007/978-3-319-46374-2_11).

[83] Schwinn, T., Menges, A.: 2015, "Fabrication Agency - Landesgartenschau Exhibition Hall," in: *Architectural Design*, 85(5), Wiley Academy, London, pp. 92-99 (DOI: 10.1002/ad.1960).

[84] Krieg, O., Schwinn, T., Menges, A.: 2015, "Neue Holztechnologien: Robotisch gefertigter Leichtbau", in: *Holztechnologie*, 2, pp. 20–26.

[85] Krieg, O., Schwinn, T., Menges, A., Li, J., Knippers, J., Schmitt, A., Schwieger, V.: 2015, "Biomimetic Lightweight Timber Plate Shells: Computational Integration of Robotic Fabrication, Architectural Geometry and Structural Design," in: Block, P., Knippers, J., Mitra, N., Wang, W. (eds.), *Advances in Architectural Geometry 2014*, Springer International Publishing, Cham, pp. 109–125 (DOI: 10.1007/978-3-319-11418-7_8).

[86] Schwinn, T., Krieg, O., Menges, A.: 2014, "Behavioral Strategies: Synthesizing Design Computation and Robotic Fabrication of Lightweight Timber Plate Structures," in: *Design Agency* (Proceedings of the 34th Annual Conference of the Association for Computer Aided Design in Architecture), Los Angeles, pp. 177–188.

[87] Schwinn, T.: 2016, "Landesgartenschau Exhibition Hall," in: Menges, A., Schwinn, T., Krieg, O. (eds.): *Advancing Wood Architecture – A Computational Approach*, Routledge, Oxford, pp. 111–124.

[88] Li, J.-M., Knippers, J.: 2015: "Segmental Timber Plate Shell for the Landesgartenschau Exhibition Hall in Schwäbisch Gmünd –The Application of Finger Joints in Plate Structure," in: *International Journal of Space Structures*, 30(2), pp.123–139.

[89] Li, J.-M., Knippers, J.: 2015: "Pattern and Form – Their Influence on Segmental Plate Shells", in: *Proceedings of the IASS Symposium 2015*, Amsterdam.

P. 102–111: ICD/ITKE RESEARCH PAVILION 2014/15

[90] Vasey, L., Baharlou, E., Dörstelmann, M., Koslowski, V., Prado, M., Schieber, G., Menges, A., Knippers, J.: 2015, "Behavioral Design and Adaptive Robotic Fabrication of a Fiber Composite Compression Shell with Pneumatic Formwork," in: Combs, L., Perry, C. (eds.): Computational Ecologies: *Design in the Anthropocene* (Proceedings of the 35th Annual Conference of the Association for Computer Aided Design in Architecture), University of Cincinnati, pp. 297–309.

[91] Schieber, G., Koslowski, V., Dörstelmann, M., Prado, M., Vasey, L., Knippers, J., Menges A.: 2015, "Integrated Design and Fabrication Strategies for Fibrous Structures," in: Ramsgaard Thomsen, M., Tamke, M., Gengnagel, C., Faircloth, B., Scheurer, F. (eds.): 2015, *Modelling Behaviour* (Proceedings of the Design Modelling Symposium Copenhagen 2015), Springer, Heidelberg, pp. 237–246 (DOI: 10.1007/978-3-319-24208-8_20).

[92] Dörstelmann, M., Knippers, J., Koslowski, V., Menges, A., Prado, M.,Schieber, G., Vasey, L.: 2015, "ICD/ITKE Research Pavilion 2014–15 – Fibre Placement on a Pneumatic Body Based on a Water Spider Web," in: *Architectural Design*, 85(5), Wiley, London, pp. 60–65 (DOI: 10.1002/ad.1955).

P. 114–123: ICD/ITKE RESEARCH PAVILION 2015/16

[93] Alvarez, M. E., Martinez-Parachini, E. E., Baharlou, E., Krieg, O. D., Schwinn, T., Vasey, L., Hua, C., Menges, A., Yuan, P. F.: 2018, "Tailored Structures, Robotic Sewing of Wooden Shells," in: Willmann, J., Block, P., Hutter, M., Byrne, K., Schork, T. (eds.): *Robotic Fabrication in Architecture, Art and Design 2018* (Proceedings of the RobArch Conference 2018), Springer, Cham, pp. 405–420 (DOI: 10.1007/978-3-319-92294-2_31).

[94] Schwinn, T., Krieg, O., Menges, A.: 2016, "Robotic Sewing: A Textile Approach Towards the Computational Design and Fabrication of Lightweight Timber Shells," in: *Posthuman Frontiers: Data, Designers, and Cognitive Machines* (Proceedings of the 36th Conference of the Association for Computer Aided Design in Architecture), Ann Arbor, MI, pp. 224–233.

[95] Bechert, S., Knippers, J., Krieg, O., Menges, A., Schwinn, T., Sonntag, D.: 2016, "Textile Fabrication Techniques for Timber Shells: Elastic Bending of Custom-Laminated Veneer for Segmented Shell Construction Systems," in: Adriaenssens, S., Gramazio, F., Kohler, M., Menges, A., and Pauly, M. (eds.), *Advances in Architectural Geometry 2016*, vdf Hochschulverlag AG ETH Zürich, Zurich, pp. 154–169.

[96] Grun, T. B., Koohi Fayegh Dehkordi, L., Schwinn, T., Sonntag, D., von Scheven, M., Bischoff, M., Knippers, J., Menges, A., Nebelsick, J. H.: 2016, "The Skeleton of the Sand Dollar as a Biological Role Model for Segmented Shells in Building Construction: A Research Review," in: Knippers, J., Nickel, K. G., Speck, T. (eds.): *Biomimetic Research for Architecture and Building Construction: Biological Design and Integrative Structures*, 8, Springer International Publishing, Cham, pp. 217–242 (DOI: 10.1007/978-3-319-46374-2_11).

[97] Sonntag, D., Bechert, S., Knippers, J.: 2017, "Biomimetic Timber Shells Made of Bending-Active Segment," in: *International Journal of Space Structures*, 32(3–4), pp. 149–159 (DOI: 10.1177/0266351117746266).6).

[98] Telford, M.: 1985, "Domes, Arches and Urchins: The Skeletal Architecture of Echinoids (Echinodermata)," in: *Zoomorphology*, 105, pp. 114–124.

P. 126–135: ICD/ITKE RESEARCH PAVILION 2016/17

[99] Solly, J., Früh, N., Saffarian, S., Prado, M., Vasey, L., Felbrich, B., Reist, D., Knippers, J., Menges, A.: 2018, "ICD/ITKE Research Pavilion 2016/2017: Integrative Design of a Composite Lattice Cantilever," in: *IASS – Creativity in Structural Design* (Proceedings of the IASS Symposium 2018), Boston, pp. 28–40.

[100] Felbrich, B., Früh, N., Prado, M., Saffarian, S., Solly, J., Vasey, L., Knippers, J., Menges, A.: 2017, "Multi-Machine Fabrication: An Integrative Design Process Utilising an Autonomous UAV and Industrial Robots for the Fabrication of Long-Span Composite Structures," in: *ACADIA – Disciplines & Disruption* (Proceedings of the ACADIA Conference 2017), Cambridge, MA, pp. 248–259.

[101] [101] Solly, J., Früh, N., Saffarian, S., Aldinger, L., Margariti, G., Knippers, J.: 2019, "Structural Design of a Lattice Composite Cantilever," in: *Structures*, 18, pp. 28–40 (DOI: 10.1016/j.istruc.2018.11.019).

[102] Vasey, L., Felbrich, B., Prado, M., Tahanzadeh, B., Menges, A.: 2020, "Physically Distributed Multi-Robot Coordination and Collaboration in Construction," in: *Construction Robotics* (4), 3–18 (DOI: 10.1007/s41693-020-00031-y).

P. 136–147: ELYTRA FILAMENT PAVILION

[103] Prado, M., Dörstelmann, M., Solly, J., Menges, A., Knippers, J.: 2017, "Elytra Filament Pavilion: Robotic Filament Winding for Structural Composite Building Systems," in: *Fabricate – Rethinking Design and Construction* (Proceedings of the Fabricate Conference 2017), Stuttgart, pp. 224–233.

[104] Menges, A., Knippers, J.: 2019, "Elytra Filament Pavilion", in: Retsin, G., Jimenez, M., Claypool, M., Soler, V. (eds.): *Robotic Building: Architecture in the Age of Automation*, Detail Special, Munich, pp. 34–37.

[105] Menges, A., Knippers, J.: 2018, "Fibrous Tectonics," in: Daas, M., Wit, A. (eds.): *Towards a Robotic Architecture*, ORO Editions, Novato, pp. 64–75.

[106] Menges, A., Knippers, J.: 2017, "Architektonisches Potential tragender Faserverbundstrukturen" (Architectural Potential Of Load-Bearing Fibre Composite Structures), in: *DBZ Deutsche BauZeitschrift*, 12, pp. 61–66.

P. 150–161: BUGA WOOD PAVILLON

[107] Alvarez, M., Wagner, H. J., Groenewolt, A., Krieg, O. D., Kyjanek, O., Aldinger, L., Bechert, S., Sonntag, D., Menges, A., Knippers, J.: 2019, "The Buga Wood Pavilion – Integrative Interdisciplinary Advancements of Digital Timber Architecture," in: *ACADIA – Ubiquity and Autonomy* (Proceedings of the ACADIA Conference 2019), University of Texas, Austin, pp. 490–499.

[108] Krieg, O. D., Bechert, S., Groenewolt, A., Horn, R., Knippers, J., Menges, A.: 2018, "Affordances of Complexity: Evaluation of a Robotic Production Process for Segmented Timber Shell Structures," in: *WCTE* (Proceedings of the 2018 World Conference on Timber Engineering), Seoul, pp. 1–8.

[109] Bechert, S., Groenewolt, A., Krieg, O., Menges, A., Knippers, J.: 2018, Structural Performance of Construction Systems for Segmented Timber Shell Structures, in: *IASS – Creativity in Structural Design* (Proceedings of the IASS Symposium 2018), Boston, MA.

[110] Menges, A., Knippers, J., Wagner, H. J., Sonntag, D.: 2019, "BUGA Holzpavillon – Freiformfläche aus robotisch gefertigten Nulltoleranz-Segmenten", in: *Proceedings of 25th International Wood Construction Conferenc IHF 2019*, pp. 129–138.

[111] Schwinn, T., Sonntag, D., Grun, T., Nebelsick, J., Knippers, J., Menges, A.: 2019, "Potential Applications of Segmented Shells in Architecture," in: Knippers, J., Schmid, U., Speck, T. (eds.): *Biomimetics for Architecture*, Birkhäuser, Basel, pp. 116–125.

[112] Menges, A., Schwinn, T., Wagner, H. J.: 2018, "Bionische segmentierte Holzplattenschalen: integrative agentenbasierte Modellierung und robotische Fertigung" in: *Proceedings of 24th International Wood Construction Conferenc IHF 2018*, pp. 239–249.

P. 162–173: BUGA FIBRE PAVILION

[113] Bodea, S., Dambrosio, N., Zechmeister, C., Gil Perez, M., Koslowski, V. Rongen, B., Doerstelmann, M., Kyjanek, O., Knippers, J., Menges, A.: 2020, BUGA Fibre Pavilion: Towards Robotically-Fabricated Composite Building Structures, in: Burry, J., Sabin, J., Sheil, B., Skavara, M. (eds.), *Fabricate 2020: Making Resilient Architecture*, UCL Press, London, pp. 234-243.

[114] Dambrosio, N., Zechmeister, C., Bodea, S., Koslwoski, V., Gil Perez, M., Rongen, B., Knippers, J., Menges, A.: 2019, "Towards an Architectural Application of Novel Fiber Composite Building Systems – The BUGA Fibre Pavilion," in: *ACADIA – Ubiquity and Autonomy* (Proceedings of the ACADIA Conference 2019), University of Texas, Austin.

[115] Zechmeister, C., Bodea, S., Dambrosio, N., Menges, A.: 2020, "Design for Long-Span Core-Less Wound, Structural Composite Building Elements," in: Gengnagel, C., Baverel, O., Burry, J., Ramsgaard Thomsen, M., Weinzierl, S. (eds.): *Impact: Design With All Senses*, Springer International Publishing, Cham, pp. 401–415 (DOI: 10.1007/978-3-030-29829-6 32).

[116] Rongen, B., Koslowski, V., Gil Perez, M., Knippers, J.: 2019, "Structural Optimisation and Rationalisation of the BUGA Fibre Composite Dome," in: Lázaro, C., Bletzinger, K.U., Onate C. Lázaro (eds.): *Proceedings of the IASS 2019 Symposium*, Barcelona.

[117] Gil Perez, M., Dambrosio, N., B. Rongen, B., Menges A., Knippers, J.: 2019, "Structural Optimization of Coreless Filament Wound Components Connection System Through Orientation of Anchor Points in the Winding Frames," in: Lázaro, C., Bletzinger, K. U., Onate C. Lázaro (eds): *Proceedings of the IASS 2019 Symposium*, Barcelona.

P. 176–187: URBACH TOWER

[118] Wood, D., Grönquist, P., Bechert, S., Aldinger, L., Riggenbach, D., Lehmann, K., Rüggeberg, M., Burgert, I., Knippers, J., Menges, A.: 2020, "From Machine Control to Material Programming: Self-Shaping Wood Manufacturing of a High Performance Curved CLT Structure – Urbach Tower," in: Burry, J., Sabin, J., Sheil, B., Skavara, M. (eds.), *Fabricate 2020: Making Resilient Architecture*, UCL Press, London, pp. 50-57.

[119] Aldinger, L., Bechert, S., Wood, D., Knippers, J., Menges, A.: 2020, "Design and Structural Modelling of Surface-Active Timber Structures Made from Curved CLT – Urbach Tower, Remstal Gartenschau 2019," in: Gengnagel, C., Baverel, O., Burry, J., Ramsgaard Thomsen, M., Weinzierl, S. (eds.): *Impact: Design With All Senses*, Springer International Publishing, Cham, pp. 419–432 (DOI: 10.1007/978-3-030-29829-6 33).

[120] Grönquist, P., Wood, D., Hassani, M., Wittel, F., Menges, A., Rüggeberg, M.: 2019, "Analysis of Hygroscopic Self-Shaping Wood at Large Scale for Curved Mass Timber Structures," in: *Science Advances* 5(9), pp. eaax1311 (DOI: 10.1126/sciadv.aax1311).

[121] Wood, D., Brütting, J., Menges, A.: 2018, "Self-Forming Curved Timber Plates: Initial Design Modeling for Shape-Changing Material Buildups," in: *IASS – Creativity in Structural Design* (Proceedings of the IASS Symposium 2018]) Boston, MA.

[122] Wood, D., Vailati, C., Menges, A., Rüggeberg, M.: 2018, "Hygroscopically Actuated Wood Elements for Weather Responsive and Self-Forming Building Parts – Facilitating Upscaling and Complex Shape Changes," in: *Construction and Building Materials*, 165, Elsevier (DOI: 10.1016/S0950061817325394).

>> IMAGE CREDITS

P. 4–5: ACKNOWLEDGEMENTS
1] ukartpics / Alamy Stock Photo (G1PJXA)

P. 10–13: ICD AND ITKE, UNIVERSITY OF STUTTGART
1] Menges / Reichert, ICD University of Stuttgart
2] Ruslou Koorts
3, 4] ICD University of Stuttgart
5] Lienhard, ITKE University of Stuttgart
6] ITKE University of Stuttgart

P. 16–21: EXPERIMENTAL ARCHITECTURE FOR THE TWENTY-FIRST CENTURY
1, 2, 3, 5, 6] Frei Otto Archive, saai | Archive for Architecture and Civil Engineering, Karlsruhe Institute for Technology
4] Conné van Grachten
7] ICD/ITKE University of Stuttgart

P. 22–23: RETHINKING ARCHITECTURE DIGITALLY
1, 2] ICD/ITKE University of Stuttgart

P. 24–25: COMPUTATION INSTEAD OF COMPUTERIZATION
1] Vitra Design Museum, Foto: Julien Lanoo
2] ICD/ITKE Universität Stuttgart

P. 26–27: RESEARCH-BASED CONSTRUCTION AND BUILDING RESEARCH
1, 2] ICD/ITKE University of Stuttgart

P. 46–55: ICD/ITKE RESEARCH PAVILION 2010
1] Roland Halbe 2010
2] Menges, ICD University of Stuttgart
3] Lienhard, ITKE University of Stuttgart
4] Eisenhardt, Vollrath, Wächter, ICD/ITKE University of Stuttgart
5] Eisenhardt, Vollrath, Wächter, ICD/ITKE University of Stuttgart
6] Lienhard, ITKE University of Stuttgart
7] Schleicher, ITKE University of Stuttgart
8] Andrea Lautenschlager
9–12] Roland Halbe

P. 56–65: ICD/ITKE RESEARCH PAVILION 2011
1, 2] Roland Halbe
3–9] ICD/ITKE University of Stuttgart
10] Menges/Schwinn, ICD University of Stuttgart
11] Roland Halbe
12–14] ICD/ITKE University of Stuttgart

P. 68–77: ICD/ITKE RESEARCH PAVILION 2012
1] Roland Halbe
2, 3] ICD/ITKE University of Stuttgart
4] Menges, ICD University of Stuttgart
5–7] ICD/ITKE University of Stuttgart
8] Menges, ICD University of Stuttgart
9, 10] ICD/ITKE University of Stuttgart
11, 12] Roland Halbe

P. 78–87: ICD/ITKE RESEARCH PAVILION 2013/14
1] Roland Halbe
2–6] ICD/ITKE University of Stuttgart
7] Prof. Oliver Betz, Anne Buhl, University of Tübingen
8–11] ICD/ITKE University of Stuttgart
12] Christoph Püschner / Fotojournalist
13] ICD/ITKE University of Stuttgart

P. 90–99: LANDESGARTENSCHAU EXHIBITION HALL
1, 2] ICD/ITKE/IIGS University of Stuttgart
3, 4] James Nebelsick, University of Tübingen
5–7] Menges/Schwinn, ICD University of Stuttgart
8, 9] ICD/ITKE/IIGS University of Stuttgart
10] Menges/Schwinn, ICD University of Stuttgart
11–14] ICD/ITKE/IIGS University of Stuttgart

P. 102–111: ICD/ITKE RESEARCH PAVILION 2014/15
1, 2] Roland Halbe
3-9] ICD/ITKE University of Stuttgart
10] Roland Halbe
11] Regenscheit, Universität Stuttgart
12] Roland Halbe

P. 114–123: ICD/ITKE RESEARCH PAVILION 2015/16
1] ICD/ITKE University of Stuttgart
2] Roland Halbe
3] ICD/ITKE University of Stuttgart
4] Telford, 1985
5-13] ICD/ITKE University of Stuttgart
14] Roland Halbe
15] ICD/ITKE University of Stuttgart

P. 126–135: ICD/ITKE RESEARCH PAVILION 2016/17
1, 2] Roland Halbe
3–10] ICD/ITKE University of Stuttgart
11–13] Roland Halbe

P. 136–147: ELYTRA FILAMENT PAVILION
1] NAARO
2] Roland Halbe
3] Dr. Thomas van de Kamp
4] ICD/ITKE University of Stuttgart
5] Dr. Thomas van de Kamp, Prof. Dr. Hartmut Greven / Prof. Oliver Betz, Anne Buhl, University of Tübingen
6–8] ICD/ITKE University of Stuttgart
9] Menges, ICD University of Stuttgart
10, 11] Victoria and Albert Museum, London
12–16] Roland Halbe
17] NAARO
18] Victoria and Albert Museum, London

P. 150–161: BUGA WOOD PAVILION
1, 2] Roland Halbe
3–12] ICD/ITKE University of Stuttgart
13] Tina Schulze
14–16] Nikolai Brenner

P. 162–173: BUGA FIBRE PAVILION
1] ICD/ITKE University of Stuttgart
2] Roland Halbe
3–8] ICD/ITKE University of Stuttgart
9, 10] Roland Halbe
11, 12] Nikolai Brenner
13] Roland Halbe
14] ICD/ITKE University of Stuttgart
15] Roland Halbe

P. 176–187: URBACH TOWER
1] Roland Halbe
2–14] ICD/ITKE Universität Stuttgart
15–17] Roland Halbe

P. 192–203: PROSPECTS
1] IBA Thueringen, Foto Thomas Mueller
2, 3] ICD University of Stuttgart
4–13] ICD/ITKE University of Stuttgart
14] Allmann Sattler Wappner Architekten
15] Menges Scheffler Architekten
16, 17] Lederer Ragnarsdóttir Oei / Menges Scheffler Architekten
18] Menges Scheffler Architekten
19] Allmann Sattler Wappner Architekten, Menges Scheffler Architekten; Jan Knippers Ingenieure

P. 206–219: PROJECT PARTICIPANTS
206 and Icon: Roland Halbe
207 and Icon: Roland Halbe
208 and Icon: Roland Halbe
209 and Icon: Roland Halbe
210 and Icon: Achim Menges, Tobis Schwinn (ICD)
211 and Icon: Roland Halbe
212 and Icon: ICD/ITKE University of Stuttgart
213 and Icon: Roland Halbe
214 and Icon: NAARO
215 and Icon: Roland Halbe
216 and Icon: ICD/ITKE University of Stuttgart
217 and Icon: Roland Halbe
218: ICD/ITKE University of Stuttgart

P. 220–223: BIOGRAPHIES
Menges/ Knippers: IntCDC University of Stuttgart, Photo: G. Koelmel
Block: Photo: Juney Lee
Burry: Photo: Swinburne Portraits
Cachola Schmal: Photo: Bernd Gabriel
Picon: Photo provided by Antoine Picon
Ramsgaard-Thomsen: Photo provided by Mette Ramsgaard-Thomsen, KADK
Sabin: Photo: Jesse Winter, 2017
Sheil: Photo: Ronan Sheil
Speck: Photo provided by Thomas Speck, Botanischer Garten Albert-Ludwigs-Universität Freiburg
Vrachliotis: Photo: Ulrich Coenen

P. 230–231:
1] ICD/ITKE University of Stuttgart

>> IMPRINT

CONCEPT:
ICD – Institute for Computational Design and Construction
University of Stuttgart
Prof. Achim Menges
Keplerstrasse 11
70174 Stuttgart, Germany
www.icd.uni-stuttgart.de

ITKE – Institute of Building Structures and Structural Design
University of Stuttgart
Prof. Dr.-Ing. Jan Knippers
Keplerstrasse 11
70174 Stuttgart, Germany
www.itke.uni-stuttgart.de

in cooperation with Bettina Sigmund, aboutarchitecture

TEXTS:
Achim Menges, Jan Knippers

CONTRIBUTING AUTHORS:
Philippe Block, Jane Burry, Peter Cachola Schmal, Antoine Picon, Mette Ramsgaard-Thomsen, Jenny Sabin, Bob Sheil, Thomas Speck, Georg Vrachliotis

PROJECT COORDINATION FOR THE AUTHORS:
Bettina Sigmund

PROJECT COORDINATION FOR THE PUBLISHER:
Alexander Felix, Freya Mohr

TRANSLATION FROM GERMAN INTO ENGLISH:
Marc Selway, Burke Barrett
COPY EDITING: Leo Stephen Torgoff

LAYOUT, COVER DESIGN, TYPESETTING:
Barbara Littig-Haas, Bettina Sigmund
PRODUCTION: Heike Strempel
PAPER: Condat matt Périgord 1.1, 135 g/m²
PRINTING: Eberl & Kœsel FinePrints, Altusried-Krugzel

ACKNOWLEDGEMENT: Achim Menges and Jan Knippers acknowledge the support by the Deutsche Forschungsgemeinschaft (DFG) under Germany´s Excellence Strategy EXC 2120/1 - 390831618.

GENDER-SENSITIVE LANGUAGE:
Gender-sensitive language is an important topic we would like to address in this publication. An ideal linguistic solution that does justice to all gender identities has yet to exist. For this reason, the gender-neutral language used in these texts refers to all gender identities.

LIBRARY OF CONGRESS CONTROL NUMBER: 2020943893

Bibliographic information published by the German National Library: The German National Library lists this publication in the Deutsche Nationalbibliografie; detailed bibliographic data are available on the Internet at http://dnb.dnb.de.

ISBN 978-3-0356-2039-9
E-ISBN (PDF) 978-3-0356-2040-5
GERMAN PRINT-ISBN 978-3-0356-2036-8

P.O. BOX 44, 4009 Basel, Switzerland
Part of Walter de Gruyter GmbH, Berlin/Boston

9 8 7 6 5 4 3 2 1
www.birkhauser.com

Working models: The collection of rejected approaches of the ICD/ITKE Research Pavilion 2012 shows that the buildings presented in the book are not the result of a linear design process, but the result of open-ended research with many aberrations and dead ends.